You Need a Schoolhouse

You Need a Schoolhouse

Booker T. Washington, Julius Rosenwald,
and the Building of Schools for the Segregated South

STEPHANIE DEUTSCH

NORTHWESTERN UNIVERSITY PRESS

EVANSTON, ILLINOIS

Northwestern University Press
www.nupress.northwestern.edu

Printed in the United States of America

10 9 8 7 6 5 4 3 2

ISBN 978-0-8101-3127-9

The Library of Congress has cataloged the original,
hardcover edition as follows:

Deutsch, Stephanie.
     You need a schoolhouse : Booker T. Washington, Julius
Rosenwald, and the building of schools for the segregated
South / Stephanie Deutsch.
         p. cm.
     Includes bibliographical references and index.
     ISBN 978-0-8101-2790-6 (cloth : alk. paper)
     1. African Americans—Education—Southern States—
History—20th century. 2. School buildings—Southern
States—History—20th century. 3. Washington, Booker
T., 1856–1915. 4. Washington, Booker T., 1856–1915—
Friends and associates. 5. Washington, Booker T., 1856–
1915—Political and social views. 6. Rosenwald, Julius,
1862–1932. 7. Julius Rosenwald Fund—Buildings. I. Title.
     LC2802.S9D48 2011
     379.260975965—dc22
                                                2011020505

♾ The paper used in this publication meets the minimum
requirements of the American National Standard for Information Sciences—Permanence of Paper for Printed Library
Materials, ANSI Z39.48-1992.

For

Sarah and Martin

Noah, Christopher, and Anna Katherine

and, of course, as ever,

for David

CONTENTS

Introduction

I married into a family with a famous forebear. *Famous* is perhaps not quite the right word, since my husband's great-grandfather—whose death in 1932 was reported in the middle of the front page of the *New York Times*—is no longer well known. As a young woman, I had never heard of him, nor had most people to whom I mentioned his name. He had been president of Sears, Roebuck, though, and that was certainly familiar. I picked out my first baby doll from the Sears, Roebuck catalog (which my West Texas father had grown up calling the wish book) and, as a child living overseas, was regularly attired in saddle shoes and pedal pushers ordered from Sears. As I began talking to people about Julius Rosenwald, I found that every now and then the name would trigger a spark of recognition. A friend of my parents, a woman whose own father had been a prominent rabbi, told me that in her house the name *Rosenwald* was highly regarded and frequently cited as an example of generosity. A well-known lawyer in Washington, an African American, reacted with awe when I told him of my connection. "Julius Rosenwald," he said. "He was really something."

And then my husband's cousin told me a story that further piqued my curiosity. She had been a young teacher at a public school in New Jersey when the newspaper wrote up her engagement to be married. The announcement mentioned that she was a great-granddaughter of Julius Rosenwald. When it was posted on a bulletin board, one of the school's janitors sought her out to tell her how important the Rosenwald name was to his family. With emotion, he said that he was so grateful for the education he and his sisters, brothers, and cousins had received in the segregated South at a Rosenwald school.

Julius Rosenwald, I learned, was an important figure, not only in the history of American business but also in philanthropy and education. Achieving great wealth in the Gilded Age at the turn of the twentieth century, he eschewed the flamboyant opulence of many other captains of industry. He did not collect European art, did not summer in a Newport cottage, did not send his name into posterity on a perpetual foundation. Rosenwald chose, instead, to give away much of his fortune to benefit American society by helping a segment of the population with which, as a Jew, he particularly identified—African Americans.

So my interest in Rosenwald led me to the story of his collaboration with Booker T. Washington. Here was a name I *did* recognize—Washington, I knew, was the author of *Up from Slavery*, the man often compared to the more radical W. E. B. Du Bois. But I quickly realized that I knew little beyond this. Why, I asked myself, was Washington's name so revered that it was on hundreds of schools all over the country, and yet his legacy today obscure enough that I, not to mention my children and others of their generation, knew little about him? What, I wondered, was the relationship between him and Rosenwald really like? Why had these two men from such different backgrounds been able to work together so effectively?

I have been attempting to answer these questions for more than ten years. I was fortunate in having met three of Julius Rosenwald's children and in being able to interview the youngest of them, William Rosenwald, who remembered meeting Booker T. Washington as a child. I have spent hours discussing Rosenwald with his grandson and biographer, Peter Ascoli. I have traveled to Springfield, Illinois, where Julius Rosenwald was born, and to Chicago, where he spent his adult life and where his papers are housed at the University of Chicago. Seeking to know Booker T. Washington, I have traveled to his birthplace in southwestern Virginia and, many times, to the place with which he is so closely identified, Tuskegee, Alabama. I have spent time with his papers at the Library of Congress near my home. I have revisited everything I knew, or thought I knew, about the time in which he lived. And finally, I have met dozens of men and women working to document and preserve what remains of the more than five thousand buildings scattered across fifteen states of the American South that resulted from the collaboration between Washington and Rosenwald. Even more than the schoolhouses themselves, these men and women, with their faith in the value of education and their devotion to their history and to their communities, are the tangible legacy of this partnership.

History has rather shortchanged both Washington and Rosenwald. Washington has long been out of fashion, often dismissed as servile, an Uncle Tom unable or unwilling to take the stands that would have led more directly to significant change for black Americans. His name is remembered, yet his importance is downplayed in history courses more focused on the activist tradition, and his reputation overshadowed by those of Frederick Douglass and W. E. B. Du Bois. His lively and moving memoir is absent from school reading lists. Rosenwald, because his name is on neither the universally known, astoundingly successful commercial enterprise he led nor on an enduring charitable foundation, has been largely forgotten, whereas the names of his contemporaries Rockefeller, Carnegie, and Ford are household words. But this is changing. Washington has recently been the subject of a fresh and stimulating scholarly look by historian Robert J. Norrell. Rosenwald's life has been admirably chronicled by his grandson, Peter Ascoli, and he has been written about as "the greatest donor you never heard of," his ideas and methods taken seriously by students of philanthropy. The historian Mary Hoffschwelle has thoroughly documented the history of the Rosenwald schools themselves.

I began this work wanting to know more about Rosenwald. I conclude it with infinitely greater knowledge of and appreciation for the way both he and Washington engaged with the difficult issues of their time. One hundred years ago, they were concerned with issues of race and opportunity, the appropriate use of wealth, the hunger for education, and the sustaining role of community. These issues are no less alive today than they were then, in my own life and in the life of our country. One hundred years after Washington and Rosenwald met, as we continue to think about and, increasingly, to discuss out loud our country's racial history—in the journalist David Remnick's words, "the longest and most painful drama this country has known"—the story of these two remarkable men of character and imagination is worth remembering.

You Need a Schoolhouse

Prologue

May 1911

Booker T. Washington and Julius Rosenwald met for the first time at lunch on a sweltering day in May 1911 at Chicago's elegant, new, lakefront hotel, the Blackstone. They had been anxious to meet each other. Washington regularly cultivated wealthy people who might donate money to Tuskegee Institute, the training school for black teachers he had founded thirty years earlier in rural Alabama. Rosenwald was such a man, extraordinarily rich and interested in using his money to promote the well-being of African Americans, though aware that he himself knew little about how best to do so. Each man knew the other might be of use to him. Each man was disciplined and determined, used to getting what he needed. We do not have a frank record from either one of his initial impressions of the other. We do know, though, that the results of the meeting between them would be extraordinary.

Booker T. Washington and Julius Rosenwald came to their meeting from different backgrounds and at different stages in their lives and careers. Rosenwald, one year shy of his fiftieth birthday, was bursting with health and vitality. He was a short, energetic man, with dark eyes and hair, not much given to introspection but gregarious, outgoing, and animated. A voracious reader of newspapers, he made up for his lack of formal education by being well informed. He had been spared major disappointments in either business or private life and the many demands on his time—from running Sears, Roebuck and Company,

3

one of the country's largest and most successful businesses, to his growing interest in using his fortune to encourage causes he cared about
and to the needs of his large extended family—seemed not to burden
him with worry but, rather, to fill him with energy. One person who
knew him said "his personality radiated vitality and versatile interest."
In a letter to his wife the previous year, Julius had described himself
as sleeping well and feeling "like a fighting cock." He was always up
early to take walks or to play tennis. He spent long hours in his office
and was often out late in the evening at fund-raising meetings, lec-
tures, or plays. His prominent position in business and his reputation
for honesty and generosity gave him influence in Chicago and beyond.
His desire to use his wealth responsibly and creatively made him open
to the ideas of social welfare and civic reform bubbling up around him.
He was developing the progressive's confidence that careful study and
the judicious application of funds could solve society's problems.

Booker T. Washington had weathered many crises, both public
and private, in his fifty-six years. He was just a few years older than
Rosenwald and slightly taller, with medium-dark skin and arresting
gray eyes, but he seemed more aged. His face was deeply lined. He had
come "up from slavery" and had endured personal heartbreak, years
of overwork, incessant travel, and both sides of fame—extraordinary
public acclaim as an educator and the most prominent black man in
America, and sharp criticism of his words and actions that often veered
off into vicious personal attacks. In the black community, he was
widely admired for his prominence and accomplishments, yet influential black leaders disparaged his program of vocational education and
criticized him bitterly for his unwillingness to more aggressively speak
out against lynching, limitations on black voting, and other signs of
intransigent racial hostility. Some described him as a traitor to his
race, overly anxious to ingratiate himself with whites. At least in part
because of this he was guarded, always keeping his deepest feelings private. His life had a disturbing double quality. Having grown up in the
country, he loved to be outside tending his chickens, riding his horse,
or gardening, yet he spent much of his time in trains and hotels, talking with people he hardly knew. He had been invited to dinner at the
White House with President Theodore Roosevelt and had drunk tea
with Queen Victoria, yet he had also, just six weeks before meeting

Rosenwald, been violently assaulted on a New York City street, receiving a wound that took sixteen stitches to close and leaving him, by his own account, "dazed and physically and mentally upset." His success and his fame, his very identity as a black American, were painfully equivocal.

Whatever doubts and anguish he held in his heart, though, on that hot May day in Chicago, Washington still had two assets that in the past had served him well—a compelling personal story and an extraordinary ability to communicate confidence and optimism. Both would strike a responsive chord in Julius Rosenwald.

CHAPTER 1

X

"No White Man . . . Could Do Better"

I was born a slave on a plantation in Franklin County, Virginia. I am not quite sure of the exact place or exact date of my birth, but at any rate I suspect I must have been born somewhere and at some time . . . My life had its beginning in the midst of the most miserable, desolate, and discouraging surroundings. This was so, however, not because my owners were especially cruel, for they were not, as compared with many others. I was born in a typical log cabin, about fourteen by sixteen feet square. In this cabin I lived with my mother and a brother and sister till after the Civil War, when we all were declared free.

Thus begins *Up from Slavery*, Booker T. Washington's famous account of his life. Like Frederick Douglass, whose own *Narrative of the Life of Frederick Douglass, an American Slave* had become a best seller in 1845, Washington was deprived even of a birthday by the peculiar institution under which he was born. Douglass wrote that he had never met a slave who knew the date of his own birth and that as a boy he felt envious of white children who could tell their exact ages and the day on which they had been born. Of his birthday, Washington knew only that it was in the spring, when the hillsides of Virginia were alive with blossoming forsythia, redbud, and apple trees. Later in his life, he celebrated his birthday on Easter. He wrote that the year was 1858 or 1859, but in fact it was probably 1856. What was sure was that when Washington was born, black people descended from Africans had been slaves of white people of European ancestry for more than two hundred years in America.

Booker grew up not on an enormous plantation but on a farm where the windowless, clay-floored log cabin he shared with his mother, sister, and brother sat just steps from the master's modest farmhouse. His owner, James Burroughs, raised tobacco, as well as wheat, corn, sweet potatoes, beans, peas, flax, and livestock, on two hundred hilly acres near the little town of Hale's Ford in the foothills of Virginia's Blue Ridge Mountains. It was, Booker later wrote, "about as near to Nowhere as any locality gets to be," and the place retains that feeling to this day. Burroughs and his wife, Betsy, had fourteen children, some of whom were grown and married, and with children of their own, during Booker's childhood. Among James Burroughs's ten slaves, Booker shows up on a property list as "1 negro boy" valued at $400. The "negro woman Jane" (worth $250) was his mother, the "negro woman Sophia" of the same value was his mother's half sister, the "negro boy John" (worth $550) was his older brother (or, possibly, half brother), and the "negro girl Amanda" (worth $200) was his younger half sister.

Normal family life, like birthdays, was denied to children born into slavery. Of his father, Booker wrote, "I do not even know his name. I have heard reports to the effect that he was a white man who lived on one of the near-by plantations. Whoever he was, I never heard of his taking the least interest in me or providing in any way for my rearing." Booker's medium-dark skin and gray eyes were certainly the legacy of a white man; children born into slavery were often "barnyard" children, fathered by the masters who owned them or by the masters' sons or nephews. Booker's brother, John, was rumored to be the son of one of the Burroughs boys. Amanda's father, though, was not white. He was Washington Ferguson, a slave on a neighboring farm, and he and Booker's mother considered themselves married. Still, that did not provide Booker with a fatherly presence, because Washington, reputed to be troublesome, was usually away, sent by his master to work for pay in the saltworks of Kanawha, to the west, beyond the mountains. He came back at Christmastime each year to regale the children with stories of life beyond the farm.

The most valuable slave on the list was Booker's uncle, Lee, his mother's half brother. He was worth $1,000. As a small child, Booker once saw Lee stripped naked and tied to a tree, whipped with a piece of rawhide. The man's cries of "Pray, master!" left an impression, Booker later wrote in his memoirs, "on my boyish heart that I shall carry with me to my grave." Powerful Lee was memorable less as a father figure than for the indignity forced on him by slavery.

Jane, Booker's mother, was the family cook and, "by the way, a good one," according to Laura, one of the Burroughs daughters. But for her own children, Jane had little time to fix meals. Slaves were denied the normal rhythms of family life. Booker wrote that he could not remember a single time that, as a child, he sat down to eat with his family. He and his sister and brother got their food "very much as dumb animals get theirs. It was a piece of bread here and a scrap of meat there. It was a cup of milk at one time and some potatoes at another. Sometimes a portion of our family would eat out of the skillet or pot, while someone else would eat from a tin plate held on the knee, and often using nothing but the hands with which to hold the food." Sometimes he scrounged corn that had been cooked for the pigs. When he was old enough, Booker was sometimes sent over to the "big house" to run a pulley that worked a huge fan to cool the Burroughs family and keep the flies away from them while they ate. His own mother and siblings never had the chance to gather for meals around a dining room table or to say a simple blessing over the food, but Booker did know what a family eating together looked and sounded like.

He also knew what a school looked like, because sometimes he went with Laura to the schoolhouse where she was a teacher, sitting behind her on the horse she rode to school so he could bring it back to the farm to work in the fields. The glimpses he caught of boys and girls in a classroom made Booker feel that the chance to study that way would be "about the same as getting into paradise." School and study seemed even more attractive when he learned from his mother that for slaves learning to read was forbidden.

Of all the myriad deprivations imposed by slavery, the banning of education was arguably the most devastating. In the words of one former slave interviewed years later, "They didn't want us to learn nothin'. The only thing we had to learn was how to work." Education, it was realistically feared, would make blacks less docile, less willing to fill their assigned role in the social order. As far back as 1680, Virginia law had prohibited blacks from gathering for any reason at all; shortly after that, Maryland mandated a heavy fine on anyone teaching blacks. Other states had determined that even allowing a slave to be taught to read was a punishable offense. In Georgia, that punishment was a fine of $100 and six months' imprisonment. A black person helping another to learn could be whipped "not exceeding fifty lashes." Mississippi went even further. There it was also against the law to instruct even the state's few free blacks. By the end of the seventeenth century, individual states were fining anyone who gave any kind of book learning to blacks. Twenty-five years before Booker's birth, when Nat Turner led a violent slave rebellion in Virginia, whites told one another that Turner had been encouraged to revolt by reading inflammatory tracts from the North. In the late 1830s, when Frederick Douglass's Maryland owner discovered that his wife had taught her young slave his ABCs, he was furious and insisted the lessons stop, telling his wife, "If you teach that nigger . . . how to read, there [will be] no keeping him. It [will] forever unfit him to be a slave." Douglass wrote in his *Narrative* that, hearing those words, he immediately "understood the pathway from slavery to freedom." Reading was denied to him because it would unfit him for slavery. Therefore, he wrote, he *would* learn to read.

Booker was five in the spring of 1861 when the irreconcilable differences between North and South over slavery and the sovereignty of the individual states exploded into war. One of his earliest memories was of waking up on his bed of rags to the sound of his mother's voice praying out loud that President Lincoln and his armies would win the war and make black people free.

Five of the Burroughs sons went off to fight for the Confederacy. Billy, the one everyone liked best, was killed in Virginia. Frank was taken prisoner and died in captivity. Ben was wounded in Pickett's Charge, at the Battle of Gettysburg in July 1863. And Edwin, the youngest son, caused some chiding laughter back home when it was learned that he had been shot in the backside. Had he been running away? Only one Burroughs son, Tom, came through the war unhurt.

The early spring of 1865 brought a steady stream of deserters from the disintegrating Confederate Army traipsing through Hale's Ford, and they brought with them the news that Richmond had fallen to Union forces and rumors that Lee would soon surrender. One morning the Burroughs slaves were told to gather in front of the master's house. James Burroughs had died at the start of the war, but old Mrs. Burroughs and the children and grandchildren still at home gathered on their porch while the slaves lined up in the yard. Then a Union soldier came; he made a short speech and read a document that, to nine-year-old Booker, seemed very long. He later understood that it was the Emancipation Proclamation. The soldier told them that they were free. They could go wherever they wanted to.

Booker remembered the tears that streamed down his mother's face as she listened to the soldier, then leaned over to kiss her three children, to tell them she had long prayed for this day and had feared she might not live to see it. "I have never seen one who did not want to be free," Booker wrote in his memoirs, "or anyone who would return to slavery."

He also remembered that the slaves' "wild rejoicing" after hearing they were free was followed very quickly by a "feeling of deep gloom." To be free meant to provide for themselves, and the men and women who had been slaves, who were uneducated children and grandchildren of illiterate slaves, had never learned to do that. Although it was something they had longed for, freedom was also a challenge. It meant leaving the only home they had ever known.

Four months after the momentous day when they learned they were free, Booker and his mother, sister, and brother said good-bye to Mrs. Burroughs, to her children and her grandchildren (after promising to stay in touch with them, which they did). Washington Ferguson had gone to live in Malden, a small town on the Kanawha River in the new state of West Virginia—it had seceded from Virginia to side with the Union. He worked in the salt furnaces and the coal mines there, although this time the money he made was his own. He sent some to Jane, and in late summer, she and her children set off in a newly

11

purchased horse-drawn cart to join him. For two weeks they bumped along, Jane riding, the children walking, cooking their food by the side of the road and sleeping where they could, often outside. One especially memorable night they found an abandoned cabin that seemed like a grand place to stay until an enormous black snake dropped down from the chimney and slithered across the floor. They spent the night somewhere else.

What awaited Booker's family in Malden, five miles from Charleston, West Virginia, was not exactly the Promised Land, although it did give them their first experience of going to church regularly. One Sunday morning, Booker was outside playing marbles with some other boys when the local black Baptist minister walked by on his way to church. Didn't some of them want to come with him, he asked. Booker recorded this story in his memoirs, seeing it as the beginning of his religious education and adding that, a few years later, the minister, Father Rice, baptized him in the Kanawha River.

The place Washington Ferguson had for his family was a dreary, crowded cabin, a "shanty" according to Booker's memoirs. It was not in the country, as their place on the Burroughs farm had been, but in a squalid village. And it became even more crowded when Jane brought home an orphaned boy a few years younger than Booker, a child whom she adopted into the family and named James.

For Booker and his brother John, freedom meant going off with their stepfather to work in a salt furnace, where they earned fifty cents a day. When they were paid, Washington Ferguson pocketed the money. They earned even more when they went down into the coal mines. Years later, Booker remembered his fright from going "a long distance under the mountain into a damp and dark coal mine." When William Davis, a young black veteran of the Union Army came to town and opened a small school, Booker's excitement was immediately quashed. He couldn't go, his stepfather said. He had to keep working. The family needed his income.

Booker had a strong early memory of a group of men in town crowded around another man who was reading to them out loud from the newspaper. He decided that he wanted to be the person in the middle of the circle, reading, telling people things they wanted to know. His mother managed to find him a reading book, "an old copy of Webster's 'blue-back' spelling-book, which contained the alphabet followed by such meaningless words as 'ab,' 'ba,' 'ca,' 'da.'" This was, Booker wrote, the first book he ever actually held in his hands, but because he had no one to explain it to him, it meant little. At last, his stepfather gave in to his nagging and said he could go to school, but only if he put in four hours of work in the mine before he went. Booker began getting up at four in the morning to go to work before school.

Later, Booker remembered that school presented challenges beyond just getting there. Everyone had two names, so he decided on the spot that his last name was Washington. He later added the exotic middle name his mother said she had wanted for him but couldn't quite say the origin of, *Taliaferro*. The second challenge was a hat; all the boys in the class wore caps, "store hats" as Booker called them. Not wanting him to be the only bareheaded boy, Booker's mother sewed together two pieces of "homespun" denim and made him a hat that he prized even though the other boys made fun of it. He later wrote, with the sense of thrift that had become part of his persona, that he was proud that his mother had not gone into debt for something she could not afford.

About the time he was learning to read the numbers and letters used to mark the barrels of salt he was packing, and attending school as often as he could, Booker had an experience that, years later, he described dramatically in his memoirs:

> One day, while at work in the coal-mine, I happened to overhear two miners talking about a great school for coloured people somewhere in Virginia. This was the first time that I had ever heard anything about any kind of school or college that was more pretentious than the little coloured school in our town.
>
> In the darkness of the mine I noiselessly crept as close as I could to the two men who were talking. I resolved at once to go to that school, although I had no idea where it was, or how many miles away, or how I was going to reach it; I remembered only that I was on fire constantly with one ambition and that was to go to Hampton.

Booker was helped in getting to Hampton Institute by a bit of good luck and by the ability to latch on to opportunity, which would prove one of his distinctive traits. When he was about eleven, he heard that the man who owned the local coal mine, one of the town's wealthiest residents, Colonel Lewis Ruffner, was looking for a servant to work in his house. Everyone said that his wife, Viola Ruffner, a "Yankee," was so fussy and strict that houseboys usually lasted only a few weeks with her. But Booker applied for the job and got it. He found that Mrs. Ruffner was indeed hard to please, just as everyone had said, and at first he thought it wasn't worth it to even try. Several times he ran away from her comfortable house by the river. But after a few weeks of other jobs, he always went back to work for her.

For Booker, the encounter was fortuitous. Viola Ruffner gave him a clean, pleasant place to live in her house, but she also gave him attention, structure, and encouragement. He learned from her fastidious ways of keeping house, from her care for the garden where she raised fruits and vegetables, and most of all from her deep love of learning. She told him about her own journey from a poor town in Vermont to her work as a governess and, later, running her own school. She trusted Booker to take her peaches and grapes to sell in town, she gave him books from her library, and she inquired about his reading. She later remembered him as a hard worker, "always ready for his book." And despite being brusque and fussy, Mrs. Ruffner had the time and the inclination to teach Booker and to care for him. Like his mother, she encouraged him to think about going to Hampton. Booker later wrote that he went from fearing Mrs. Ruffner to considering her a good friend. Her inclination to educate, the generosity and trust that she showed Booker, and even her fussiness helped shape the hardworking, conscientious man he was becoming.

Just as he was learning to trust and respect Mrs. Ruffner, Booker was learning that not all white people were as well intentioned. One night a brawl in town involving a black man and a white man escalated, and an angry, racially divided crowd gathered. Mrs. Ruffner's husband, well known as sympathetic to blacks, ran to the scene and was urging calm when a brick hurled from the mob hit and seriously injured him. Years later Washington wrote that watching this scene, it was hard not to feel that "there was no hope for our people in this country." He remembered that during slavery there had been much talk of "patrollers," groups of armed men who operated at night, breaking up meetings

14

of black people, preventing them from traveling without permission, and supervising their activities. More recently, the Ku Klux Klan had emerged, "bands of men who had joined themselves together for the purpose of regulating the conduct of the coloured people," Booker wrote years later, "especially with the object of preventing the members of the race from exercising any influence in politics . . . but they did not confine themselves to this, because schoolhouses as well as churches were burned by them and many innocent persons were made to suffer. During this period not a few coloured people lost their lives."

Viola Ruffner wasn't the only person who encouraged Booker's ambition to go to Hampton Institute, the school in eastern Virginia for freedmen, as former slaves were called. His older brother John gave him a few dollars he had saved, and people in town, amazed to think one of their own was going off to a faraway boarding school, contributed a "nickel, a quarter, or a handkerchief" toward his expenses. Finally, when he was sixteen, he set off, afraid that he might never again see his mother, who was "rather weak and broken in health." He had few possessions, little money, and no certainty about what might await him at the end of the three-hundred-mile trip across Virginia to Hampton.

Booker traveled by train, by stagecoach, and for long stretches on foot. On the way he had what he later identified as his "first experience in finding out what the colour of my skin meant." The manager of the small hotel where the stagecoach stopped for the night refused to even consider giving him a room. He kept warm by "walking about" and staying focused on the goal of his trip. In Richmond he stopped for several days, working at the docks unloading pig iron from a ship and sleeping at night under a wooden plank sidewalk. Another eighty miles beyond there he arrived at last, dirty and tired, at the imposing square, red-brick building that was Hampton Institute.

The entrance exam he faced there was unusual. Former slaves had had so little opportunity for schooling that it was useless to test how much they knew. It was their attitude that determined whether they could get in to Hampton. The head teacher, a white woman named Mary Mackie, told Booker that the classroom next door to hers was dirty, and she indicated a broom. This was an exam that Booker must immediately have realized he could pass. Mrs. Ruffner's training had assured him of that. The room Booker swept—and he did it three times to make sure—was perfectly clean. Mrs. Mackie ran her handkerchief over the desks and windowsills, but she could find no dirt. She told Booker that he was admitted to Hampton and that he could work as a janitor to help pay for his education there.

Years later, Booker T. Washington often said that the greatest person he ever knew was General Samuel Chapman Armstrong, the man who founded Hampton Institute a few years after the end of the Civil War. Armstrong had grown up in Hawaii, the son of a Christian missionary who ran a school there. He had been educated at Williams College in western Massachusetts and had volunteered for the Union Army, where, at a young age, he became a general and was put in command of a unit of black troops. Their courage impressed him, and at the end of the war he went to work for the Freedmen's Bureau, the government agency set up to ensure the welfare of former slaves. He bought an old federal hospital in the town of Hampton, near Newport News in Virginia, and on April 1, 1868, he opened a school there. He called it Hampton Normal and Agricultural Institute—"normal" meaning that it was a school for training teachers (so they could establish "norms" of learning) and "agricultural" because the former slaves were mostly from rural areas and farming was what they relied on and needed to learn more about.

At Hampton, students studied traditional academic subjects like reading, geography, and mathematics. They also learned carpentry, sewing, shoe making, and printing—trades that allowed them to contribute work to help pay for their room and board and that some would pursue as careers out in the world. The daily schedule was demanding. It included not just classes, study halls, and practical work but also mandatory prayers, room inspections, and military-style drills. There was a strict code of behavior and discipline. Hampton was orderly and rigorous; it was the kind of environment Booker had come to like at the home of Mrs. Ruffner.

At Hampton, Booker came under the influence of another energetic, dedicated white woman. Miss Nathalie Lord, from Portland, Maine, taught elocution and, seeing Booker's natural talent for public speaking, gave him extra coaching in the subject. Soon he had formed the After Supper Club so that students could fill twenty minutes or so after the evening meal with formal discussion of issues of concern. He became part of the Hampton debating society. His first public debate was on the execution of Major John André, an English officer hanged in 1780 for conspiring with Benedict Arnold to hand West Point over to the British. Years later, one of Booker's classmates remembered his speeches as "convincing and unanswerable." Miss Lord also taught Sunday school and introduced Booker to the study of the Bible, which, despite his churchgoing in Malden, was new to him. He began to read it as Scripture and, also, he wrote later, as literature. Years later, his daughter would remember him starting each day by reading the Bible.

When Booker graduated from Hampton in June 1875, no one from his family was there to applaud his accomplishment. His mother, who had died during the summer after his second year, would not see her nineteen-year-old son honored as one of two graduates chosen to speak at the ceremony. "Should the United States annex Cuba?" was the question he was asked to address. Booker argued against U.S. intervention in Cuba, delivering what the *New York Times*, which covered the graduation, called "a very terse, logical and lawyer-like argument." To a young woman who graduated with him, Washington looked on the day of his Hampton graduation like "a conqueror who had won a great victory."

It took the young conqueror a few years to discern his calling. Initially, he went back to Malden; rented a small, rough cabin; and for a few years ran the school there. The work was challenging. There were between eighty and ninety students of all ages, many of whom he had known since childhood. By day he taught them reading and writing, as well as algebra (which he said he never really understood until he taught it), and at night he worked with adults who wanted to make up for the education they never had received as children. He preached the virtues he had learned from Mrs. Ruffner, which had been reinforced at Hampton—order, hard work, thrift, cleanliness. He stressed, as he would often in later life, simple rules that nonetheless were new to many of his students—like the importance and value of regular use of the toothbrush. Washington encouraged his brothers, John and James, to follow his example and go to Hampton. And he spent time with Fanny Smith, a girl he had known since they were children and in whom he took a particular interest. Although she had no money, he urged her, too, to aim for Hampton.

In Malden, Washington noted, the joy among blacks at welcoming an educated man back to the community was "almost pathetic." Everyone wanted him to do something. He went to the African Zion Baptist Church, taught Sunday school, and served as a church secretary, taking minutes of meetings and assisting the pastor in other ways. He started a debating society and took speakers to match skills with similar groups in Charleston and elsewhere. He set up a library. And he became active in politics. White leaders asked him to make speeches to black groups urging them to vote in support of the effort to make Charleston the capital of the state of West Virginia. It was not a controversial issue (Charleston easily won the election in 1877), but it gave Washington an opportunity to practice public speaking. It also allowed him to adopt a theme he would return to often throughout his career—the idea that, in public matters such as this one, there was no difference between the interests of blacks and the interests of whites.

Young Washington knew he wanted a career beyond teaching at the little school in Malden. Two professions that would build on his obvious gift for public speaking—ministry and law—attracted him, but after exploring each, he decided that neither was right. His mind was given less to the abstraction of legal thinking than to practical matters. As he said in *Up from Slavery*, "I have always had more of an ambition to *do* things than merely to talk *about* doing them." Similarly, while he was a church-attending Christian, he was not drawn to dogma or theology, preferring what he called practical religion. (In later life he would be accused of having Unitarian tendencies.) He spent a semester at Wayland Seminary in Washington, D.C., and a few months reading law books, but when General Armstrong invited him back to Hampton as a graduation speaker in the spring of 1879, Washington accepted. A reporter who covered his speech, "The Force That Wins," described Washington as "a remarkable man" and went on to say that not many speakers can "manifest such dignified ease upon a public platform, and hold so mixed an audience in such close attention. The Institution that can develop such a man, and send him out, may well take great credit to itself for doing good work."

When Armstrong suggested that Washington join the Hampton faculty, Washington accepted. He went to work as a teacher in the night school, which prepared students for the regular classes, and began using part of his salary to contribute to the expenses of his brother John and of his friend from Malden, Fanny Smith. Then he took on the assignment of teaching Indian youths who had been captured out west in conflicts with the U.S. Army over land rights and who were being sent to school. Washington became the sponsor of their dorm, "the Wigwam." Accompanying one of these students on a trip, Washington learned a refinement of racial rules he hadn't encountered before. Despite the fact that the color of their skin was about the same, his young Native American charge could be served in the dining room on the steamboat they took, but he could not. The same thing happened at a hotel in Washington, D.C.

In 1881, General Armstrong received a letter asking if he could recommend "a well qualified white man" to become principal of a school being started by the state of Alabama for the training of Negro teachers. In response Armstrong wrote recommending Booker T. Washington, "a very competent, capable mulatto, clear headed, modest, sensible, polite and a thorough teacher and superior man. The best we ever had here . . . I know of no white man who could do better." The commissioners accepted the recommendation. "Booker T. Washington will suit us," they replied. "Send him at once."

In June 1881 Washington traveled to Tuskegee, the Alabama town forty miles east of the state capital, Montgomery (which briefly had served as the capital of the Confederacy). "I think I shall like it," he wrote to a friend at Hampton. He went on to clarify the pronunciation of the name ("with a hard g, accent on KE") and called it "a beautiful, quiet little town." With a population of two thousand, Tuskegee was certainly small, a typical southern town with, at its center, a statue of a Confederate soldier on a small square rimmed by shops and offices, porch awnings and benches. The surrounding countryside was hilly, leafy, and green. His early letters did not mention the fact that the town, which had once been a thriving center of the cotton trade, was actually struggling. Sporadic violence against them combined with economic depression and a changing, increasingly industrialized economy had driven some of the area's blacks away.

The school Washington had come to build was the brainchild of a local black merchant who had been raised in slavery and was completely without education himself. Lewis Adams was a tinsmith and harness maker so he knew everyone in town. When two Democratic candidates for state senate had asked him to support them and to use his influence to urge other blacks to do the same, he agreed despite the fact that, like most blacks, he usually voted for the Republican Party of Abraham Lincoln. What he wanted in exchange, he said, was for the state to create a school to educate black teachers. The deal worked, and the governor appointed Lewis and two local white merchants as commissioners of the new school, allotting them $2,000 annually to pay salaries for teachers. The balance of the school's expenses, as was typical in the South, was left to the resourcefulness of the commissioners and to the community. Despite inadequate funding for all public schools, and particularly those for black children, many people were beginning to see providing education as a way to retain the black workforce.

Despite his fashionable handlebar moustache, twenty-five-year-old Booker T. Washington initially struck the commissioners as awfully young to be the founding principal of a school. The more they saw of him, however, the more they were impressed with his "manly bearing." His height and build were average, his face handsome, but it was his energy, the intensity of the focus, that impressed them. On his first Sunday in Tuskegee, Washington spoke at both black churches, the Baptist and the Methodist, urging the people of the congregations to send their sons and daughters to see him about enrolling in the school. He conscientiously made the rounds of the white storekeepers, introducing himself and talking about his work. And he traveled out into the countryside to see how black people were living there. He knew the area he was going to was poor, but even so he was shocked to see little children running around naked and dirty. Some of the children attended school for a couple of months each year in small church buildings surrounded by the seemingly endless cotton fields, where whole families worked the rest of the time. To anyone who would listen, Washington talked about the school he was going to open. Writing back to his white friend James Marshall, the treasurer at Hampton, he noted, "The colored people here are very anxious that the school shall be a success and are willing to do what little they are able to do for it."

For the opening day of the new school, Washington chose the Fourth of July, 1881. Despite the fact that enrollment was hard to determine because some students attended class so irregularly, Washington wrote that he had about thirty students, "an earnest and willing company of young men and women," many of whom had already been working as teachers and were in their twenties and thirties. He was less enthusiastic about the church building where he met with them. It was so dilapidated that on rainy days he had to have a student hold an umbrella over his head while he heard others say their lessons. Three months later, though, Washington found what he thought was a perfect permanent location for the school—an old farm on a hundred hilly acres just out of town referred to locally as "the old Burnt Place," a property that included no main farmhouse but did have a stable, a kitchen, and a henhouse. He wrote to James Marshall at Hampton asking for a loan of $200 until the state appropriation came through. Marshall wouldn't use money from Hampton's coffers, but he did send a check from his own personal account, and with that Washington purchased the property.

There was a lot of work to do, not only to get the buildings ready to hold classes but also to begin the farming that, according to Washington's plan, would help support the school and provide additional valuable training for the students. Working side by side with them, Washington cleaned the farm's cabins and henhouse. Each afternoon after classes, he and his students cleared land and prepared fields for planting. It wasn't what everyone who had enrolled in the new school thought "education" was going to be all about, but Booker T. Washington's enthusiasm and conviction were infectious. And physical work was part of his philosophy. He felt that, more than anything, black people needed to be able to support themselves. The book learning they had been denied in slavery and that so many of them craved had to go hand in hand with occupations that would bring them the income that would allow them to build their own homes, raise families, and gain the respect of their neighbors. Trades—carpentry, laundry, cooking, sewing, farming—were to become as much a part of the

Tuskegee education as English and math. They would, as well, allow students a way to pay all or part of their tuition.

The concept of vocational education was not unique to the founders of Hampton and Tuskegee. It was, in fact, part of a progressive trend. Many educators of white children were interested in opening up secondary education to make it more egalitarian and practical, less exclusively focused on the upper class who would attend elite universities. Not everyone, they argued, needed to study the classical curriculum with its emphasis on Latin and Greek, philosophy, and ancient history. Modern languages and practical subjects were becoming more common; vocational training was being adopted as an alternative to classical education in some public school systems. Students from Tuskegee and other vocational or "industrial" schools would go on to work as teachers, or they would become carpenters, bricklayers, farmers, and cooks. The goal was not college; it was employment.

By the end of his first summer in Tuskegee, Washington had hired a striking young woman he knew from Hampton to come down and work with him as "lady principal"; to be in charge of the female students; and to teach math, astronomy, and botany while he taught rhetoric, grammar, composition, and "mental and moral science." Olivia Davidson had been a brilliant student at Hampton, and she had received a scholarship that allowed her to do further study at Framingham State Normal School in Massachusetts. Arriving at Tuskegee in the fall, she found a fast-growing school with seventy students but few supplies. "Think of it," she wrote to a friend. "A Normal school without even a Dictionary or map of the U.S.!!" The students, she noted, lacked not only book learning. They were from "the most ignorant families" and "uncultivated in manners and habits." They needed, she said, "so much training." On a trip out into the countryside near Tuskegee she encountered a "camp meeting," where she had "a most novel and interesting time. There were a great many people there and these with their strange costumes, customs, wild religious services, songs and shoutings, together with the mules, oxen, and strange vehicles of every description, made up a scene which having once seen one can never forget."

Olivia herself was beautiful and self-assured, and in addition to her talents as a teacher she brought a flair for fund-raising. She was willing to go door-to-door in the town of Tuskegee telling people about the school and asking for small contributions. She began organizing festive suppers at which local families, both black and white, would gather outside for bake sales and entertainment provided by students reciting poems and speeches. These dinners didn't just raise money; they gave people the chance to get to know the students and to see what was happening on the hillside where the new school was coming into being. In the spring of her first year there, Olivia traveled back to New England, where she had studied, to Boston and the towns around it, and talked about the new school. The area that had nurtured abolitionist preachers and writers produced significant financial donations to Tuskegee.

Washington decided that he, too, would try some northern fundraising despite the fact that he had spent very little time in the North (just one summer working as a waiter at a hotel in Saratoga, New York). He was not familiar with social habits there. In Northampton, Massachusetts, he looked all day for a black family to lodge with before, finally, going to a hotel and, to his surprise, being offered a room. Northern customs did not dictate the strict separation of blacks and whites in many social situations that he was used to in the South, where the rules said that no black could ever go to the front door of a white person's house or fail to remove his hat and step aside when he passed a white person on the street. There was no written code. It was just something people knew.

When he was talking about Tuskegee to potential funders, Washington's strengths came to the fore—his natural optimism and enthusiasm and his way of being forceful without being "bumptious," a word some whites used to describe blacks they found insufficiently deferential. He could talk about what was happening in Tuskegee in a way that made people want to donate money to it.

One of Washington's most important early decisions was to begin manufacturing bricks at Tuskegee. Clay found on the land he had bought for the school had once been used for that purpose, and the old farm included a defunct kiln. Learning how to make bricks, though, turned out to be much more challenging than he had imagined. It took many tries and many failures—whole batches of bricks that crumbled, a kiln that collapsed, grumbling by students and faculty—but finally his determination was rewarded. Students would soon be successfully manufacturing distinctive red-orange Tuskegee bricks.

The school's first year ended with a memorable closing ceremony attended by students, parents, and townspeople from Tuskegee. Recitations by students (none of whom had yet done enough work to graduate) were followed by the laying of the cornerstone for the school's first substantial building and a luncheon served, according to the account written by Washington and Olivia Davidson, "in true picnic style, on the grounds, under the trees, from bountifully filled baskets." In the afternoon, there were speeches. The pastor from a large black church in Montgomery thanked God for "what I have witnessed here today," and the white Macon County superintendent of education assured the crowd that "the time is near when public education will be recognized as a measure of public economy."

Attention to public relations and an emphasis on white support were part of the distinctive Tuskegee identity already emerging at the end of this first difficult but exhilarating year.

The following summer, Washington traveled back to Malden and married Fanny Smith, who had just graduated from Hampton. Together, they returned to Tuskegee and set up their home in the large house where the school's four teachers boarded. Soon, the couple had a baby girl whom they named Portia Marshall Washington—Portia after the wise lawyer in Washington's favorite play, *The Merchant of Venice*, and Marshall after the Hampton treasurer who had lent the money to purchase the Tuskegee property. To Marshall, Washington wrote that the baby "adds much to our happiness." That happiness, however, did not last. On a school outing in the winter of 1884, Fanny fell out of a wagon and was seriously injured. The following spring she died, leaving Washington responsible for his baby daughter and a school with more than a hundred students and a faculty that had grown to ten.

He quickly fell in love again, this time with Olivia Davidson, the first person he had hired to teach at Tuskegee and the one he always said was more responsible than any other for the school's early success. Olivia (her middle name was America) had been born the same year as Booker, and like him, she was the child of a slave mother and a white father. After Emancipation, her mother moved to Ohio, to a town where blacks had set up a private school, and Olivia was well educated there. Despite her delicate features and frail body, she was strong-willed. Having become an intense advocate of education for black people, she traveled south with one of her brothers to teach the freedmen in Mississippi. There, Olivia's idealism came up against the ugly reality of racial fear and hatred: bigots opposed to education for blacks murdered her brother. She carried on, though, attending Hampton Institute, then continuing her education in Massachusetts before accepting Washington's offer of a job at Tuskegee. In August 1885, at the home of her sister in Ohio, she and Booker were married.

Before her marriage, Olivia had had times of breakdown, perhaps from tuberculosis, but she had always recovered and brought energy, sophisticated intelligence, and dedication to her work. The year after her marriage, she gave birth to a son, Booker T. Washington Jr. (though, adopting the pet name Portia used, Olivia often called him "Brother"). In February 1889, Olivia and Booker had a second son whom they named Ernest Davidson (but called by his middle name, Dave). One night as Olivia was recuperating from his birth, a fire broke out in the Washington home. Her husband was away on one of his fund-raising trips up north. Olivia took the infant in her arms and, with the other two children, ran through the night to safety with a neighbor. But after that she became seriously ill. Washington followed the recommendation of friends to take her to a hospital in Boston for consultation, and he spent the spring of 1889 alternating time at her bedside with fund-raising visits in the surrounding area, keeping in touch by letter with his trusted assistant Warren Logan about Tuskegee business. Late in April he wrote to General Armstrong, "As hard as it is I guess it is best for me to look the matter in the face and say that at present she is not gaining and without a change soon can not last much longer." Three days later he wrote to Warren Logan: "I cannot be away from Mrs. W. very long." Olivia never recovered, and on May 9 she died. "She literally wore herself out," Washington wrote later, "in her never ceasing efforts on behalf of the work that she so dearly loved."

Washington returned to Tuskegee to bury his second wife next to his first in the hillside graveyard there. On her headstone he placed the inscription, "She lived to the Truth." To General Armstrong at

Hampton, Washington wrote of his "deep, deep affliction." He went on to say, "Few will ever know just what she was to Tuskegee and to me. But I cannot trust myself to write more now. I want to tell you about it sometime." Olivia had been a real partner, both professionally and personally, and her loss was a crushing blow.

John and James Washington had both completed their studies at Hampton and had come down to work at Tuskegee, bringing their wives and James's baby, named for his uncle Booker. They were a cheering presence, and they and others of the close-knit Tuskegee family helped Washington care for his three children until he could find a nurse. But as a young man not yet thirty-five years old, Booker T. Washington bore, in addition to his professional and personal responsibilities, a heavy load of sorrow.

A month after his second wife's death, Booker T. Washington was invited to Nashville, to the graduation at Fisk University, a college that had been founded by missionaries in an old army barracks at the end of the Civil War to educate freedmen. It had become nationally known as an educational institution and for the Jubilee Singers that toured the country and, indeed, the world singing spirituals and raising money. At Fisk, Washington met a young graduate named Margaret Murray. She had been recommended to him as one of the promising students he should consider for a position at Tuskegee. Maggie, as she was called, was lively and intelligent with a strong personality. She had grown up poor in Georgia, one of ten children of a black mother and an Irish father. She was attractive, plump, and short, just four feet, eleven inches tall. Washington lost no time in inviting her to come teach at Tuskegee, and by the time she had been there a year, he had asked her to become the new lady principal. He trusted her with responsibility for everything having to do with the female students.

He also paid attention when, during his northern travels in the summer of 1892, Maggie wrote telling him that his little boys did not seem to be getting much attention from their nurse. Once, before she put a stop to it, she wrote, "Davidson had run in the drizzling rain for more than an hour." It obviously worried her because she fussed about the children playing out in the rain again in another letter. Maggie had already confided to Washington that she did not particularly want children of her own, yet she was becoming attached to his little boys and was trying to win affection from a reluctant Portia, who, she wrote, "tells me her nose bleeds every night and often her stomach is sick." Clearly, the children needed a mother. And a feeling of mutual regard had been growing between "My dearest Booker," as she addressed him in her letters, and Maggie, who wrote of missing him while he was away and complained that his letters to her were too short. In August, Washington wrote to a friend: "Miss Murray and I are to be married October 12th. In this way both of us think we can be more valuable to the cause to which we have dedicated our lives." Maggie's letters were rather more sentimental, but she, too, was absorbed with their work. She wrote to him that she wanted to go on teaching. "I love to work in the classroom, and I want to make some money too because I shall need many things for the house and the children that you will not know of. I like a pretty home." The marriage was to be a long one, based less on passion than on convenience but, nonetheless, providing Washington and his children with affection, stability, and calm.

In May 1892, Washington had brought to Tuskegee as the speaker for the school's eleventh commencement the most distinguished black man in America, Frederick Douglass. The seventy-four-year-old Douglass was famous not just for the widely read narrative of his escape from slavery as a youth but also for his career as a journalist; as an eminent resident of Washington, D.C., where he had served as city recorder of deeds; as the U.S. envoy to Haiti; and as a staunch, eloquently persistent defender of freedom and equality—not just for black people but for women as well. His sons had fought in the Union Army; he had heard Abraham Lincoln deliver his second inaugural address, had shaken his hand at the Executive Mansion, and had praised him at the dedication of a park in the slain president's honor near Douglass's home in Washington, D.C.

At Tuskegee on the day of the graduation, people flocked in from the surrounding countryside "in wagons, in carts, in ox-teams, on horseback, on mule back and on foot . . . by noon the School grounds were filled almost to overflowing." Before a crowd of five thousand people, Douglass made a speech that, in essence, he had given many times before. In "The Self-Made Man" he praised as the keys to success for black people living in the wake of slavery the values that Washington always promoted—hard work, thrift, and unflagging energy. A newspaper account of the speech reported that, "so far as it touched upon race questions," its tone was "calm and dispassionate." It was different from the speech Douglass had given a few days earlier at Atlanta University, a school for blacks, where he had alluded to what had happened earlier that spring in Memphis. There an argument over a game of marbles between a white boy and a black boy had escalated into a fight. Three black men had been arrested, then dragged from jail in the middle of the night and shot to death by a Memphis mob. Twelve hundred black leaders, including Washington, had met in Ohio to sign a petition drawing attention to the danger to public safety represented by such mob violence. But in the rural South, on his home turf, Washington was not confrontational, and Douglass's speech struck much the same note. "Let us alone, and give us a fair chance," he said in conclusion, addressing the whites in the audience, then adding for emphasis, "but be sure you do give us a fair chance."

Just a year later, Frederick Douglass would publicly doubt that American blacks were getting that fair chance, and shortly after that, Booker T. Washington would be offered the opportunity to articulate his own views. The national spotlight would come to rest on him.

CHAPTER 2

X

Peddler's Son

Growing up in the years after the Civil War a few blocks from the center of Springfield, Illinois, Julius Rosenwald and his brothers, sisters, and cousins had a lot of company and considerable freedom. They could chase the clumsy pioneer wagons that rattled through town on their way west and observe the exotic-looking Indians who sometimes came into the clothing shop run by their uncles and father. They went to the local public schools, and early on, they got used to working. Julius did odd jobs like carrying satchels for businessmen and pumping the organ at the local Congregational church. On Saturdays, he helped out in the store, fetching things as needed and sometimes even waiting on customers.

In the taunts of other children, though, Julius occasionally heard echoes of the prejudice that had pushed many Jews toward their decision to leave their own countries and come to America. Julius's father, Samuel Rosenwald, who noted the remarks his children heard in a letter home to Germany, had arrived in Baltimore, Maryland, on a May afternoon in 1854, two years before Booker T. Washington was born. Settlers from Great Britain, France, and Spain may have been the earliest colonizers of the American continent, but in the first half of the nineteenth century, in one of the great population influxes in its history, millions of immigrants from the lands that today are Germany and Austria were settling the young United States. These settlers were motivated by what some scholars call the push-pull of circumstances. People were pushed away from Prussia, Hanover, Westphalia, and other German lands by poverty, by a potato rot like Ireland's, and by a rigid society that required long military service and made it hard to get ahead financially or socially. For Jews, like Samuel, the push was stronger still. They left to escape special taxes and laws restricting where they could live, when they could marry, and what professions they could choose. These burdens, based on age-old prejudice, had limited the lives of Jews in Europe for hundreds of years.

Pulling settlers to America was opportunity—fertile land that was plentiful and cheap, low taxes, and a shortage of workers. What's more, a new land offered Europeans freedom from the Old World's rigid class structure. No one knew or cared about who their parents and grandparents were. German newspapers and magazines of the time were full of advertisements for steamers crossing the Atlantic and for inexpensive land in America; they carried pages of letters about life there. A resident of Iowa was quoted saying, "One hardly realizes that one is in America because one hears German everywhere . . . Here people are not divided into classes as in Germany. One person is as good as another." Another writer noted, "The land is so 'fat' that the laborer can always count on a good harvest. There are so few workers that they have to pay them well . . . The paradise of America is Illinois."

As were many Jews who came from countries where they were forbidden to practice law or medicine, and where they could not own land and farm, Samuel Rosenwald was from a family of shopkeepers. Trade was what he knew, so in America he quickly took a path followed by many Jewish newcomers—he became a peddler. The Gimbel, Straus, Mack, Goldwater, Flexner, Filene, Rich, Kuhn, and Guggenheim families, among many others, can all trace family fortunes back to men who started out as peddlers. (Some non-Jews also became peddlers, of course: John D. Rockefeller's father worked for a time as a peddler; so did the father of Louisa May Alcott and, many years later, the mother of the Lebanese American writer Khalil Gibran.) In Europe people looked down on traveling salesmen, but in America, where homesteads were far flung and settlement was sparse, people didn't just tolerate peddlers selling pots and pans, needles and threads, and all kinds of small household items; they welcomed them. The 1850 U.S. census listed ten thousand peddlers in the country (in contrast with the seventy-two pawnbrokers on the preceding line and the fifty-six pen makers on the one that followed). With credit from Jewish shopkeepers and a large amount of energy, a peddler could begin to support himself quickly. So Samuel, who had arrived with almost nothing, soon put a pack on his back and set off from his home base in Baltimore to sell his wares through Maryland and Virginia.

Many of the four thousand Jewish residents of Baltimore were, like Samuel, German-speaking immigrants. Their community was well established, with a Greek-style synagogue at the corner of Lloyd and Watson streets; a Jewish burial ground; and a benevolent society to take care of the sick, widowed, and orphaned among them. "In as much as we know," the Baltimore American newspaper reported in 1856, "no Jew has ever asked for assistance from the general charity fund. The Jews take care of their own poor and contribute to the poor of all religions." An early history of Baltimore's Jews wrote that "in those early days there was little difference between those who needed charity and those who gave it, and the fewness and homogeneity of the Jews in Baltimore strengthened the feeling of brotherhood created by common faith and traditions." For thousands of years this had been the teaching of the Jewish faith and the custom of a people often isolated among neighbors who disdained them. Jews took care of one another, teaching their children to tithe by giving a portion of their income to the community for the benefit of the poor, to practice tzedakah, or charity. It was Jewish tradition to be grateful for beggars because they presented an opportunity to benefit the poor.

Samuel Rosenwald had good luck in Baltimore when he met four brothers—Julius, Edward, Louis, and Simon Hammerslough. They came from the same part of Hanover as he, and they, too, were Jews. The eldest, Julius, had come to America when he was just thirteen years old; the others had arrived one by one, welcomed by the older relatives who had already settled in Baltimore. They were doing well, selling dry goods—clothing and groceries. And they had a sister, Augusta, a small, sturdy woman five years younger than Samuel. His gruff nature was attracted to her more cheerful disposition, and in August 1857, they married.

For a few years, Samuel and Augusta were unsettled. The Hammersloughs sent their new brother-in-law to look after stores they were trying to launch, first in Peoria, Illinois, then in Talladega in central Alabama. But Samuel and Augusta didn't like Alabama's hot weather or the rats and fleas that infested the town. They had never before lived in a society based on slave labor, and they found it disturbing. Their first child died in infancy. Soon they had a new baby, a little boy named Benjamin, and they were glad to be needed again back in Illinois, where, suddenly, the Hammersloughs' shop was overwhelmed with business. In the spring of 1861, the newly inaugurated president called for army recruits to put down the Southern Rebellion, and the volunteers pouring into Springfield all needed uniforms.

By the time Julius Rosenwald was born, on August 12, 1862, his parents were comfortably established in Springfield. It was a busy town of 9,300 residents, with wooden sidewalks and straight streets evenly intersecting each other. The train depot where the prominent local lawyer and former congressman Abraham Lincoln had said good-bye to his neighbors before heading to Washington to become president in March 1861 was about three blocks from Capital Square. The Capitol Clothing House, the shop where Samuel Rosenwald worked for his brothers-in-law, stood on the north side of the square facing the imposing state capitol building. At the edge of town, flat prairie land stretched out to the sky, seemingly forever.

Springfield was a lively place for trade, a fast-growing town connected by railway to Chicago in the north and St. Louis to the south, on the regular route of the many wagon trains headed west. Even before the start of the war, the Hammerslough brothers' store was competing successfully with several other clothing shops in town. In 1858 R. G. Dun & Company, a credit-rating business also called the Mercantile Agency, wrote that the Hammerslough brothers were "Jews of good habits and appear to be making money." It also made the colorful but crude observation that Louis was of the "pizzle-clipped tribe in which but few of us have any confidence." Customers, though, did not share any lack of confidence on the part of the credit assessors. The following year the assessors considered that the brothers had a "splendid trade" and were "making money fast." Abraham Lincoln had been a client, becoming friendly enough with Julius Hammerslough that the clothier had traveled to Washington in 1861 to see his neighbor and customer inaugurated as president.

In April 1865 word came that the southern surrender had brought to an end four ghastly years of war. A week later, people in Springfield were shocked to learn that an actor had entered the theater box where Abraham Lincoln was watching a play and had shot him dead. Julius Hammerslough joined a delegation of Springfield citizens that traveled to the capital city to accompany the slain president's body on its sad, slow train journey home for burial. The Capitol Clothing House sold thirty thousand mourning badges and was draped in black bunting, with the martyred president's picture in the window under a sign that read "Millions bless thy name."

The Rosenwalds soon outgrew their first home and moved to a pleasant wooden house across Eighth Street and down the block from the house where the Lincolns had lived. It wasn't as big as the Lincolns', but the house was of recent construction, with front and side porches and bay windows on two stories. There was also a shed and a carriage house on the large, shady lot. Julius and his older brother, Benjamin, were soon joined by more children—Morris, Samuel (who died of the croup when he was five), Selma, Sophie, and Louis. A white hired girl helped Augusta with the cooking and the cleaning, the entertaining of visitors from back east, and the care for this lively brood.

There were about a dozen Jewish children in Springfield, and they all went to religious school together in a room above Salter's Grocery. Julius Hammerslough, who had been one of the first Jews to settle in Springfield, was the founding president of the congregation, which soon began raising money for a proper building and wrestling with the question of what form of worship they would follow there. Most members thought Reform Judaism was more suited to life in America than the Orthodox faith in which many European Jews had been reared. The young congregation made the decision to switch to Reform— to have prayers in English and German, as well as Hebrew; to have organ and choir music; and to seat men and women side by side rather than in separate sections as traditional synagogues did. Men would not even have to cover their heads for worship. Samuel Rosenwald took a turn as president of the congregation and then joined the building committee. The few Jewish families of Springfield raised $7,500 (which would be at least $150,000 today, and probably more) so they could build an imposing brick temple on North Fifth Street. In March 1876 Brith Sholom was dedicated.

The switch from Orthodox to Reform Judaism did not, of course, alter the lessons that Julius and his brothers learned as each turned thirteen and prepared for his bar mitzvah. As Jews had done for thousands of years, they learned then that Jewish life is governed by laws believed to come from God, rules written in the first five books of Hebrew scripture, the Torah. These laws include the Ten Commandments and other directions about how to worship God and how to live together with other people of the same faith; they emphasize the importance of life in community. Julius learned that no law is more important than the injunction to practice *tzedakah*—to act justly, to be fair in all business and private dealings. *Tzedakah* also means that charity and care must be offered to neighbors in need, that the mitzvah that is not simply a favor but the care and sharing to which everyone has a right. Just as Julius's father had benefited from help when he arrived in Baltimore, so Jews had always and would always practice *tzedakah* toward one another. Helping others to become self-sufficient so they would not need further assistance was considered one of the most blessed forms of giving.

His shop was not Samuel Rosenwald's only interest in Springfield; he was something of a community leader. An early history of Sangamon County profiled him as a "representative citizen." It said that in politics he was "rather independent" and claimed to have cast his first vote for Buchanan for president of the United States (which would mean he had voted within two years of arriving in America). By 1869 he was a charter member of the Springfield Board of Trade. He joined two different benevolent brotherhoods, one the Eames Lodge of the Independent Order of B'nai B'rith.

In 1868 Samuel Rosenwald was able to buy out his brothers-in-law when Edward and Julius Hammerslough moved to New York and Louis Hammerslough left Springfield for Kansas City. Samuel moved the business to more spacious quarters across Capital Square and reopened it as "S. Rosenwald, the C.O.D. one price clothier," meaning that this was a modern business in which there was no bargaining or bartering. Everything had just one set price. A few years later, Samuel wrote to relatives in Bünde, Germany, that he was doing well. "It has taken a long time," he said, "but my dear wife and I have been very economical; otherwise, we would not have gotten so far."

One day in October 1874, twelve-year-old Julius answered an ad in the Springfield newspaper that called for "live, active, energetic boys" to sell a brochure describing the new memorial that was soon to be dedicated at President Lincoln's grave. The celebrations brought to town military bands; divisions of Civil War veterans; members of the Lincoln family; General William Tecumseh Sherman; and his friend, the general who had won the war and who was then president of the United States, Ulysses S. Grant. In the enormous crowd that gathered for the ceremonies, Julius made $2.50 selling the brochure, "peddling" as he called it. He later recalled observing Grant sitting in his carriage. "He was the first man I had ever seen with kid gloves on his hands," Julius told an interviewer many years later. "They were yellow in color and I looked so long that I have never forgotten them." The merchant's son was picking up the eye of a clothier and the ways of the salesman.

Indeed, in the spring of 1879, when he was sixteen, Julius made a practical decision. He had been attending the local public schools, and his name was sometimes listed in the Springfield newspaper's honor rolls of students who had been "neither absent nor tardy . . . and whose deportment and scholarship are good." But his uncles, Julius and Edward Hammerslough, were manufacturing clothing in New York City as well as selling it retail, and when they offered Julius the opportunity to come and learn from them, he took it.

In later years, Julius Rosenwald often said that he was sorry never to have completed high school; even as a well-known man he did not feel he could accept the honorary degrees that were offered to him because he had not attended any university. What he had instead of college, though, was a similarly formative experience—six years of working side by side with his enterprising uncles, of learning every aspect of the clothing business from them, of tasting independence from his parents, and of forming lasting connections to friends and peers in similar lines of work. And no less than any college freshman, Julius experienced the excitement and stimulation of new surroundings. New York was a far cry from quiet Springfield; it was an enormous, sprawling city with elevated trains, electric lights, telephones, theaters, and restaurants—more enterprises of every kind than Julius had ever seen.

The business he went there to learn—the manufacture, buying, and selling of ready-made clothes—was a hot one in the 1880s. People like Julius's uncles were making a lot of money in what they themselves often called the rag trade. The production of uniforms for the Civil War had given a boost to the standardization of sizes necessary for bulk sales, and the invention of the sewing machine had opened the way for mass production. Large numbers of immigrants willing to work long hours for low wages made possible the crowded city sweatshops, where workers lived and worked in the same cramped quarters and where much of the merchandise was manufactured. As the country's population grew, and more and more disparate folks sought to become part of the middle class, many people preferred the appropriateness and anonymity of store-bought clothing to the homemade garments their parents had always worn. In fact, there was so much and such varied merchandise available that people began to use a new word to describe the process of looking around stores and deciding what to buy: *shopping*.

Working as a stock clerk for his uncles, taking samples of clothes they manufactured out on the road to show to stores, and eventually opening his own small shop, Julius learned the ups and downs of the trade. His brother Morris joined him, as did their cousin Julius Weil, and they all moved from Uncle Edward's luxurious home on East Fifty-eighth Street to a boarding house where they met Mo Newborg, Harry Goldman, and other young Jewish men getting started in business. They opened their own shop, Rosenwald and Brother, just off Broadway on Broome Street in Greenwich Village, and struggled to compete with other nearby stores. In a letter to relatives in Germany, Samuel Rosenwald admitted that his sons were "only doing fairly well."

A casual conversation with another clothes merchant dramatically changed that. One of the partners in a firm that sold summer clothing to the Hammersloughs showed Julius sixty telegrams asking for goods he did not have, especially lightweight summer clothing for men—crinkled seersucker suits and linen coats and pants. There simply wasn't enough merchandise available, he said, to meet the need. This stuck in

Julius's mind; he woke up in the middle of the night thinking about it. Why not, he asked Morris, start their own business for the manufacture of summer clothing? Morris liked the idea; so did their uncles. They suggested the new business should be in Chicago—far enough from New York to keep Julius out of direct competition with his uncles but large enough and young enough to be a city of opportunity, a return to the Midwest of his childhood, a dynamic place to live and work.

The grand funeral procession for Ulysses S. Grant and the enormous crowds that turned out to watch its slow progress up Fifth Avenue in August 1885 may have been among Julius's last sights in New York before heading to Chicago.

Julius had been a boy when he left Springfield; when he returned from New York to Chicago, he was a man. At twenty-three, he was on the short side, with dark eyes and wavy, dark hair and the generous moustache that was fashionable at the time. He was pleasant looking without being striking; serious but not dour; an energetic, self-confident, deceptively ordinary-looking young man.

Chicago was a big, bold town extending for many miles along the dazzling blue waters of Lake Michigan. Despite the brutally cold weather that accompanied it, this location where the prairie, the lake, and the Chicago River came together was a key to the city's spectacular growth. Chicago was a hub of communication between the East Coast and the western parts of the country, the biggest nexus of railroads in the world. A fire had destroyed much of it in 1871, but Chicago had recovered to become the second most populous American city, rebuilding with the country's first skyscrapers in the spare, linear, modern style that Louis Sullivan, Dankmar Adler, and Daniel Burnham would make famous. The city was a magnet for immigrants, businessmen, and the curious, with gigantic grain elevators, acres of lumberyards, and the brand new stockyards full of pigs and cows on their way to market that had quickly become a tourist attraction despite their nasty odor.

The city soon became infamous, too, known for poverty and crime; for vast slums where many of the city's immigrants lived; and in the spring of 1886, Julius's first year there, for the Haymarket riot. In the wake of a one-day strike against McCormick Harvester Company, some workers were demonstrating for reforms like an eight-hour workday and the right to join trade unions when a bomb went off. In the chaos that followed, gunshots rang out. Seven police officers and two bystanders were killed. Eight men, union leaders, were quickly arrested; they may or may not have fired the shots, but they were quickly tried and found guilty in an atmosphere of hysteria and fear. Four of them were hanged. Many people became convinced that pushing for reforms in working conditions and agitating for unions to represent workers were little different from preaching violence and revolution. It would be two decades before the need for reforms regulating the workplace—the eight-hour day, the right to organize, limitations on child labor—would begin to be widely accepted.

Such concerns do not seem to have been much on Rosenwald's mind as he launched his new clothing company, Rosenwald & Weil (Julius Weil was a cousin on his mother's side of the family). Remembering this time later, he wrote, "I will never forget how bitter cold St. Louis was when I was on my first trip to sell clothes intended for the hottest summer weather and the welcome I received seemed to me even colder than the weather, but as time went on, the prospects grew brighter and results comparatively satisfactory." Samuel Rosenwald sold his Springfield shop and left the town where he was a respected community leader to come up to Chicago and help with the new venture. He lent his sons $2,000 (which was about what a successful merchant could hope to earn in a year) and invited them to come live with him and his wife in the house they had purchased on Wabash Avenue. It was on the city's South Side, in a pleasant neighborhood of sandstone row houses on tree-lined streets where many middle-class Jewish merchants and professionals lived.

A mile north of the Rosenwalds' new home was Temple Sinai, a gathering place for the religiously liberal and culturally German Jewish community it had been created to serve. A brilliant, dynamic rabbi was breathing new energy into what had been a small congregation there. Emil Hirsch, the son of a rabbi, had come to the United States from Luxembourg as a teenager, had played football at the University of Pennsylvania, had returned to Europe for graduate study, and then had served briefly at a synagogue in Baltimore. At Chicago's Sinai Temple he took a radical and controversial step when he changed the day of worship from Saturday, the traditional Jewish Sabbath, to Sunday so that the Jews of his congregation would be working and worshipping on the same days as their Christian neighbors. He downplayed many traditional Jewish practices and stressed ethical conduct. Rabbi Hirsch preached that modern Judaism was more like the Unitarian religion than it was like Orthodox Judaism, practical rather than mystical, anchored in the moral choices of this world rather than in the hope of the next. Men and women must love their fellow human beings, Hirsch preached, and not focus their energy on the complicated and, in his view, antiquated practices of Orthodoxy. He encouraged members of his congregation to have Christmas trees in their homes to emphasize that Jews share in the spirit of goodwill that the holiday celebrates. Hirsch's teaching and style suited Samuel Rosenwald, who soon began making regular contributions to charitable funds at Sinai. It was not long before he requested membership there.

In the close-knit German Jewish community, it was inevitable that Julius would meet the Nusbaum family. They lived nearby, and they, too, attended Sinai. Emanuel Nusbaum was born in Prussia and had been a peddler and shopkeeper in upstate New York. After his wife's death, he had moved to Chicago with his son, Aaron, and seven daughters—Sarah, Miriam, Augusta, Lena, Florence, Hannah, and Therese. Julius was taken with the one who shared his mother's first name, Augusta, whom everyone called "Gussie." When he met her (in 1888, when he was twenty-six and she was twenty), she was helping her widowed father care for the younger girls. This devotion to family was among her attractions. So was the fact that she was a spirited, intelligent young woman with wavy hair; a determined chin; and a rich, attractive voice. On April 8, 1890, Julius and Gussie were married. After a honeymoon trip to New York and Boston, they settled in with his parents.

Julius and Gussie quickly had two children—a son to whom they gave the German name Lessing in honor of a close friend and a curly-haired daughter they called Adele. They moved into their own house, but they continued to spend a lot of time with their parents, sisters and brothers, cousins, and soon nieces and nephews. Almost every Sunday, there was a big family gathering. After dinner the Rosenwalds gathered to talk and to read aloud letters from family or friends who were traveling.

Most of Julius's time, though, was taken up with the business of Rosenwald & Weil. He often had to be away from home, taking samples of clothing on the road to sell to retailers in smaller cities and towns, some as far away as Albuquerque, Colorado Springs, El Paso, and Phoenix. Regularly, he traveled to New York to purchase fabrics and merchandise and to consult with his uncles. Gussie hated these separations and wrote to her husband every day when he was away, calling him "my darling" or "my sweetheart" and signing her letters "Your own Frau." (Having grown up surrounded by the language, they both used a lot of German words and expressions in their letters. Julius once said a large meal left him feeling like a "gestopfe Ganz," a stuffed goose.) Gussie complained about being lonely when Julius was away and described her determination to stay contended and busy, to make time not just for housework and cooking but also for German lessons, reading, and playing the piano.

One worry that cropped up from time to time in her letters was money. Julius and Gussie had enough, for sure, but with a growing family and business always uncertain, they had to be careful. When they had been married for two years, Gussie wrote to Julius that his father had stopped in to see her and had suggested that they were spending too much, that they should be more careful in the future. In another letter, she reported that she wanted a mink cape like one a friend had; then, after her husband wrote that he had "almost fainted" at the price of it, she wrote that she had changed her mind. "A real nice [cloth] coat" was going to be just fine, she said in her next letter. She urged her husband not to bring gifts back from his travels for anyone, "not even me." She said it was "an extravagance we can't afford at present." Gussie wrote about wanting to cut back their expenses a bit "since there is the Future of our children to look after. It is our duty to try and save so as when they are old enough we can try and give them the very best education and this is why all extra expense worries me."

Week after week, Julius and Gussie listened to sermons at Sinai, where Emil Hirsch preached that religion is as much "a power for social readjustment" as a vehicle of personal enlightenment. The message of religion, Hirsch consistently told his congregation, "is for *this* world . . . If present conditions are not as they should be, a kingdom of God, these conditions are an accusation against us. They ought to be answered by us." To Hirsch, Judaism was and always had been "the outcry for justice . . . dissatisfied with conditions in which justice is denied to the Jew and the non Jew." The special obligations of those who had great wealth was a favorite topic. For Julius and his family this was stimulating food for thought, but it also had a straightforward application for them. Julius's father, his father-in-law, and his brother-in-law Aaron Nusbaum all supported Sinai's annual charity drives. Julius was not a wealthy man, but he could certainly afford small, regular donations. Years later, Mo Newborg, one of his friends dating back to their time together in New York, remembered that Julius had confided to him a dream of someday having an annual income of $15,000—"$5,000 to be used for my personal expenses, $5,000 to be laid aside, and $5,000 to go to charity." The dream was to be realized beyond Rosenwald's wildest imagining.

CHAPTER 3

X

A Lucky Chance,
a Daunting Task

In the summer of 1893 Chicago was alive with the excitement of a world's fair commemorating the four hundredth anniversary of Christopher Columbus's arrival in America. The endless words of boosterism and praise of their city that had been published by Chicagoans as they vied with New York for the right to host the fair had earned it a nickname, "the Windy City," which was more than meteorological. The World's Columbian Exposition that opened in the summer of 1893 was spectacular. The country's foremost urban planners and engineers had transformed a barren, swampy lakefront area close to the Rosenwalds' neighborhood into a glittering city of elegant white, classically inspired buildings on miles of artificially engineered canals, lagoons, and ponds. Fountains, statuary, and enormous shrubs lined wide, curving walkways. The entire six-hundred-acre fairgrounds, four times the size of the Paris world's fair of a few years earlier, was dazzling at night when thousands of electric lights—quite a novelty—outlined the buildings and bathed the fountains in color as beams from huge searchlights swept the sky.

Pavilions offered extraordinarily varied displays on the arts and industries of thirty-six states, three territories, and nineteen foreign countries. Frederick Douglass, who had been consul general in Haiti,

43

was on hand as the commissioner of the Haiti display, where he was frequently surrounded by white visitors wanting to shake his hand. There was the enormous Woman's Building, designed by a young female graduate of the Massachusetts Institute of Technology, showcasing a mural by the American painter Mary Cassatt and statues by the San Francisco artist Alice Rideout. When Gussie toured the fair with her father, she commented that she had seen models of the ships that brought Columbus to America.

The summerlong fair offered, as well, speeches on topics from philosophy and religion to literature and drama. Frederick Jackson Turner, a professor at the University of Wisconsin, presented the lecture "The Significance of the Frontier in American History," extolling the vitality demanded by exploring and settling a new land, and attributing much of the strength of the American character to it. In the passing out of existence of the frontier, he saw the culmination of the first stage of American history. Some would hear in his words an invitation for the United States to expand territorially. Turner himself noted that "since . . . the fleet of Columbus sailed into the waters of the new world, America has become another name for opportunity" and implied that modern times would bring new areas of endeavor and creativity.

The mile-long carnival on a strip of parkland called the Midway Plaisance (which gave the name *Midway* to amusement parks all over the country) featured a Parisian department store; a natatorium; and the fair's answer to the Eiffel Tower (which had been the star of the Paris fair), an incredible, two-hundred-fifty-foot-tall amusement-park wheel created by a young bridge engineer named George Ferris. There were re-creations of Irish villages; of an eighteenth-century street in Vienna; and of a Cairo scene complete with minaret, souks, and belly dancers. And from the French colony of Dahomey (which became present-day Benin) there were sixty African Pygmies in grass skirts, curiosities displayed to show what Europeans were up against in their "civilizing" mission. The *New York Times* said the Pygmies were "as degraded as animals" and noted disdainfully that they had "many characteristics of the American Negro."

The glorious story the fair's many exhibits told did not include the progress that had been made by America's black men and women in the fewer than thirty years since their liberation from 250 years of slavery. They had been excluded from the fair's planning, although they received a rather ambiguous nod with a special event planned for the end of the summer. Colored People's Day would, ostensibly, be like the German Day that, in June, had brought out thousands of people to celebrate Germany and its contributions to America. At least in part because his grandson, a violinist, had been invited to perform there, Frederick Douglass had somewhat reluctantly agreed to be the featured speaker at Colored People's Day, despite the strong disapproval of his friend, the fiery, young black journalist Ida B. Wells, who felt that blacks should boycott the event. She feared it would demean rather than hold up blacks. She herself did not attend, but she heard about what happened.

A then-unknown twenty-one-year-old black poet named Paul Laurence Dunbar opened the proceedings with "Columbian Ode," a poem from *Oak and Ivy*, the book he had recently published at his own expense, which concluded:

> The schoolhouse tow'rs where Bruin had his den
> And where the wigwam stood the chapel stands;
> The place that nurtured men of savage mien
> Now teems with men of Nature's noblest types.
> Where moved the forest foliage green
> Now flutters the stars and stripes!

Douglass then began to speak. When hoots of derision from whites in the audience interrupted the speech, the old man departed from his carefully prepared text and angrily extemporized. "Men talk of the Negro problem," he said. "There is no Negro problem. The problem is whether the American people have loyalty enough, honor enough, patriotism enough to live up to our own Constitution." He concluded: "We Negroes love our country. We fought for it. We ask only that we be treated as well as those who fought against it." It was a powerful performance, and the applause that greeted it more than covered over noise from any remaining hecklers. Booker T. Washington was in the audience and later wrote, "No one who listened to this masterful plea for justice for the Negro race can ever forget the inspiration of that hour."

Ida Wells was less inspired than appalled. She rushed into print twenty thousand copies of an eighty-one-page pamphlet that she and Douglass had been planning but that had been slowed down by lack of funding. *The Reason Why the Colored American Is Not in the World's Columbian Exposition* had a forceful introduction by Douglass, who exhorted Americans not just to take pride in the achievements documented by the fair but also to acknowledge the "repentance" and "shame" appropriate to the way the promise of American democracy was being withheld from its black citizens. Wells, who had been investigating and documenting instances of mob violence, wrote on lynching, including the grisly details of an event that had occurred earlier that summer in Kentucky—the mutilation and murder of an almost certainly innocent black man. She pointed out that Russia's serfs, who had been liberated at the same time as America's blacks, had been provided with three acres of land and some tools. "But to us," she wrote, "no foot of land nor implement was given. We were turned loose to starvation, destitution and death." Wells called the pamphlet "a clear, plain statement of facts concerning the oppression put upon the colored people in this land of the free and home of the brave." It was handed out free to anyone who cared to take it.

The reality of Colored People's Day—Dunbar's patriotic poem, Douglass's dignity, Washington's optimistic remarks—contrasted sharply with a lithograph about the fair that appeared in *Puck* magazine. It showed grotesquely caricatured blacks, some wearing grass skirts and carrying spears, and others lining up for watermelon looking like dandies from minstrel shows. It was titled *Darkies Day at the Fair.*

As that summer of 1893 wore on, neither the rousing Sousa marches the bands played on the Midway nor the lively ragtime of an unknown piano player called Scott Joplin could quite drown out some uneasy background music. When the fair closed in October, an astonishing twenty-seven million people had visited it, but outside its gates, unemployed men were milling around demanding that the city create more jobs. On the fair's very last day Chicagoans were shocked when a crazed man shot and killed their popular mayor, Carter Harrison, in the front hallway of his own home. The year that followed brought Chicago an uneasy hangover from the fair's festive intensity, as the national economy slumped. In November, an English newspaperman and moral crusader named William P. Stead held a huge public meeting and invited Chicago's civic leaders in order to thunder at them, as one observer said, "at white heat ... [like] one of the Hebrew prophets" about their inactivity in the face of the terrible poverty he observed in the city and the ignorance, illness, and degradation that went with it. Stead poured his outrage into a five-hundred-page report that came out the following spring as a book titled *If Christ Came to Chicago*.

Troubling times continued the following year when workers producing railroad cars in the company town of Pullman outside of Chicago went on strike and federal troops were called in to ensure that the mail trains could still run clashed with demonstrators on the abandoned grounds of the World's Columbian Exposition. Four demonstrators died in the melee, and a fire raged through the fair's empty buildings, burning most of them to the ground. Many people were uneasy, scared of what they saw as a dangerous radical movement inspired by foreign anarchists and revolutionaries.

One person who was not feeling the pinch of the economic slump was Gussie's brother, Aaron Nusbaum, who had profited enormously from the fair. He had landed a profitable business deal after he did a favor for one of Chicago's richest men, the owner of a department store that carried his name, Marshall Field, and who was on the planning committee for the World's Columbian Exposition. His reward to Nusbaum for helping him locate a trainload of merchandise that went astray was not cash but an opportunity—the concession to sell flavored soda water to visitors at the fair. By the time the fair closed, Nusbaum had made $150,000 (several million dollars in today's money). Since then, he had been looking for a way to invest this small fortune. Such an opportunity appeared in the summer of 1895, when he went to visit a young man named Richard Sears. Nusbaum was representing the Bastedo Tube Company, which made a device for sending money, receipts, and change through overhead tubes between floors of department stores. Sears, however, had problems more pressing than how to move receipts between floors.

Sears told Nusbaum that his tremendous success had overwhelmed him. He was from a small town in Minnesota, where he had begun his career as a teenaged railroad agent. Finding a box of watches unclaimed at the station where he worked, he had offered to buy them cheaply from the manufacturer. Then he had advertised them for sale in a local newspaper and had sold them all by mail, making a nice profit. Since then he had experimented with other products—including baking powder—and he had concluded that he could entice people to send away for just about anything. Twice a year he published a two-hundred-page catalog with colorful, folksy descriptions that he wrote himself of items he was selling—clothes, jewelry, watches, sewing machines. He purchased enormous quantities of these goods and so kept his prices low. And orders poured in; sometimes as many as two thousand arrived at his downtown Chicago office in one day. Richard Sears said that he was working from seven in the morning until eleven at night, but he could not handle all the orders. He admitted to Nusbaum that, often, he didn't even have on hand the merchandise he advertised, and what he did have was stocked so haphazardly he couldn't find it. His office was chaotic; his eighty-member staff was disorganized; his own understanding of business finance was minimal; and the whole situation was making his partner, a watch repairman named Alvah Roebuck, so uneasy that he wanted out. Richard Sears needed cash to invest in his company, and he desperately needed the help of an astute business partner.

In August, Nusbaum went to see his brother-in-law, Julius Rosenwald, and told him that Sears had offered him the chance to become that partner. Aaron had agreed to pay $75,000 for a half interest in Sears, Roebuck and Company, but he was having second thoughts. It was a huge investment—more than $1 million in today's terms. Another brother-in-law had turned Aaron down, so he had gone to Julius. Did he want to go in with him and become a part owner of Sears?

Rosenwald already had a lot on his mind. His father's powerful presence in the family had been suddenly diminished when he suffered a stroke that left him paralyzed and bedridden. His mother was caring for her husband at home. Gussie could not help much because in May she had another baby, a little girl to whom she and Julius gave the fashionable name Edith. Rosenwald was now the father of three. In addition to increased family responsibilities, he had to worry about the economy; it was bad nationwide, which made business flat and uncertain. Nonetheless, in the midst of all that, he had expanded by becoming a Chicago distributor for a New York clothing manufacturing firm run by his friend from his days in New York, Mo Newborg. While Gussie wondered whether they could really afford the extra girl she had hired to help her care for the new baby, Rosenwald was traveling back and forth to New York, working out the details of his new company.

Still, Julius Rosenwald immediately recognized what has since been proved true beyond anything he could have imagined—mail order was a concept with a future. He knew the limitations of the small country stores where so many people had to shop for clothes and everything else and the high prices that these stores often charged. He knew that as manufacturing boomed, new products were appearing all the time and that, when they did, people wanted them. The Chicago-based company Montgomery Ward was making a success with a mail-order business that catered to farmers and members of the farmers' fraternal order, the Grange. And, finally, he knew that Richard Sears had bought a large number of suits from Rosenwald & Weil and owed him money. Rosenwald could accept Nusbaum's offer without having to come up with the full amount for his share in cash. He later wrote that buying into Sears was "a decision made and acted on in five minutes." That it proved such a spectacularly sound one was "a lucky chance."

On August 13, 1895, Richard Sears, Aaron Nusbaum, and Julius Rosenwald signed the papers that made them partners. Sears remained the company president and owner of half the stock; he had bought back Alvah Roebuck's share and had paid for the right to continue using his name. Nusbaum became treasurer and general manager. And Rosenwald, like his brother-in-law, a quarter owner of the company, said he would join the other two in running Sears as soon as he could free himself of his commitments to his other businesses.

By the time Julius came to work at Sears, Roebuck and Company at the end of the following year, the economy had improved, and Congress had given mail order a nice boost when it created Rural Free Delivery, expanding and improving mail service to areas outside of cities. The ever-thicker and more enticing Sears catalog would soon be on kitchen tables in farmhouses all across the country. And thanks to Richard Sears's ingenuity, it would be just a little smaller than the Montgomery Ward catalog. People would tend to place it on top.

That same summer, of 1895, Booker T. Washington was asked to speak at the ceremony that would open the Cotton States and International Exposition, a huge fair in Atlanta similar to the Chicago World's Columbian Exposition but with a focus on the South and the progress it had made in business, agriculture, and the arts since the devastation of the Civil War. Unlike the Chicago fair, it would feature a separate "Negro Building." Washington had sidestepped the issue of whether contributions by blacks should have been included in the various pavilions rather than shown separately by turning down the invitation to be in charge of planning for the segregated display. He said he was too busy. But the speech was another matter: it was an honor and an opportunity. His audience would be large, and it would include important civic and business leaders. He would be the only black among the speakers. What he said would be noticed. Like Rosenwald when he decided to buy into Sears, Washington could not know that this speech would be, for him, a life-changing event.

He knew that it was going to be hard for him to strike the tone he so valued, one that was honest and strong, true to the aspirations of blacks, yet inoffensive to white southerners. Certainly, some of the audience would be eager to hear from him, and some would be simply curious about how a black man would conduct himself and what he might say. There would be others, though, who would not consider allowing blacks out of the inferior social, economic, and political position they had always occupied in the South. Those people would be extremely sensitive to any hint of presumption of equality on his part. Tuskegee depended on the goodwill of whites, both its neighbors and its many donors, and Washington knew it would be unwise to risk offending them. Blacks themselves would be in a segregated seating area. There, men and women who had struggled mightily in the years of their freedom to create stable lives for themselves and their families would be listening as well, looking to him for leadership, seeing in the presence on the stage of Booker T. Washington the validation of their own hopes for becoming real citizens, and looking to him for leadership. The speech was a challenge as much as an opportunity.

As Washington traveled to Atlanta with his wife and the three children (Portia was twelve, Booker Jr. was eight, and Davidson was six), they passed through Tuskegee, where Booker had a quick conversation with a white farmer who joked that he certainly had gotten himself into a "tight place." Washington later said he felt "as I suppose a man feels when he is on his way to the gallows." The night before the speech, he could not sleep.

September 18 was a sunny, hot day in Atlanta. The procession to the fairgrounds took several hours, and by the time he got there, Washington recalled later, "the heat, together with my nervous anxiety, made me feel as if I were about ready to collapse." His new friend, William Baldwin Jr., a white trustee of Tuskegee Institute, was so uncertain about how the crowd might react to the speech that he paced around outside the pavilion rather than going inside to listen. When the speakers for the opening ceremony walked on stage, a huge audience cheered. One man remembered that the warm applause quieted as Booker T. Washington walked out on the stage and took his seat. "A sudden chill," he wrote, "fell upon the whole assemblage."

When his time came to speak, Washington displayed no nervousness. Despite the afternoon sun that was shining brightly in his eyes, he delivered his five-minute speech in a steady voice. Noting that black people made up a third of the population of the South, he talked about friendship and mutual aid between white people and black people as a goal that would benefit all southerners. He mentioned the importance for people who had been slaves to learn the skills of running their own farms and businesses. And speaking of the progress blacks had already made in the transition from slavery to independence, he alluded to the help of "Northern philanthropists, who have made their gifts a constant stream of blessing and encouragement."

Then Washington told a story—a parable that he and others had often used about a ship that was lost at sea and had run out of drinking water. It signaled for help to a passing ship. The word came back from the other vessel: "Cast down your bucket where you are!" To the surprise of the thirsting crew, the water around them, flowing from the mouth of a huge river, was fresh. Help was actually right there where they were. Repeating this image again and again, and alluding obliquely to the influx into all parts of the United States of workers from abroad, and the labor disturbances many had come to fear, Washington urged his white listeners to "cast down your bucket among these people who have, without strikes and labor wars, tilled your fields, cleared your forests, built your railroads and cities and brought forth treasures from the bowels of the earth and helped make possible this magnificent representation of the progress of the South." Unlike recent arrivals "of foreign birth and strange tongue and habits," he said, blacks had again and again proved themselves "patient, faithful, law-abiding and unresentful."

The subject that was trickiest for Washington—because it was so intensely, irrationally emotional for many white southerners—was that of social relations between the races, but he did not shy away from it. Again, he used a vivid image, one he had used before (and that President Rutherford B. Hayes had used in a speech at Hampton in 1880 when Washington quite likely heard it). "In all things that are purely social we can be as separate as the fingers," he said, holding up his hand with his fingers spread wide apart, "yet one as the hand in all things essential to mutual progress." Then he dramatically closed his hand into a fist. He wanted people to know he was not there to push for changes that scared many whites; he was not calling for an end to the customs that decreed, for example, that whites not entertain blacks in their homes. "The opportunity to earn a dollar in a factory just now is worth infinitely more than the opportunity to spend a dollar in an opera house." Affirming his belief that "racial animosities and suspicions" would slowly disappear and be replaced by "a determination to administer absolute justice . . . a willing obedience among all classes to the mandates of law," Washington expressed confidence in the rosy future of "our beloved South."

The man who had noted the quiet that greeted Washington's appearance on the stage described what happened at the end of the speech: "When the Negro finished, such an ovation followed as I had never seen before and never expect to see again." Cheers, whistles, shouts, and applause filled the hall. The governor of Georgia rushed across the platform to shake Washington's hand. Writing in the *New York World*, the Canadian journalist James Creelman noted that "most of the Negroes in the audience were crying, perhaps without knowing just why." He quoted the white editor of the *Atlanta Constitution* as exulting, "That man's speech is the beginning of a moral revolution in America." Creelman himself said it had "electrified the audience, and the response was as if it had come from the throat of a whirlwind."

Initially, reaction to Washington's speech was overwhelmingly positive. A young professor at Wilberforce University in Ohio, a college friend of Margaret Washington's named W. E. B. Du Bois, wrote a brief note congratulating Washington on his "phenomenal success" and calling the speech "a word fitly spoken." Mary Stearns, a wealthy white Bostonian who had helped Olivia Davidson financially and who corresponded regularly with Washington, ranked it with Lincoln's Gettysburg Address and emotionally assured him that "Olivia was with you yesterday." A black teacher from Tennessee, William J. Cansler, wrote congratulating Washington, calling him "our Moses destined to lead our race out of the difficulties and dangers which beset our pathway and surround us on all sides." Frederick Douglass had died six months before the Atlanta speech, and Cansler concluded his letter by assuring Washington, "Upon you has fallen the mantle of the illustrious Douglas[s]." Washington's good friend T. Thomas Fortune, a prominent black journalist in New York, also made the comparison, writing, "It looks as if you are our Douglass and I am glad of it." He also asked Washington if he couldn't "see your way to using the term Afro American."

But later, in the light of unfolding events, some blacks acknowledged feeling uneasy about Washington's apparent willingness to accept inferior social status, reduced access to the ballot box, and even worse on their behalf. They began to distance themselves from Booker T. Washington, and one of them, W. E. B. Du Bois, would derisively dub the speech "the Atlanta Compromise," a name it has retained in many minds.

Washington's optimism was certainly genuine, but the rosy picture of race relations he had evoked was negated the very next day when his twelve-year-old daughter witnessed an ugly episode. Portia left Atlanta by train headed to Boston, where she was in school, chaperoned by R. W. Taylor, a Tuskegee graduate who had returned to teach there and who assisted Washington with northern speaking and fund-raising duties. Portia and Taylor took seats on the train facing each other, with Taylor riding backward. When the conductor came around, he ordered

Taylor to sit facing forward. "I told him that I preferred riding back wards," Taylor later wrote to William Baldwin, a Tuskegee board member and president of the Southern Railway. The conductor responded that he cared nothing for the passenger's preference. He punched his tickets and then, abruptly, grabbed him around the neck, struck him in the face, and kicked him "until passengers from different parts of the car ran around him and the disgraceful scene was closed." Taylor said he had been "humiliated, disgraced."

A week later William Baldwin wrote to Washington saying the conductor had been suspended from duty pending an investigation and that Baldwin himself would "take proper steps to see that such a disgraceful scene will not occur again." And he congratulated Washington on his speech, noting, "I have heard nothing but praise for your speech and your philosophy."

The following spring, Washington was invited to Harvard's commencement, where he would be the first black man ever to receive an honorary degree from the country's most prestigious university (which would also be honoring Alexander Graham Bell for his invention of the telephone). The prolonged applause that greeted him there was a powerful indication of his new fame. With the humor that he often used to defuse racial tension, he began his remarks by telling the majority white crowd that in front of them he felt like "a huckleberry in a bowl of milk."

But in the wood-paneled magnificence of Harvard's Sanders Theatre, he continued with deadly serious words of tragic prescience. "In the economy of God there is but one standard by which an individual can succeed . . . This country demands that every race shall measure itself by the American standard . . . During the next half-century and more, my race must continue passing through the severe American crucible," he told the crowd. "We are to be tested in our patience, our forbearance, our perseverance, our power to endure wrong, to withstand temptations, to economize, to acquire and use skill; in our ability to compete, to succeed in commerce, to disregard the superficial for the real, the appearance for the substance, to be great and yet small, learned and yet simple, high and yet the servant of all. This, this is the passport to all that is best in the life of our republic, and the Negro must possess it, or be debarred." With the fervor of a preacher, Washington affirmed that the time was coming when "both races in the South, soon shall throw off the shackles of racial and sectional prejudice and rise . . . as we all should rise, above the clouds of ignorance, narrowness and selfishness, into that atmosphere, that pure sunshine, where it will be our highest ambition to serve man, our brother, regardless of race or previous condition." The phrase "our republic" told the privileged white men of his audience that Washington and they shared the same national identity. His focus on service reminded them of the radical inclusiveness and humility of the Christian message. They would remember that Christ himself had been identified as the suffering servant.

With his forceful personality, optimistic attitude, and ingratiating manners, Washington was, himself, the engine driving the impressive early growth of Tuskegee Institute, which by 1900 had fourteen hundred students and a hundred instructors (among them the brilliant agronomist George Washington Carver) and was one of the largest educational institutions in the South, one of the few to offer coeducation. While his Sunday evening chapel talks and his impromptu visits to the school's dining halls encouraged his students and faculty, and a steady stream of personal letters thanked small donors, the way he cultivated people of power and affluence brought the school national recognition and essential financial support. On his frequent trips north, he sought out meetings with wealthy individuals so he could tell them about Tuskegee's work, always emphasizing the most recent developments— the new buildings being raised by student labor, the success of the student-run farm, progress at the model school. He met Robert Ogden, a wealthy white trustee of Hampton whom General Armstrong had told about Tuskegee and who, in 1901, brought a train car full of prominent, wealthy men to see it and other southern schools, both black and white. He cultivated William H. Baldwin, general manager of the Southern Railway, who became a good friend, and the banker George Foster Peabody, who became an active trustee. He brought Julia Ward Howe, the author of "The Battle Hymn of the Republic," to visit and, in 1899, even entertained the president of the United States, William McKinley, with a parade and pageant in his honor. The American flags that flew on campus for that occasion were the first that had been seen in the town of Tuskegee since before the Civil War.

But despite all the undeniably good things happening at Tuskegee, as the nineteenth century gave way to the twentieth, conditions for black Americans were getting not better but worse. Grimly determined reaction was eroding the unruly, uneven hopefulness of the Reconstruction years, when former slaves had taken their first steps toward freedom, leaving their places of bondage, voting in large numbers, electing representatives to Congress, and eagerly sending their children to newly established public schools.

Beginning in 1889, all the southern states rewrote their constitutions, creating various ways to keep blacks from exercising the voting rights they had been ensured by the Fourteenth and Fifteenth amendments: literacy tests, poll taxes, property requirements, character assessment, grandfather clauses restricting voting to descendents of men who had voted three generations earlier, primaries for whites only, ballots that were deliberately made confusing. Often the changes were justified as necessary to clean up the dirty politics that, depending on one's point of view, may have been the result of the Democrats' desperate attempts to hold on to power as large numbers of blacks (who generally voted Republican) entered the electorate. In Virginia a delegate to the constitutional convention noted ironically that, by rewriting its constitution, his state was denying the rights of blacks "to prevent the Democratic election officials from stealing their votes." The future Alabama senator Tom Heflin told the constitutional convention, "I believe as truly as I believe that I am standing here that God Almighty intended the negro to be the servant of the white man." And the president of the convention asserted that, in fact, the "true philosophy of the movement was to establish restricted suffrage and to place the power of government in the hands of the intelligent and virtuous." This did not include poor whites or females of either race any more than it did blacks.

An 1898 challenge to the new constitution of Mississippi made it to the Supreme Court but lost there. The *Boston Evening Transcript* editorialized that disfranchisement was "the policy of the Administration of the very party which carried the country into and through a civil war to free the slaves." An article in the *Nation* placed the disfranchising movement in the context of the brief 1898 American war with Spain and the subsequent annexation of Puerto Rico, the Philippines, and Guam, reporting that it was "an interesting coincidence that this important decision is rendered at a time when we are considering the idea of taking in a varied assortment of inferior races in different parts of the world." The implication was clear—the countries being annexed included nonwhite people who were not being invited to become voters. By 1902, when Virginia changed its rules, black voting throughout the South had dropped dramatically, and withholding the vote from the vast majority of southern black voters had become more or less an accepted policy, producing occasional outrage in the press and discussion in Congress but no effective challenges.

In 1896, racial fairness was dealt another blow when the U.S. Supreme Court affirmed the right of states to maintain laws enforcing separation of blacks and whites in railroad cars and other public places. "If one race be inferior to the other socially," the Court opined in *Plessy v. Ferguson*, "the Constitution of the United States cannot put them upon the same plane." This view treated the inferiority of the black race, or at least the widespread assumption that inferiority existed, as a fact that could not be legislated away. Soon, the legal regimen of separate but equal would extend to a whole range of facilities—hotels, restaurants and public schools, water fountains and restrooms. The two races, kept apart for long years mostly by custom, could be required to stay that way by laws made and enforced by white people and seldom, if ever, providing anything close to equal facilities for blacks.

All these dispiriting changes, which collectively created the system of racial segregation informally called Jim Crow, were taking place against a background not just of prejudice but also of horrifying anti-black violence. Even in places where they could legally vote, blacks had often been kept away from the polls by intimidation and scare tactics. The Ku Klux Klan, created by veterans of the Confederate Army just after the Civil War to keep newly liberated blacks "in their place," had been largely suppressed in the 1870s (although it would reemerge in the twentieth century), but in states with large percentages of black people, white people's irrational fear of them lingered. Many poor whites felt threatened by real or imagined competition from blacks. Black churches and schools often mysteriously burned down. Even in the town of Tuskegee racial feelings could be explosive. Early in the summer of 1895 a black lawyer who had interacted in a friendly way with a visiting white preacher had been confronted by an angry mob and injured in a shootout. He escaped and ran to the Tuskegee Institute, to the door of Booker T. Washington's home. Washington was able to make sure the man was spirited away to safety, and later that night, when the mob showed up outside his house, he dispersed it by claiming that he had turned the man away. There was some criticism of him in the black press for this, but he ignored it. As always, he was treading a fine line between factions.

Mobs were not always so easily routed. Starting the year after Tuskegee's founding, librarians and students had been collecting newspaper clippings about lynching—the brutal form of vigilante "justice" meted out by mobs against individuals accused of crime, real, assumed, or imagined. When the archive began, more whites than blacks were lynched each year, but as time went by, the victims, more and more, were black men. Often, they were accused of being insolent to a white person or, worse, of raping a white woman. They were chased down by mobs or dragged from jail cells, sometimes tortured, and then killed, hanged from a tree or burned alive, mutilated and jeered at while crowds of otherwise normal-seeming white people looked on. The mob leaders were never arrested and never prosecuted. The newspaper articles and reports that piled up in the Tuskegee archives showed a hundred or so such crimes for each year. In 1895, the year of Washington's Atlanta speech, 113 blacks were reported lynched in the American South.

"Whites' pursuit of superior status over blacks provides the most basic explanation for the relentless discrimination and exploitation of African Americans in the United States," wrote the historian Robert Norrell. But the cultural breakdown that permits mob violence comes from an even deeper, more complex source. Slavery had been disastrous for both races. It deprived blacks first of their homeland, language, and culture, then of the right to live and learn as others did. Family ties were hard or impossible to maintain; schools were nonexistent. Slavery encouraged whites to blind themselves to the immorality of the arrangement that allowed many of them to grow rich and to think of their black slaves as intrinsically inferior. The excruciating upheaval of rebellion and war left the South humiliated and in ruins; it created feelings of guilt and resentment for many whites and economic devastation for members of both races. Even one positive legacy of Reconstruction—the public school systems that some states created at that time—was subverted by whites who were unwilling to send their children to school with blacks and, in many cases, actively hostile to any education at all for them. The 1890s were a time of economic downturn and widespread unemployment. And always, and perhaps most fundamentally, the human capacity for fearing and despising the "other"—be he or she black, Jewish, or poor; a speaker of a foreign tongue; or just in some way different or strange—was and is a tragic constant.

CHAPTER 4

X

"You Need a Schoolhouse"

In the summer of 1899 in South Georgia, two thousand frenzied whites burned to death a twenty-one-year-old black man at the end of a manhunt encouraged by incendiary newspaper accounts of the murder of his employer and the supposed rape of the employer's wife. The murder later appeared to be self-defense; the rape charge, denied, was never proved. The place where the man, Sam Hose, was killed became a gruesome pilgrimage site. His knuckle bones were offered for sale in an Atlanta shop. When asked to comment on this ghastly episode, Washington relied on a familiar catechism. Rather than speak out in general against the horror of lynching, he told a reporter that there was a "permanent cure for such outrages" and that it was to be found in education. In another interview he made note of the fact that "peace and harmony between the two races" depended not just on widespread education for blacks but on education for whites as well. "I have invariably found," he said in an interview, "that it is the ignorant and poorly educated white people who are inclined to turn up their noses at the negro ... [T]he ignorant and poor white man, whether North or South, seems to have a certain amount of contempt for the negro, while the prosperous and intelligent white man is much more inclined to treat the negro in the way that one man treats another."

Similarly, in a letter to two New Orleans newspapers in 1898 arguing that limitations in the new state constitution on voting must be fairly applied to the ignorant of both races, Washington wrote, "Any law controlling the ballot that is not absolutely just and fair to both races, will work more permanent injury to the whites than to the blacks." Sounding a theme that was dear to his heart, he wrote, "I beg of you, further, that in the degree that you close the ballot-box against the ignorant, that you open the schoolhouse."

The formulation of the question varied, but the answer Booker T. Washington gave was almost always the same. When he was asked what the greatest need was for black Americans, he always replied not rights or greater freedom but education. Rights, he said, mean little without the capacity to understand and make use of them. The first step up the ladder of self-improvement, inevitably, he felt, was education.

Washington did speak out powerfully against white racism, though, in October 1898. At a celebration in Chicago marking the end of the war with Spain, in front of a crowd of sixteen thousand people that included Rabbi Hirsch of Temple Sinai and President William McKinley, Washington noted that the military victory of the United States had been achieved with the help of black troops. "There remains one other victory for Americans to win," he said, "a victory as far reaching and important as any that has occupied our army and navy. We have succeeded in every conflict, except the effort to con-quer ourselves in the blotting out of racial prejudices . . . Until we thus conquer ourselves, I make no empty statement when I say that we shall have, especially in the Southern part of our country, a cancer growing at the heart of the Republic, that shall one day prove as dangerous as an attack from an army without or within." Washington softened the effect of these strong words by ending his speech with an affirmation of patriotism. "Whether in war or in peace, whether in slavery or in freedom, we have always been loyal to the Stars and Stripes," he said, prompting such wild cheering that, according to a newspaper account, it made "the very columns of the massive building tremble."

The *Atlanta Constitution*, ignoring his prediction of trouble to come, accused him of grandstanding. "When he escapes from the enthusiasm of Chicago and returns to the regular performance of routine duty in Tuskegee," the paper wrote, "he will take a more practical view of the situation."

A year later, in an interview with the *Memphis Commercial Appeal*, Washington noted, "Within six years almost as many people were lynched in the Southern states as the number of soldiers who lost their lives in the Spanish American war in Cuba." Asked if he foresaw a time when a black man would be president of the United States, he replied, "I should hope so."

With his relentless schedule of speeches and fund-raising tours added to the work of running Tuskegee, with the stress of living in the tension between hope and realism (or, as the historian Robert Norrell has put it, being always "on a tightrope between candor and survival"), Booker T. Washington was worn out. In 1899, Tuskegee's trustees collected a fund to send him and Maggie on a four-month vacation trip to Europe, where neither of them had ever been. During the weeklong Atlantic crossing on the liner *Friesland,* and for several weeks after that, Washington slowly shed his exhaustion by sleeping for fifteen hours each night. He was not too tired, though, to appreciate the pleasure of being at sea; the relief of being comfortably accepted in social situations on the ship; and once he arrived in Europe, the beauty and charm of Holland's quaint cities and canals, the history and hubbub of Paris and London. "Art . . . gayity [*sic*] . . . beggars . . . cheating . . . excitement," were among the traits of Paris he listed in notes for a speech. "Greatness of London, law and order (cabs), Parliament (no humor), [and] no soda fountains (no ice)" were on the list of observations about England.

Everywhere, Washington's fame was apparent from the prominent people who were eager to meet him. In The Hague it was Seth Low, the president of Columbia University, who was there as part of a delegation to an international peace conference. In Paris, former U.S. president Benjamin Harrison had a dinner for the Washingtons. In England, they met the author Mark Twain and saw the American suffragist Susan B. Anthony, whose friend and neighbor Emily Howland was an educator and a frequent correspondent of Washington's. And they were honored to be invited to meet the person who literally personified the age in which they all lived, the dignified old woman who had been sovereign of England for sixty years—Queen Victoria. She invited Dr. and Mrs. Washington to tea at Windsor Castle. "Seeing the Queen" was the last item on Washington's list in his notes. In a thank-you note to one of the contributors to their trip, Maggie said that they had "feasted our souls in England's hospitality and beauty" and that they had enjoyed tea in the banquet hall with "the dear old Queen."

Every Sunday evening at Tuskegee, students and faculty attended a chapel service where, when he was on the campus, Washington did his own style of preaching. He spoke about events of the past week, introduced visitors, and encouraged positive attitudes and habits— cleanliness, sobriety, thrift, and reading. He recommended newspapers, magazines, books of history and biography, as well as the Bible. He also talked to the students about the lives that many of them would lead when they became teachers.

"You need a schoolhouse," he said in one talk. Describing the conditions he had faced himself and that he knew many young men and women would experience as they went out from Tuskegee into the rural South, he said, "You cannot teach school in log cabins without doors, windows, lights, floor or apparatus. You need a schoolhouse and, if you are in earnest, the people will help you."

He reminded Tuskegee students that men and women whom they did not know were donating money to the institute because they were convinced of the importance of its mission (and he spent a great deal of time writing personal thank-you letters to each one of them). The education they were receiving, he told them, would benefit not just them, and not just the individual students they would teach, but whole communities. "Go out and be a center," he continued, "a life-giving power as it were to the whole community, to give life where there is not life, hope where there is no hope, power where there is no power."

The turn of the century saw Washington's fame increase with the publication of his autobiography. He wrote it at the request of *McClure's* magazine and with the help of a white journalist, Max Bennett Thrasher, who did public relations work for Tuskegee and who often traveled with Washington. While riding on the train together, the two men batted around ideas. Thrasher took notes; Washington wrote them up. The work that resulted from this collaboration, *Up from*

Slavery, was published in installments in *McClure's* from November 1900 to February 1901.

Washington used simple language and a straightforward style to tell the story of his life. His chapter titles were vivid: "A Slave Among Slaves," "The Struggle for an Education," "Teaching School in a Stable and a Hen-House," "Anxious Days and Sleepless Nights," "Two Thousand Miles for a Five Minute Speech." It was typical of the time in which he was writing that Washington said much about his work and public life and little about his private feelings. Of the two wives he had lost, of Portia and his young sons, he said little. He dedicated the book to his third wife, Margaret, and to his brother John Washington, "whose patience, fidelity and hard work have gone far to make the work at Tuskegee successful." The book was also typical of the time in its emphasis on character and hard work as the building blocks for success. Throughout the book, Washington sounded a characteristic note of optimism. "Despite superficial and temporary signs which might lead one to entertain a contrary opinion, there was never a time when I felt more hopeful for the race than I do at present." It is hard to imagine that this was true, but it was Washington's official line.

Thirty thousand copies of *Up from Slavery* were sold in its first two years, and it was translated into a dozen languages. Mary Mackie, the woman who had admitted Booker to Hampton, wrote to him that her sister, a teacher, was reading the book aloud to her students and that it "sets forth more graphically than any article that I have read the transition of life from slavery to freedom. It reads like a romance." A review by the prominent novelist and *Atlantic Monthly* columnist William Dean Howells praised it, saying that its author "has lived heroic poetry, and he can, therefore, afford to talk simple prose."

Since its publication, *Up from Slavery* has never been out of print. It brought Washington even more fame and recognition than he had before. People not only knew of his work but also felt that they were acquainted with the man himself. Wealthy men read the book and found their sympathies aroused. Booker T. Washington, they discovered, was a self-made man; he had come from humble beginnings, had worked hard and single-mindedly to achieve his goals, and had succeeded. It helped them to see that, in some ways, he was not unlike themselves.

When a youthful Theodore Roosevelt became president in September 1901, after a self-proclaimed anarchist shot William McKinley, one of his first acts was to write to Washington. "When are you coming north?" he asked. "I must see you as soon as possible. I want to talk over the question of possible future appointments in the South, exactly on the lines of our last conversation."

Roosevelt and Washington had met on several occasions, and as vice president, Roosevelt had been planning to visit Tuskegee. Despite the obvious, wide differences in their backgrounds, the two men shared much. They were both moralistic and energetic, and they loved the outdoors. Roosevelt was from a wealthy, distinguished New York family, a willful, exuberant man of strong intellect and wide-ranging experience and interests, the same age as Washington. He had become a popular hero as leader of the Rough Riders, the regiment that captured San Juan Hill outside Santiago during the war in Cuba. Roosevelt valued Washington's knowledge of southern society, in which he was anxious to shore up support for the Republican Party. He would rely on Washington's guidance when he wanted to appoint blacks to federal jobs. And Washington was attracted by Roosevelt's personal charisma and by his political power.

In October 1901, Washington traveled to the capital city and, at Roosevelt's invitation, had dinner at the White House with him; his wife, Edith; and their children. A newspaper pointed out the next day, "Washington is probably the first American negro to dine with a president of the United States and his family" (although it was reported that President Cleveland once entertained a black friend at the White House board). Soon the press, especially in the South, was inflamed with negative commentary. Some writers complained that the president and Washington had planned the dinner for the express purpose of flouting the long-established norms of social behavior that kept the races apart. According to the Memphis *Scimitar* it was "the most damnable outrage ever perpetrated by any citizen of the United States." The *Richmond Times* interpreted the invitation to mean that "the President is willing that Negroes shall mingle freely with whites in the social circle and that white women may receive attentions from Negro men." The pronouncements of Senator Ben Tillman of South Carolina are painful to quote: "The action of President Roosevelt in entertaining that nigger will necessitate our killing a thousand niggers in the South before they learn their place again." The Mississippi governor James Vardaman was still raging crudely about the incident two years later. Reporters pestered Washington with requests for interviews about the dinner, but he refused them all.

The uproar did not change the outcome of the dinner, though, which was to increase Washington's prestige in many quarters and his behind-the-scenes influence with the president. The day after the dinner, in fact, Washington wrote to Roosevelt suggesting a black man of his acquaintance who could offer insight into conditions in Mississippi. Shortly after that, Washington and Roosevelt were together again when both received honorary degrees at Yale University. They remained on cordial terms and exchanged frequent letters, but the relationship would prove to be a tricky one, and there were no more invitations for Washington to dine at the White House.

The increasing prominence of Washington's public profile paralleled heightened skepticism of him in certain sectors of the black community. One place where he came in for repeated criticism was a new weekly newspaper, the *Boston Guardian*, whose editor, William Monroe Trotter, an acerbic black Harvard graduate (and the first black to earn a Phi Beta Kappa key), used the paper to push for better conditions for blacks and to relentlessly criticize Washington. In 1902, Washington was infuriated to read in one of Trotter's editorials implied criticism of his daughter, Portia, for not returning to Wellesley College, where she had enrolled the year before. Washington's children, the editor wrote, "are not taking to higher education like a duck to water, and while their defect in this line is doubtless somewhat inherited, they justify to some extent their father's well known antipathy to anything higher than the three R's for his 'people.'" Trotter's dismissive remark was a crude caricature of Washington's attitude toward higher education for blacks. Washington's sons were, in fact, not in college because they were too young. And his emphasis on the value of the industrial education offered at Tuskegee and elsewhere had never been a rejection of university education.

It was true that Portia was leaving Wellesley, where she had enrolled after being unhappy as a student at Tuskegee. As the daughter of the founder she felt conspicuous there; she struggled with chemistry, taught by the famous scientist George Washington Carver, and hated her dressmaking course. She told an interviewer in Boston that her father was "very anxious to have me attend college. He believes in college education of girls where it is possible for them to have it and my mother, you know, is a graduate of Fisk University." But having escaped to Wellesley, she found that she was not fully prepared for the academic work there and was socially isolated in the all-white school. She later transferred to Bradford Academy, a Massachusetts private school that admitted her because of the fame of her father (despite a precedent of accepting neither blacks nor Jews). She did well there pursuing her real interest, which was music.

Public opposition to Washington continued the next year when W. E. B. Du Bois, then a sociology professor at Atlanta University (he had been offered a job at Tuskegee but had declined), published a slim, eloquent book of essays called *The Souls of Black Folk* that criticized the Tuskegee founder, "the most distinguished southerner since Jefferson Davis," for his "silent submission to civic inferiority" and for not using his prominent position to push harder for black access to colleges and universities. The emphasis on industrial education, Du Bois wrote, was admirable, but it was not enough, and it demeaned blacks by not assuming that they, like others, could aim higher than careers as artisans and manual laborers. Washington's attitude, Du Bois asserted, was making blacks once again into "a servile caste." No amount of their own effort could change their status unless whites accepted them and also worked for change. "We have no right," Du Bois wrote, "to sit silently by while the inevitable seeds are sown for a harvest of disaster to our children, black and white." For a short while longer Du Bois and Washington remained on more or less friendly terms despite their differences, but that would soon change.

Monroe Trotter's opposition to Washington was less elegant and thoughtful than Du Bois's. In July 1903, Washington addressed the National Negro Business League, of which he was president, at a meeting held at a black church in Boston. Having packed the audience with his supporters, Trotter confronted Washington with a mocking tone and hostile questions, the last of which was, "Is the rope and the torch all the race is to get under your leadership?" But the words were scarcely heard in the midst of heckling, booing, and rowdy disorder that erupted when Washington was introduced. It became so bad that Trotter was arrested and charged with disturbing the peace (for which he subsequently served thirty days in jail). Washington finally completed his planned speech, but the episode was a nasty indication of the growing opposition to him and his leadership.

Still, he managed to get Du Bois to come to a small conference he quietly put together in January 1904 in New York City, a meeting he hoped would affirm his role as spokesman for those who wanted to articulate a shared vision of future action to promote black progress. The meetings were heated, and although the final resolution signed by the conferees expressed support for "industrial" education, it also affirmed the absolute necessity of the right to vote and of the repeal of laws restricting the rights of blacks. But when it came time to move forward with the conference's proposal for ongoing meetings and committee work, Du Bois withdrew. Instead, in the summer of 1905, Du Bois gathered together a group of thirty black intellectuals (that included Monroe Trotter) for a meeting in Canada to found the Niagara Movement for the purpose of, among other things, publicly pushing for black voting rights and opposing the leadership of Booker T. Washington. The declaration of principles issued at the end of the meeting stated, "We refuse to allow the impression to remain that the Negro American assents to inferiority."

In fact, far from silently assenting to inferiority, Washington had privately paid for a legal challenge to Alabama's competency requirement for voting. A black Alabaman, Jackson W. Giles, had claimed that he was being denied the right to vote because of his difficulty in registering in the wake of changes made in the state constitution in 1901. The case of *Giles v. Harris* went all the way to the Supreme Court but lost there. The Court found that the rights that were abridged were political rather than legal in nature and that it was, thus, a question for the state legislature to answer. On another occasion, Washington paid to have his personal lawyer, Wilford H. Smith, take the case of a convicted black man to the Supreme Court, where it was overturned on the grounds that the defendant's "peers" included none of the qualified blacks who had been in the jury pool. It was only Washington's closest associates, however, who knew of these activities.

While Washington's moderate stance was drawing fire from black intellectuals, he continued to win the admiration and support of prominent
whites. Among these was America's (and, possibly, the world's) richest man, Andrew Carnegie. He had worked his way up from childhood
poverty in Scotland to an extraordinary fortune in American manufacturing. Believing that wealthy men had a responsibility to use their
money to benefit others, Carnegie once said, "The man who dies rich,
dies disgraced." More than a thousand public library buildings all across
the country were the result of this philosophy. Washington's work at
Tuskegee had attracted Carnegie's interest, and Carnegie had donated
first a library and then, impressed with how low the cost had been (students had made the bricks and constructed the building), he followed
up with a pledge of $10,000 for the school's operating expenses, had
covered the costs of Washington's New York conference, and had made
a major gift to Tuskegee's endowment fund. Part of it, he said, was to be
used for the personal expenses of Booker T. Washington. Embarrassed
by this arrangement, Washington asked Carnegie to change the terms
of his gift to say that funds for his benefit would be distributed to him
at the discretion of the Tuskegee trustees.

Becoming a wealthy man had never been Washington's main goal,
but he could now live as one. In the summer of 1904 he paid for a trip
to Europe for his brother John and for Lewis Adams, one of the original
trustees of Tuskegee. That summer Washington and Maggie took a second trip to Europe. The following year he sent Portia, who had become
a serious musician, to study piano in Berlin (albeit with frequent
fatherly letters reminding her to keep her expenses down). He sent
Booker Jr. briefly to Phillips Exeter Academy in New Hampshire where
his namesake charmed everyone but also, like many another child of
the middle class, got into trouble for neglecting his studies; smoking in
his room; and on one occasion, coming back to his dormitory through
the window after curfew. His father stayed in close touch with Booker
Jr. via letters, gently urging him to be careful with his money, to spend
time on Sunday reading the sermons he sent him, and to attend to
his studies, signing himself "Your papa, BTW." He also sent him the
tennis racquet and balls, the football and the protective headgear
his son requested, even indulging him in the motorcycle he wanted.
"Be careful," he wrote Booker Jr. in May 1907, "and do not make the

mistake of spending too much time on your motorcycle. I want your mark to be higher this month even than it was last month." Booker Jr. entered Fisk University in 1908. Meanwhile, Washington's younger son, Davidson, now called Dave, studied at the Tuskegee model school, then went to an academy in Ohio. He was not a good student, and his father wrote to the school's principal that he had "never learned to study and he has been made a pet and a baby of by everyone in our family and on the school grounds." Still, Washington wrote his son encouraging letters. "Try to write legibly," he wrote in one. "There are many words on your present letter that I can hardly make out. I think it would be better for you to use paper that has lines on it." In another he urged him to attend church regularly and even to teach Sunday school. "Be sure to take plenty of good open air exercise every day," Washington wrote to Dave. "Do not try to take more than two studies, otherwise your health will break down." Dave did, eventually, graduate from Tuskegee and go on to college.

And Washington built himself a gracious home, the Oaks, across the road from the Tuskegee campus. The trustees insisted that the house be a large one because it was there that the Washingtons entertained the school's many visitors. And, in any case, Washington felt that appearances were important. "I have found," he wrote in *Up from Slavery*, "that it is the visible, the tangible, that goes a long way in softening racial prejudices. The actual sight of a first class house that a Negro has built is ten times more potent than pages of discussion about a home that he ought to build or, perhaps, could build." The Oaks was designed by Robert Robinson Taylor, the first black man to graduate from Massachusetts Institute of Technology, who also designed many of the striking buildings on the Tuskegee campus. Students made the bricks; built the walls; hewed the beams and sills and doors of the house's wide porches, elegant parlor, large dining room, low banisters (to accommodate Margaret Washington's small stature), and five bedrooms for the family, with more on the third floor for students who lived in and cared for the house. A large office for Washington occupied a corner of the second floor. It was the first house in Macon County to have electric lights and featured, as well, a sauna students designed on the basis of Washington's description of one he had seen in Europe. The walls downstairs were painted deep burgundy, the Tuskegee school color, and were topped with a wide painted frieze of European scenes.

The Oaks stood on three acres, surrounded by trees that George Washington Carver had selected and gardens where Washington loved to get back to his rural roots by tending vegetables, chickens, and pigs. "There are no peas, no turnips, no radishes, no beets or salads, that taste so good as those which one has raised and gathered with his own hands in his own garden," he wrote in an article for the *Outlook*, the weekly illustrated newspaper published by the liberal theologian Lyman Abbott to which he often contributed. Washington wrote that he liked his time in the garden so much that "I frequently find myself beseeching Mrs. Washington to delay the dinner hour that I may take advantage of the last bit of daylight for my outdoor work." Flowers, he wrote, did not "contain enough of the industrial or economic element" to appeal to him; those he left to his wife.

In the summers, the Washington family often spent time on the Massachusetts coast in a house lent to them by William Baldwin, a Tuskegee trustee who had become a real friend. Baldwin's father had been a wealthy Boston businessman, an abolitionist, a reform-minded Unitarian, and a supporter of the Young Men's Christian Association. Once, walking through a Boston train station, Baldwin Sr. had offered to help a black man carrying several heavy bags. When he learned that the man was Booker T. Washington, he gave him a letter of introduction to his son, who was general manager of the Southern Railway. Baldwin Jr. visited Tuskegee and liked what he saw. He joined the board of trustees and immersed himself in details of the school's management.

Baldwin, like his father, had a lively mind and a wide range of interests. It was he who first suggested the creation of a national board to focus on the need for improving public education in the South. When John D. Rockefeller Jr., fired with enthusiasm after visiting the South on the train trip Robert Ogden had organized, set up the Southern Education Board (later the General Education Board) to look for ways to do this, and funded it with $1 million from his father, he invited Baldwin to be its first chairman. Baldwin started with the paternalistic attitude, not unusual among whites at the time, that accepted inferior social status for blacks as a matter of course. The black race, this assumption was, had yet to achieve the evolutionary stage of development that whites had attained. Equality between the races was simply not possible. But as Baldwin dug into the issue and spent more time at Tuskegee and with Washington, he began to revise this notion. In 1903, he wrote to an associate that "very interesting meetings with Mr. Washington" had left him concerned about the ferocious hostility to blacks in the South, hostility he saw as springing from the "fear on the part of the ignorant white people that the negro will get on top." To Washington he wrote that he had spoken with other members of the board. "My talk was based on my meeting with you and I began by saying that I had seen you and your family and that I noted the anxiety and sense of responsibility which you have in view of the increasingly strained relationship between the two races in certain parts of the country. I went right to the bottom of it. I talked right out plainly about all the things that one seldom talks [about] with Southern men." If the southern states were not prepared to provide public education for blacks, Baldwin wrote to one of his fellow members of the General Education Board, they might need help from the federal government. It was, he felt, an urgent priority at the national level. In 1904 Baldwin wrote to a friend predicting a difficult time ahead. "Race hatred," he said, "is gathering fast."

The next year McClure's magazine ran an article by the journalist Carl Schurz titled "Can the South Solve the Negro Problem?" Schurz argued that "white ignorance and lawlessness are just as bad as black ignorance and lawlessness," and he suggested that "neither white nor black can override the rights of the other without endangering his own." Washington made sure his friend Baldwin saw it. Baldwin wrote to Robert Ogden, his colleague on the Tuskegee board, that in the future he planned to be more forceful and open in his support for black schools.

Washington and Baldwin got together frequently at Tuskegee, where Baldwin took an interest in every aspect of the school, especially everything to do with finances and budgeting. They also saw each other at Baldwin's home in New York. "It seems to me," Washington wrote later of this friendship, "that the most pleasant and profitable hours I have ever known were spent with Mr. Baldwin in his library in Brooklyn . . . as soon as dinner was over, we would spend three or four hours in his library, sometimes not breaking up our conference until after midnight."

But early in 1905, William Baldwin died unexpectedly at the age of forty-two. The *New York Times* eulogized him for his interest in social and labor problems. One writer said, "He is of more importance in the solution of the race problem in the United States than any other man." Baldwin's son wrote to Washington that his father had told him that thinking about the work the two of them were doing together at Tuskegee and their conversations about it was one of the main things that had made him hope to get well.

To Portia, studying piano in Berlin, Washington wrote in 1906 that she should not let her mind "dwell too much upon American prejudice, or any other racial prejudice. The thing is for one to get above such things. If one gets in the habit of continually thinking and talking about race prejudice, he soon gets to the point where he is fit for little that is worth doing." Even to his daughter Washington chose not to give in to the bitterness to which he must have felt entitled. He did not deny the existence of racial prejudice; he simply asserted his unwillingness to let it affect him.

A few years later, Washington had a chance to show Portia what he meant. Father and daughter visited the Washington Monument together, and as they were leaving, he signed the guest book. The guard used a racial epithet to say that the invitation to sign the book did not extend to blacks. Then, having looked at the signature and realized to whom he was speaking, the guard tried to apologize. Whatever he was feeling, Booker T. Washington said nothing. He just walked away.

This is the earliest-known picture of Booker T. Washington, capturing him at about the time of his graduation from Hampton Institute. A classmate described him as looking on that day "like a conqueror who had won a great victory."

Students built the impressive campus of Tuskegee Institute from bricks they manufactured. When the American flag started flying there it had not been seen in that part of Alabama since before the Civil War.

Classes at Tuskegee, as at Hampton, were coeducational before that was the norm elsewhere. Here, a history class studies the settlement of Jamestown. By the end of the nineteenth century, Tuskegee was one of the largest educational institutions in the South.

Young Julius Rosenwald was in many ways a typical Chicagoan—a first-generation American son of German immigrant parents, with tremendous drive and energy. He was also atypical in that he was Jewish and already comfortably middle-class when he arrived in the city.

There are few images of Booker T. Washington and Julius Rosenwald together. This one shows them at Tuskegee in February 1915. Washington would die later that year.

Booker T. Washington's third wife, Margaret, was an educator who played a large role at Tuskegee. Here she is with Washington and the children, Davidson, Booker Jr., and Portia, about the time of the speech in Atlanta that made her husband famous.

The Oaks, the Washingtons' large house across the road from Tuskegee Institute, was built by student labor and staffed by students. In 1914 Ella Flagg, a visitor from Chicago, wrote that the home was "beautiful, far more beautiful than I ever hope to have."

Booker T. Washington grew up in the country, and he always liked outdoor work. Here, he feeds his chickens with, according to the picture's original caption, "green stuff" he raised in his garden.

Julius Rosenwald grew up in Springfield, Illinois, in this comfortable house across the street from the home that had been Abraham Lincoln's.

The enormous Sears, Roebuck and Company headquarters, completed in 1906, was financed by one of the country's first Initial Public Offerings, suggested by Rosenwald's friend Henry Goldman and underwritten by Goldman, Sachs. The plant covered forty acres and included, besides the offices, gardens, and the clock tower seen here, athletic fields for the employees, a printing plant, a power station, and a railroad depot from which orders were shipped.

This picture shows the Rosenwalds at about the time Julius and Booker T. Washington met. Their son William, here seated on his older brother, Lessing's, knee, would remember Washington's visit to their home throughout his long life.

It was their mutual interest in the work of the YMCA that originally brought Washington and Rosenwald together. Here they are at the dedication of Chicago's black YMCA building in 1913. Rosenwald is at the center, speaking; Washington is at the far left.

Visitors at Tuskegee were sometimes entertained with outdoor meals the students prepared and served.

When it opened in 1898, the Tuskegee chapel was the first structure in Macon County, Alabama with electric lights. It was destroyed by fire in 1957 and replaced a few years later with a striking modern building.

One of the first Rosenwald schools was at Chehaw, close to Tuskegee. When Rosenwald visited it in November 1915, just before the death of Booker T. Washington, he was greeted, he said in a letter to his wife, with bonfires and "the usual yelling and singing."

Little Zion

Washington brought a scrapbook of photographs of the schools with him to Chicago in 1914 to help convince Rosenwald to continue and expand the school building program.

The NAACP staged the Silent March in 1917 in New York City to protest disenfranchisement and anti-black violence, especially lynching. The sign at the front of the marchers reads, "The first blood for American independence was shed by a Negro, Crispus Attucks." Julius Rosenwald began supporting the NAACP with donations and service on the board of the Chicago chapter in 1912.

In 1926 members of the white supremacist Ku Klux Klan paraded down Pennsylvania Avenue in Washington, D.C.

Rosenwald school agents went out into communities to encourage and facilitate applications to the school-building program. Seated in the middle of this group is Robert Moton, the second principal of Tuskegee Institute, who said of the relationship between Booker T. Washington and Julius Rosenwald, "It was a fortunate day" for black people when the two men "met and trusted each other."

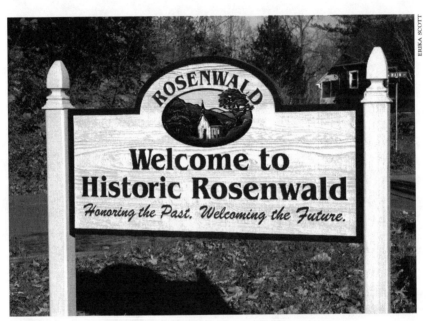

It is in Brevard, North Carolina, that Rosenwald Lane and Main Street intersect in a neighborhood now called Rosenwald.

CHAPTER 5

X

An American Citizen

In 1910, the *Chicago Tribune* asked several people which books had most influenced them, and Julius Rosenwald, identified as one of the city's leading citizens, named two. They were *An American Citizen: The Life of William Henry Baldwin, Jr.* and Booker T. Washington's *Up from Slavery*. The busy years since he first bought into Sears, Roebuck and Company had not just brought Julius Rosenwald wealth and increased responsibility. They had enormously widened his world.

The situation that greeted Rosenwald when he went to work at Sears in December 1896 was, if anything, even more chaotic than it had been the summer before. The company had moved its offices to the six-story Enterprise building, which occupied a full block in downtown Chicago. But with sales twice what they had been the year before and new lines of merchandise constantly being added, space was always an issue. Every possible room was filled with stock and product samples; they overflowed from boxes on the floor or took up space in the hallways. There were no telephones, so young boys ran all over the building with messages. On the packing crates that served as desks stood baskets of unanswered correspondence, much of it complaining about merchandise that had been ordered but not received. A visitor to the Sears office at the time said it was the "busiest place I had ever seen . . . like Saturday evening [in retail] all the time."

There were similarities in background between Julius Rosenwald and Richard Sears, and initially these masked the great differences between them. The two men were the same age; both were from modest, Midwestern backgrounds; neither had completed high school. They had married at about the same time, and both were devoted to their wives and children (Sears had two sons and two daughters). In addition, both men were by nature cheerful and optimistic. More so even than Rosenwald, Sears had an outgoing, compelling personality that drew people to him. He was a big, handsome, exuberant man.

At an early age Sears had discovered that he liked answering ads in newspapers, sending away for things and then receiving them in the mail. The amount of "trinkets and notions" (his sister's words) he received as a child had been a joke in his family. As he grew older, he came to love the challenge of selling, of enticing buyers with lively, well-written copy. He once published an ad making an "astonishing offer" for "an upholstered parlor set" of a sofa and two straight-backed chairs, all for the amazing price of ninety-five cents. A drawing showed three elegant pieces of furniture; tiny text revealed that it was, in fact, "miniature." The people who sent in money received furniture suitable for a child's dollhouse. Complaints were filed, but Sears was never prosecuted. This episode notwithstanding, he was for the most part honest. He simply approached selling with imagination and gusto.

Rosenwald, however, was practical. When he arrived at Sears, one of the company's major problems was that orders were being botched. People would order one thing but receive something else. A joke making the rounds at the time featured a Sears clerk boasting to an employee of Montgomery Ward, the older, better-established mail-order company, "Heck, we get more goods *returned* than you folks ship out." This was especially true in the clothing department, where the Sears cash-on-delivery policy meant that customers could return anything without payment if it wasn't satisfactory. Enormous amounts of clothing were, in fact, sent back. Richard Sears relished exciting customers' interest, but to him the mechanics of responding to orders were a bore. Rosenwald, having come of age looking customers in the eye across the counter of a store, knew the importance of giving people what they wanted. He thought like a shopkeeper, and in fact, he always referred to his office at Sears as "the store."

Still, the amount and variety of merchandise for sale in the Sears catalog was extraordinary, and as the American economy rebounded from the 1893 recession, people had more money to spend on it. Orders poured in. By the end of the century, Sears had twenty-four department managers and relationships with small factories that could charge low per-item costs because Sears was ordering so much. Besides clothing for everyone from Baby to Grandpa, the company sold groceries, guns, stoves, books, stationery, fishing rods, jewelry, veterinary fever reme-dies, musical instruments for marching bands, bicycles, gravestones, pig forceps, perfume, and electric belts advertised to cure everything from headache to nervous anxiety. The catalog was famous not just for its enormous variety of merchandise but also for the folksy style in which it was written. "Don't be afraid that you will make a mistake," said the instructions on how to place an order: "We receive hundreds of orders every day from young and old who never before sent away for goods. We are accustomed to handling all kinds of orders. Tell us what you want, in your own way, written in any language, no matter whether good or poor writing, and the goods will be promptly sent to you."

In 1899, Sears's sales totaled $10 million and, for the first time, sur-passed the receipts of Montgomery Ward. Julius was working so hard that he complained in a letter to his brother Louis that during the Christmas season, "I am in the store almost every night and, conse-quently, see very little of anyone in the family."

The different work styles and personalities of the three Sears own-ers—Sears, Rosenwald, and Aaron Nusbaum—would soon lead Julius to a stark choice: family loyalty versus his own, unfettered business interest. Richard Sears and Julius Rosenwald, it turned out, had com-plementary talents. Sears was personable and charming, constantly overflowing with ideas for new lines of merchandise and creative mar-keting schemes. Rosenwald was straightforward, sometimes to the point of being brusque. Some of his coworkers called him "the great objector" because of all the questions he raised about new plans and the way he criticized some product lines. To Rosenwald business was not a results-driven game as much as it was a process of establishing trust—trust between himself and the staff members with whom he worked and trust between the company and its customers. He did not want to generate more orders than he could reliably, accurately fill, and he steadily pushed for more clarity in catalog descriptions and fewer questionable products like patent medicines and the electric belt.

Aaron Nusbaum, in contrast, often offended people with his arrogant manner and ruthless policies, like firing people for a few weeks to save on the payroll, then rehiring them as needed. In 1901, a rift developed among the owners. According to one version of what happened, Sears decided he would leave the company he had founded rather than continue to work with Nusbaum. A history of Sears, Roebuck suggests that, at this point, Julius "felt himself ready for both business and emotional maturity." Indeed, Julius's and Gussie's fathers had both recently died; his brothers Benjamin and Louis had moved away from Chicago; and Julius, at almost forty years of age, was being looked to by his sisters and brothers as the head of his large family. He had worked hard and was beginning to see a strong financial return for his efforts in a business that, he firmly believed, had a promising future. Not for the last time in his career, Julius decided what to do using not sentiment but hard-nosed business sense. He saw Richard Sears as the inspiration behind the company's astonishing success; he recognized that Sears was familiar with the farmers who made up a large part of the company's customers and that he had a knack for communicating with them. Nusbaum's skills, though real, were less unusual, and his personality made him hard to work with. Despite the fact that Nusbaum was his wife's brother, Julius decided to break with him and stick with Sears.

Sears and Rosenwald offered Aaron $1 million for the share of the company he had bought for $37,500 six years earlier. Aaron accepted, but when the day came to sign the sales agreement that Rosenwald's lawyer, Albert Loeb, had drawn up, he changed his mind. Aaron wanted $1.25 million. Richard Sears and Julius Rosenwald were furious. But they were committed to the company's future and were sure that they wanted Nusbaum out of it. They agreed to his conditions, including his insistence that, until he had been fully paid, they would limit the total they would pay to their employees in salaries to $100,000 a year. Even their own dividends would be withheld until Aaron had been paid in full.

This parting was a bitter one on both sides. Aaron eventually left Chicago, spent a good deal of time in Europe, then moved east and changed his last name from Nusbaum to Norman. Gussie tried more than once to contact her only brother, but he always returned her letters unopened. He never again spoke to either Gussie or Julius.

Between Sears and Rosenwald a relationship developed that was friendly but never extremely close. Richard Sears took to calling Julius "J. R.," as did many of his family and friends, but to Julius, his partner always remained "Mr. Sears." The tone of the letters they exchanged when each of them traveled was often light and friendly. "I regretsky to reportsky," wrote Rosenwald in 1905, showing his characteristic love of word play, "that the snow is still on the ground and in consequence some of our buggy orders are snowed under." They discussed only one subject in their letters, though, and that was business.

In December 1903, the income at Sears, Roebuck and Company was so high that the three owners (Albert Loeb had taken Aaron's place) decided to pay off Aaron Nusbaum in full and to distribute some of their company's extraordinary profits. Before this, Rosenwald had received only his salary, which, although it had risen to $6,000 a year, did not reflect the company's startling growth. (As a comparison, that same year, when Rabbi Hirsch had threatened to leave Sinai for Temple Emanu El in New York, Temple Sinai convinced him to stay by raising his salary to an extremely generous $12,000 a year, twice what his friend Rosenwald was making.) At a special board meeting on the last day of 1903, Richard Sears and Julius Rosenwald awarded themselves dividends of $2 million each—something roughly equivalent to $50 million in today's terms. Suddenly, Julius Rosenwald was rich.

He was also, now, the father of five. In May 1902, with Lessing aged eleven, Adele ten, and Edith seven, Gussie had another baby, a girl they called Marion. By the end of that year, she was pregnant again, and in August 1903 the youngest Rosenwald child was born, a bright little boy Julius and Gussie named William but dotingly called "Billy."

With this large family, the Rosenwalds needed a bigger house, and in 1904 they bought a two-acre corner lot on Ellis Avenue in Hyde Park, the gracious, leafy neighborhood about two miles south of where they had been living, a few blocks from the campus of the new University of Chicago. Professors lived in the neighborhood, as well as many prosperous members of the Sinai congregation. Julius's brother Morris had already moved there with his wife, Mae; so had his sister Selma and her husband, Sig Eisendrath. Soon Julius's business partner, Albert Loeb, with his wife and their four boys, would live just around the corner, and Julius would buy a house for his mother on nearby Greenwood Avenue. A prominent firm, Nimmons and Fellows, designed the house for the Rosenwalds in the restrained, linear prairie style that was becoming popular in Chicago. *Architectural Digest* magazine ran an article on it and described the house as "plain and even severe in treatment." The article reported that it had "dignity without the slightest pretension." Still, it was big—there were ten bedrooms; an enormous kitchen; rooms for staff; a billiards room; a wide, screened porch; and, on the third floor, a ballroom. In the sunny yard were a tennis court, a garden, and a modern necessity: a two-car garage.

Less than a week after moving into the house that spring, forty-two-year-old Julius left for his first trip to Europe, sailing from New York on a German liner with a group from Chicago. Gussie stayed home with the children. Bubbling over with excitement, Julius's letters to her were deaf to the resentment the good times he described might stir up in her. He described stimulating new experiences—crossing the ocean; conversing with a group of Russians on the ship; driving by automobile through France, Switzerland, and Germany. He loved Paris and said that he was looking forward to being there again someday with his family and that he hoped his children would speak French and would learn European history. From the Loire Valley he wrote that the car had regular breakdowns and flat tires (motoring was an adventure in those early days of the automobile), that his face was becoming sunburned from being outside so much, that his favorite chateau was Chenonceau, and that the only thing marring the trip was that he was "getting the old French royalties so terribly mixed." His sister Selma and their mother joined him in Germany. His mother wrote home that she had shown pictures of her son's new house to the relatives in Bünde and, "of course, they thought it was a palace."

When the time came to make donations to the 1904 relief fund at Temple Sinai, Rosenwald raised his contribution from his usual $50 to $3,000 and immediately became the largest donor to it in Chicago. He accepted a position on the board of one of the relief fund's charities, the Chicago Home for Jewish Orphans, and became what he called a *schnorrer*, someone who went to visit other members of the temple and encourage them to follow his lead and make large donations, too. He made his first major gift outside of his synagogue when, at the suggestion of Rabbi Hirsch, he donated $6,000 to the University of Chicago for the Bernays library, a collection of German-language books.

Still, despite his public generosity and his big house, Rosenwald did not easily throw off the thrift that had always been part of him. From Europe he wrote to Gussie, "I was a little extravagant . . . I bought a trunk for myself . . . not quite as nice as yours but something I've wanted for some time." He also reported to Gussie on the lace bedspreads she had asked him to buy in France. He wrote that he had decided against it because they were $125 each and "the duty will bring them up to $225."

As Rosenwald began to give away money, he turned first to the community he knew and the tradition that had nurtured him. He contributed to a new building for Michael Reese Hospital, which catered to Chicago's well-established German Jewish population, and he joined the board of the Chicago Hebrew Institute, which offered assistance to Jews among Chicago's large population of recent immigrants. Rosenwald was quickly elected president of the board and took on a major role in finding a new building and then raising money to purchase it. Consistently, it was not only money that he donated but also the time it took to go to meetings, to write letters and make visits encouraging others to contribute, to have the endless conversations that were part of promoting the institute's work.

The need was great as immigrants poured into Chicago, many of them Jews fleeing a rising tide of anti-Semitic violence in Russia, Poland, and other countries of Eastern Europe. There, harassment of Jews was not just tolerated but also often officially sanctioned. In 1903, the *New York Times* reported on a "frenzied and bloodthirsty mob" that terrorized Jews in the Moldovan city of Chisinau, then called Kishinev and part of the Russian Empire, during the week of Easter, when accusations were made that Jews had murdered a Christian child. What began as boys throwing rocks at Jewish homes gained steam and turned into three days of rioting in which more than forty Jews were killed, almost a hundred people were wounded, and seven hundred homes were looted and destroyed. The paper reported, "The general cry 'kill the Jews' was taken up all over the city." Two years later, in October 1905, violence again erupted in Chisinau and in many other places across Russia.

American Jews, secure against such violence themselves, organized meetings to protest anti-Jewish violence and to raise funds to help the victims. In May 1905, a meeting at the Star Theater in Chicago featured speeches by the increasingly prominent lawyer Clarence Darrow and by Jane Addams, the heiress who had purchased a shabby mansion in downtown Chicago and turned it into Hull-House, a place where she herself lived and where immigrants found kindness, as well as English lessons and other forms of assistance. The largest contribution to the fund raised from participants in the meeting came from Julius Rosenwald. To one of his uncles Julius wrote, "Of course a very small fraction of the money collected will be collected from non-Jews but the general opinion seems to be that this wonderful outpouring and response by the Jews of this country will be a great stride toward lessening the prejudice that exists."

In the fall of 1904, Julius Rosenwald and Richard Sears bought a forty-acre tract of prairie land five miles west of downtown Chicago for the new plant their thriving business required. Rosenwald was in charge of working with the architect. He hired the firm that had built his house and a contractor, Louis Horowitz, who made an attractive bid, he later said, because he immediately liked and trusted Julius Rosenwald. Amazingly, the work was completed in just over a year, and the result was spectacular. The operations of Sears were housed in five sleek, modern buildings dominated by a 250-foot clock tower (that held water for fire protection) and surrounded by formal flower gardens and shrubs. The massive administration building held an employees' restaurant, a hospital, the largest branch of the Chicago Public Library, and a savings bank for employees. There was a printing plant, where the catalogs were produced, an advertising building from which they were mailed, a power station, and a railroad depot where orders were shipped out. And the merchandise building, which the 1908 catalog called "the largest ever erected" for such a purpose, held the vast array of goods ready to be shipped out and the conveyer belts, chutes, and baskets required by the brilliant and original system that had been devised for filling orders.

The schedule system was a simple but very successful idea that the manager Otto Doering created. It broke orders down into their components and assigned each one a specific number and time to be retrieved from the warehouse before gathering everything together again for shipping. The new system solved the problem that had undermined Sears's efforts to become more efficient. Several years before Henry Ford introduced the assembly line in his auto factory, this innovative use of modern technology was transforming operations at Sears. The combination of the modern plant and the new operating system made possible a major expansion of business.

But the building was also larger and more elaborate—and thus more expensive—than had originally been planned for. So, in the spring of 1906, Richard Sears and Julius Rosenwald went to New York to discuss the possibility of getting a loan from Julius's old friend Harry Goldman, the senior partner at a young investment firm called Goldman, Sachs. Goldman suggested a different approach. Why not, he asked, take the company public? He had just completed the first deal of this kind for a general merchandising company (what we now call an initial public offering, or IPO). Goldman suggested selling common stock based on the enormous tangible assets of the company and offering "preferred" stock to the company's partners, with the value of that stock resting on the company's widespread good reputation and solid future prospects. By midsummer the partners had agreed to the idea. Richard Sears and Julius Rosenwald each received $4.5 million for the stock they already had, and their salaries were raised again, this time to $9,600 a year. Rosenwald became a millionaire many times over.

This bold sale was a moment of triumph, yet it was also a challenge. The very next year, Sears experienced its first serious business slump. In the summer of 1907, as Rosenwald toured Europe with his family, the fun and relaxation of travel had to compete with the long, typewritten letters he received every few days from Richard Sears. For the first time ever, his partner wrote, sales had fallen.

The Rosenwald entourage included Gussie; all five children; a governess for the "babies," as they were still called (Marion was five, and

William was three); and a maid who did the packing and unpacking and cared for their clothes. The trip took them to Paris; to the spa towns of Baden-Baden and Ragaz; to Marienbad, where Julius and the children went mountain climbing; to Munich and to Bünde, the birth-place of Samuel Rosenwald. Gussie wrote home about how intoxicated she was with Paris after her first "spin" down the Champs-Élysées in an automobile and about the laughs she, Julius, and the children were having. "When Jule gets excited he starts to talk German to our chauf-feur who does not speak or understand anything but French," she wrote in one. Edith, she commented, amused them all with her tendency toward "good repartee just like her daddy & the Rosenwalds in gen-eral." Gussie's only frustration as they toured galleries and historical sites was realizing "how little we all know."

Responding to Sears's letters, Rosenwald wrote reassuringly from Europe. "You know, I am too optimistic to believe for a moment that any signs point to a permanent decline in our business." He suggested that some prices might have been raised too much, that some of the new product lines did not appear to be successful. By late August, Sears was writing back with his own analysis of the problem—neglect of the customers—and his plan to counter it. He wanted to initiate a complex customer profit-sharing plan, a series of premiums shoppers could earn with purchases and redeem for discounts and special products. Sears's letters were long and manic. "I am handing you these things wildly as they come to my mind," he wrote in one, "and it will be a somewhat incongruous mass, but out of it you can pick such little fragments of information as may be of interest to you."

In fact, a national financial crisis was part of the problem, and by 1908 the discussion of what to do was gaining urgency. Julius Rosenwald and Richard Sears pushed for opposite approaches. Sears wanted expansion. He had argued for and, over Rosenwald's strenu-ous opposition, got a branch office for the company in Dallas. Then he proposed aggressive new plans to increase advertising and to encour-age sales in other ways, not just through the customer profit-sharing program he had already instituted but also with another plan he called Iowaizing (because it had worked well in Iowa). This involved send-ing large numbers of catalogs to good customers and having them solicit orders from their neighbors. Rosenwald's approach was the opposite. He favored cost-cutting measures, price stabilization, budget tightening. The crisis crystallized essential differences between the two men.

Harry Goldman had described Richard Sears as a "mail order Barnum" and said he "could sell a breath of air." A history of the company touched on the wellspring of Sears's business personality when it said that success generating orders "intoxicated" Sears. Rosenwald, in contrast, was soberly cautious. As it turned out, many members of the staff, although they were personally devoted to Sears, agreed with Rosenwald about how to handle the business crisis.

The situation came to a head in the fall of 1908. After a two-hour private conference with Rosenwald, Sears surprised everyone by leaving the office complex he had once described as "the most beautiful place I have seen in three weeks travel." He sold his company stock to Harry Goldman (Julius declined to buy it because he didn't want to look like he was profiting from his partner's departure), gave ill health as the reason for his retirement, and left. Sears retained the title of company president, but he attended no board meetings and never once returned to the Sears plant. Indeed, his health had suffered from his many years of overwork. Six years after he left the company he had created, Richard Sears died at the age of fifty-one.

Many years later, Rosenwald would tell a new employee with an interest in company history that he felt Richard Sears had never really had confidence in the long-term viability of the mail-order business. Rosenwald said that he himself had early on come to believe in the essential soundness of the concept and to understand that its survival depended on putting meaning into the words Sears was beginning to use in its advertising, "Satisfaction guaranteed or your money back."

As Julius Rosenwald took over as president of the company, Sears, Roebuck was proving that his confidence was justified. The company employed thousands of people and owned sixteen factories that manufactured Sears-brand goods. The enormous, lavishly illustrated catalog full of clever descriptions of everything from lace boleros ("the swellest and most stylish") to firearms (the $8 hammerless revolver "will surely prove a death blow to competition") was working its way into American folklore as "the wish book." And there was tremendous growth still to come.

On Saturday, August 15, 1908, the *Chicago Tribune* announced that the Illinois capital, Springfield, was "in the hands of a mob and the throes of a race war." The next day, the paper's front page was taken up with news of the violence in Rosenwald's hometown. A drawing showed blacks fleeing a mob, with the memorial at Lincoln's grave in the background. "The declaration of martial law and the presence of eight thousand militiamen in the city have failed to check the mob spirit in Springfield," the paper reported. "Negroes have been chased through the streets by angry mobs intent on taking their lives." It had started, as such episodes often did, with a white woman's accusations against a black man. The weather was steamy; tempers flared. A crowd gathered that then became a mob; the police were powerless against it. An eighty-year-old black man, reported to have "once been a friend of Abraham Lincoln," was hit in the head with a brick and then hanged in his own front yard near the statehouse, not far from where Samuel Rosenwald's store had been. The black section of town was destroyed. There were no arrests.

For Julius Rosenwald—who had grown up roaming the streets of Springfield, a Jew well aware of the vulnerability of despised groups, who had just raised money for the victims of mob violence in Russia—this was a particularly personal indication of the dire state of race relations in the United States. And it was not a unique episode. In 1898 in Wilmington, North Carolina, a white mob had destroyed the office of a black newspaper, killed at least ten people, and chased hundreds of blacks out of town. In 1906 thirty people died during four days of racially charged rioting in Atlanta. And a few months after that, violence broke out in Brownsville, Texas, when a black army unit, one that had served with distinction in Cuba, was posted there. The townspeople did not welcome the black troops, who were regularly insulted and excluded from bars and parks. Finally, a fight broke out between soldiers and townspeople. A riot resulted, and a white bartender was killed. When the dust settled, President Theodore Roosevelt, despite his reputation for taking an interest in black welfare, sought no formal charges and encouraged no attempt to determine guilt or innocence. No less a figure than Booker T. Washington pled for lenience for the soldiers or at least a delay in a case where guilt was anything but clear, but the man in the White House, reputed to be his friend and ally, ignored him. One hundred sixty-seven black soldiers, some with as many as twenty years of service, were given dishonorable discharges that only fifty years later would be overturned—posthumously.

The Great Migration that would pull millions of blacks from their rural southern homes and attract them to northern cities with promises of better jobs and enhanced opportunity was just beginning. Blacks were still a small percentage of Chicago's population, and Rosenwald knew little about them. He was familiar with one young black man who, years later, would remember him well. Claude Barnett (who would go on to a successful career in journalism) worked as what he himself called "a houseboy and general factotum" at Richard Sears's home in the Chicago suburb of Oak Park between 1902 and 1904. He remembered that Julius Rosenwald occasionally came there to have a meal with Sears and had suggested to him that, after he quit working for Mr. Sears, he should go down and get a job at "the store." Barnett did and was employed for a time in the grocery department, packing and shipping sugar. "So far as I know," he wrote later, "I was the only colored employee who was not a janitor."

As he became more aware of the racial climate, Rosenwald considered pushing his own company to hire more blacks. According to Edwin Embree, who became president of the Julius Rosenwald Fund in 1928, Rosenwald encountered more resistance to this than he had expected. Fearing he might create antagonism rather than increased opportunity, he backed off and looked for other ways to address the increasingly painful issue of American race relations.

In 1908, when his oldest son, Lessing, went off to Cornell University in upstate New York, Rosenwald stayed in close touch with him via letters. When he couldn't write himself, he would have a secretary at Sears send a typewritten note saying, "Your father is too busy to write now but wants you to know that everything here is fine." When he did write, Rosenwald was both affectionate and a nag. In February 1909 he wrote, "I received your expense account and I can't help but feel that you are in a great many ways loose with your money. When you think you want a thing, try to get along without it for a while and see if you don't save buying a good many things that you now buy on impulse."

Another time, Julius wrote that "a baseball glove at $3.50 is a terrible extravagance." He feared his son's college friend, Armand Deutsch, the son of a Hyde Park neighbor, might be encouraging him to spend too much money or to drink (Lessing had mentioned in a letter that he had been to a "saloon"). Julius cautioned his son, writing, "To what extent you are influenced will depend on your own strength of character." In another letter, he wrote, "Every time you spend your money foolishly, you weaken your character."

Good character. It was the trait most admired, most respected, most sought after by men and women of Rosenwald's time. In his emphasis on thrift, sobriety, and hard work, he—like Booker T. Washington—was reflecting not just his own personal attitude but also a cultural heritage, part of the American ethos. The Puritans had prayed, "May my character not my circumstances chiefly engage me"; even while striving for financial security, they had feared the effect affluence would have on them. And in a country that prided itself for rewarding people on their merits rather than according to class, it was character that was considered the decisive factor in success. The Horatio Alger books so popular in the second half of the nineteenth century emphasized the material rewards to hardworking boys of good character. *Little Women*, never out of print from 1869 to the present, tells of four sisters whose mother's priority for them is not worldly success but modesty, self-respect, and hard work. The virtues of humility, thrift, and generosity that nineteenth- and early-twentieth-century children learned at church and synagogue were reinforced by the McGuffey readers they used in school. "Never be afraid to do good, but always fear to do evil," advises a third-grade story about a boy rescuing a friend who has fallen in a river. "Humble modesty is more often right than a proud and boasting spirit," says another. Such lessons were the essence of the age.

Rosenwald felt that the way he dealt with his rapidly increasing wealth was a test of his own character. He didn't want affluence to make him soft or to spoil his children. He was quite willing to spend large amounts for his family's luxurious European trips, but when he traveled for business by train, he slept in upper berths rather than private Pullman cars, and he chose the least expensive rooms in hotels. He made a point of not having a valet (although Gussie had a lady's maid, and the house on Ellis Avenue, well run by a German couple, was certainly not understaffed). He gave his children small allowances. William, who as a young boy, received ten cents a week, once complained to his father that he wished he were the son of the Standard Oil tycoon, John D. Rockefeller. When his father asked why, he said, "Because then maybe I'd get a quarter." Julius laughed and told him that, in fact, old Mr. Rockefeller was a good deal richer than he was and even stricter. Rockefeller's four children shared one bicycle.

Just as in our own age many seek guidance in self-help literature and pop psychology, people in the early twentieth century sought inspiration in books about the admirable lives of people of strong character. In the fall of 1910, Julius was given such a book by his friend Paul Sachs, *An American Citizen: The Life of William Henry Baldwin, Jr.*, by John Graham Brooks. The book did not describe the exciting events of an adventurous life but, rather, the way one man answered a question he himself found vital, a question of great interest to Rosenwald: is it possible to succeed in business without sacrificing personal morality and idealism? Baldwin, president of the Southern Railway, made it his stated goal to use his influence and his wealth for the good of his workers. At a time when many people feared and despised unions, he supported them, believing that unions gave workers a vehicle by which they could help themselves. He encouraged (and donated money for) libraries on the railroad lines so workers would "have some place to go in the evenings and will not have to patronize saloons." He supported the YMCA movement, with its varied services for men and boys of meager means. And a large part of the book dealt with a subject especially dear to Baldwin—his work as a member of the board of Tuskegee and his relationship with Booker T. Washington.

"It is a glorious story," Rosenwald wrote of the book in a letter to his daughters Adele and Edith. He described it to them as being about "a man who really *led* a life which is to my liking and whom I shall endeavor to imitate or follow as nearly as I can. We have a great many views in common but he, being college-bred and much of a student, had powers of analysis which I lack." Baldwin, he wrote, had "made great study of the Negro problem along common sense, helpful lines."

Rosenwald also sent a copy of *An American Citizen* to his son at Cornell and, in letter after letter, asked if he had yet read it.

CHAPTER 6

⚹

Lunch at the Blackstone

It was a chance encounter on a train and their mutual connection to the YMCA movement that led to the meeting, which later seemed so inevitable, between Booker T. Washington and Julius Rosenwald. On one of his northern trips, Washington fell into conversation with Wilber Messer, a white minister and the general secretary of Chicago's YMCA. He asked Messer if he could suggest a wealthy person from Chicago who might have an interest in serving on the board of Tuskegee. Messer named Julius Rosenwald. He then ensured that the two men would meet by inviting both to speak at the annual YMCA dinner in Chicago in May 1911.

The Young Men's Christian Association movement had come to Boston from England in the fervent years before the Civil War, and it was dedicated to the physical, mental, and spiritual well-being of young men, especially those who were particularly vulnerable because they were newly arrived in town from rural areas. The well-known evangelist Dwight Moody worked with the YMCA in Chicago, where, as elsewhere, it focused on offering safe lodging and wholesome recreation to young working people, along with Bible study. Wilber Messer had worked with the prominent Chicago industrialist Cyrus McCormick to raise money for the state-of-the-art YMCA building that opened in 1893 with electric lights, bowling alleys, a swimming pool, a gymnasium, a photography club, and an observatory. By the turn of the century, the YMCA was a highly regarded national organization. It was officially opposed to racial discrimination, yet following the mood and, increasingly, the laws of the times, YMCA facilities were segregated. The new Chicago building was for whites only. Many cities had black YMCA organizations, but their activities took place in houses or rented rooms. Young blacks, in Chicago and elsewhere, were excluded from the swimming pools and gyms of the YMCA's modern new buildings.

The YMCA, with its emphasis on discipline, sobriety, and self-improvement, was very much in line with the thinking and the personal traits of both Washington and Rosenwald. "No philanthropy in Chicago is a greater power for good," Julius had said of it in 1908 as it kicked off a fiftieth-anniversary fund-raising drive. Sears, Roebuck had made a large donation to the YMCA's anniversary fund and had requested that the Y open a branch near its new plant, providing recreation and dormitory facilities for Sears employees. Six hundred of them signed up for membership as soon as it opened. Rosenwald praised it, saying the officers at Sears had felt a "clubhouse" would be "undemocratic" but that a YMCA building was for everyone. That he was aware that the new Sears branch of the YMCA was, in fact, actually not for everyone, is clear from his response to a request for a contribution to a new YMCA building in his own neighborhood, Hyde Park. "I think that the duty of contributing the necessary funds for this building should rest upon the shoulders of my wealthy Christian friends," he wrote in response to a solicitation, "but tell your Wilber Messer, your general secretary, when the Association decides to erect a YMCA building for Negroes in Chicago, I shall be glad to contribute toward that project."

Messer lost no time in scheduling a meeting, with astonishing results. In December 1910, sitting in Rosenwald's Sears office with William Parker, another YMCA official, and Jesse Moorland, the very capable coordinator of black YMCAs, Messer asked Rosenwald if he would consider a contribution of $25,000 for a black YMCA building in Chicago. Yes, Rosenwald said, he would make the donation, provided that $75,000 more could be raised from the local community, both black and white. Then, rather enjoying his guests' surprise, he added that he wanted to extend this challenge to any large city in the country that could meet these conditions. "Well, I guess you can't build more than one a month," he joked. "But I hope you can."

Rosenwald's willingness to overlook the YMCA's occasionally anti-Semitic practices was typical of his pragmatic approach and, perhaps, an indication of the fact that he himself had personally experienced very little prejudice. When he moved beyond his own almost exclusively Jewish social world, his prominence in business gave him special entrée. His own focus was always less on what he and others could not do than on what they could.

On a snowy New Year's Day, 1911, Rosenwald was at the Odd Fellows' hall on State Street in downtown Chicago for the rally to kick off the ten-day drive to raise money for a black YMCA building. Five hundred black male volunteer fund-raisers jammed the hall and cheered the speeches made to encourage them in their efforts. Such drives—short, intense, and involving a large number of volunteers—were a trademark of YMCA fund-raising. A white banker named N. W. Harris, who had followed Julius's lead by donating $25,000, made a speech rather windily calling Julius's gift "the most important benefaction the colored race has received since the Emancipation Proclamation."

When Rosenwald rose to speak, it was his first time addressing a large black audience. He drew a parallel, awkward at first but one he would refine as he used it over and over in the years to come, between blacks and Jews as members of despised and persecuted races. He said that, because he was Jewish, he could not be admitted to the city's University Club. "I do not want you to feel I have an ax to grind," he said. "I couldn't get in even if they admitted Jews. I am not a university man." The humor of the remark was probably lost on the audience of people whose problems were more fundamental than the inability to get into a club or go to university. But when Julius spoke about the ghastly conditions facing Jews in Russia, he made his point more clearly. "I belong to a race that in times gone by did not have a fair chance in life," Rosenwald said. "I feel a peculiar sympathy with a race that does not have a fair chance under the existing conditions of American life." The men of the audience registered their approval with loud applause.

When the speeches were over and the cheering had subsided, individuals came forward to give their contributions. One elderly man said that the donation he was making was the savings of his lifetime's work as a janitor. It was $1,000.

The Rosenwalds went to Europe again in early 1911, traveling to Paris, the Swiss Alps, and Venice, which Julius enjoyed despite the fact that by the time he got there he was tired of being a tourist. Of St. Mark's Basilica and the Doge's Palace he wrote to his mother that they were built "a hell of a long time ago. I don't know how long—the old dates and history are beginning to get on my nerves. I went on a strike to-day and wouldn't go to any more churches. I like to look at the people and the little streets and the shop windows and the quaint buildings, the bridges and the scenery generally is great."

Rosenwald was supporting the candidacy of a young professor from the University of Chicago named Charles Merriam, who was running for mayor on a plank of fighting city corruption, and he was anxious to get back to the campaign. Because they were having work done on their house and because Adele and Edith were at a German boarding school, Gussie stayed behind. Julius wrote to her that Merriam's campaign managers sent him to make speeches in "the 'black belt' and in the Jewish wards" and that on one occasion he spoke for twenty-five minutes extemporaneously. When the election came, though, Merriam lost, and Julius confessed in a letter, "I've never felt worse about anything except once and that was when I thought my reputation was endangered." Leaving aside the interesting question of when and why he had felt his reputation threatened, Gussie responded that she was surprised at how hard Julius seemed to be taking the defeat. "You are spoilt, my dear," she wrote to him, and "are accustomed to having your efforts meet with success."

Gussie had a few other tart things to say to her husband during their long separation that spring. She had received a letter from her chauffeur mentioning several problems with her car, which seemed to be the result of lack of servicing. Gussie wrote that she thought Julius had attended to the car. "I have been accustomed to depending upon you & now that you are so deep in outside work I must learn to think for myself & not bother you." She had already complained that she was feeling "homesick and blue" and wanted Julius to return to Europe so the family could be together and all go to England in

June to observe the festivities that would mark the coronation of the new king.

"I can't under any circumstances come back before June," Rosenwald responded. "I've got to get into business again." But a few days later he wrote her a warm letter on their twenty-first wedding anniversary. "What I am of Jew or citizen, any honors which have come to me, would not have come about but for your cooperation and helpfulness." In May he was back to business: "I have my hands full again. The 15th I must preside at the annual meeting of the American Jewish Council and the 18th I will talk for a few minutes at the YMCA dinner together with Booker T. Washington and some others and the same day I am going to give a luncheon in honor of BTW."

Two months before meeting Rosenwald, Booker T. Washington was assaulted on a street in New York City. His attacker, who later said that he had been alarmed by the sight of a black man lurking around the lobby of his apartment building late in the evening, chased him down the street and beat him over the head with his walking stick. Washington tripped and fell. Police called to the scene initially refused to believe that the distraught and bleeding man was the famous educator. At a nearby hospital it took sixteen stitches to close the wound in his head. Washington denied his attacker's accusation that he had been drunk and had made inappropriate remarks to the man's wife. Such behavior would have been quite out of character for the fastidious Washington. Still, it was not clear just why he had been in the apartment lobby; the person he said he was seeking did not live there, and the neighborhood was not a desirable one. The disturbing (and never fully explained) episode generated a lot of publicity, some of it sensational, implying that Washington had been at the building to meet a white woman and, later, much of it sympathetic (although, as one of Washington's biographers has noted, a devastating fire that killed 146 young female workers at the Triangle Shirtwaist factory a week later pushed it from the headlines in New York and elsewhere). Washington received much private sympathy from friends and colleagues, but if nothing else, becoming himself a victim of violence was a powerful reminder to him of the extreme racial animosity he tried so hard to minimize.

Rosenwald invited forty-five prominent Chicagoans to join him for lunch to meet Booker T. Washington at the elegant new Blackstone Hotel that overlooked Lake Michigan from its site on Michigan Avenue. The twenty-five men who gathered there on an unusually hot May 18 included Julius's brother Morris, his Sears colleague Albert Loeb, and his YMCA associates Wilber Messer and William Parker. Harris, the banker who had helped with funding the black YMCA building, was there, as was H. H. Kohlsaat of the *Chicago Record-Herald* newspaper. The guests were a cross-section of Chicago's civic leadership, and they were all white men. The man the luncheon honored was the hotel's first black guest.

"Whether it is because I belong to a people who have known centuries of persecution, or whether it is because I am naturally inclined to sympathize with the oppressed," said Rosenwald in introducing his guest, "I have always felt keenly for the colored race." He went on, using the honorific Washington had adopted since receiving his honorary doctorate from Harvard, honestly but with a certain lack of tact, to say that it was reading the biography of William Baldwin that had really excited him on the subject of relations between the races. "I had, of course, read Dr. Washington's *Up from Slavery* and later writings, but interesting as they were, they did not for some reason or other make the impression upon me that did this book." Dismissing as "unworthy of serious discussion" the issue of deportation of blacks back to Africa, which some had, in fact, seriously considered as a possible solution to the country's racial situation, Julius said that the essence of the problem was that "two races must occupy one country." Rosenwald called Washington a "wise, statesmanlike leader" but the attitude of assumed superiority so typical of the time did creep into his remarks. "He is helping his own race to attain the high art of self-help and self-dependence and he is helping the white race to learn that opportunity and obligation go hand in hand, and that there is no enduring superiority save that which comes as the result of serving." His ending was gracious, though. Rosenwald assured his listeners that Washington's rise from slavery "is prophetic of the widening opportunities of his people. Happy the race which follows his sane, wise and earnest leadership! Happy the nation which . . . knows and honors a Washington whether he be George or Booker!"

Washington's remarks at the lunch were brief, but he had the chance to say more that evening at the long, stifling dinner honoring the anniversary of the founding of the YMCA. This was a larger affair, with four hundred guests, both black and white, at a less elegant hotel, the Auditorium. After a dinner of cream of asparagus soup, fricassee of chicken, followed by Neapolitan ice cream and cakes, and several rousing songs, including "The Song of Chicago" sung to the tune of "Marching Through Georgia" and "Come, Chicago" to the tune of "John Brown's Body," there were speeches. The Reverend Charles Gilky of Hyde Park Baptist Church, who had been a luncheon guest, spoke in the evening on the role of the YMCA movement in character development. Then it was announced that Julius Rosenwald had donated $50,000 for a YMCA hotel for men and boys in Chicago and had personally solicited several other major gifts toward its completion. After all that, Rosenwald introduced Booker T. Washington.

Washington elicited laughter when he began his remarks by saying that he was ready to go back to Alabama, where at least it was not so hot. He then picked up on the idea Rosenwald had used earlier in the day of inferior and superior races, one offensive to modern ears and also to many blacks at the time. Washington made reference to it often by assuring his listeners that any inferiority in blacks was not intrinsic but was the result of 250 years of slavery. The defect thus created could be overcome. Only the "best" people, he said, are willing to come into contact with an "inferior" race: "The little fellows, the weaklings, are always afraid to come in contact with an unpopular race or with an unpopular cause. It is so in the South, it is so in the North." With that bit of flattery to his hosts, he moved on to praise for the YMCA's work in Chicago, particularly the campaign for the YMCA for blacks. Washington explained that blacks were willing to support their own YMCA building because they learn the habit of giving from their financial support of the black church. "We inherited no church houses since we became a free people—within forty five years we have erected 35,000 church buildings and in 90% of cases the money with which to erect these buildings has come out of our own pockets. And, Mr. Rosenwald, if you had not done anything else through this movement than to give the white people of this city of Chicago a chance to know the kind of colored people they have . . . it would have paid for itself."

Washington reported on Philadelphia and Atlanta, where fund-raising was under way for "Rosenwald" black YMCAs.

Washington then reaffirmed the confluence of interests between the country's white and black populations with a not-so-subtle putdown of his own—of recent immigrants. "In the fundamental elements of citizenship, the Negro in America is more like a white man than any other race. We understand your ideas of civilization . . . We dress like you do. We do not dress like some of these other fellows that come into this country . . . We don't hold onto a foreign tongue like some people do." Washington often alluded obliquely to the competition for jobs between black and foreign-born workers. In his Atlanta speech he had invoked the loyalty and familiarity of the black worker as opposed to the foreigner. He subtly used stereotypes—the radical foreigner, the loyal black. He knew that *foreign* might evoke thoughts of not just Italian, Greek, or Russian workers but also of the fear of radicals, revolutionaries. The "loyalty" he spoke of might also be heard as docility.

Enthusiastic applause greeted Washington's remarks. Then, again, Rosenwald spoke. "I don't believe that I am entitled to any credit for any of these things that they have referred to," he said. "I have such a good time doing anything of this kind that I do not feel any thanks is due me." He said that he was particularly gratified by the work he had been able to do with the YMCA because "it has a tendency toward bringing together the two races which have to live side by side. And in my opinion there is no problem which faces the American people that has more importance than this problem of how to have these two races live congenially and try to uplift each other."

Sometime during the course of this very full, very warm day, Washington asked Rosenwald if he would consider becoming a member of the board of Tuskegee Institute. Julius said that he wanted to visit before he made up his mind.

Two weeks after Washington's visit the *Chicago Tribune's* front page carried a small article at the bottom of the page under the headline "Six Negroes Are Lynched." It said that a mob had taken the men, accused of murder, from their jail cells. Under the headline, smaller type read, "Bogus telegram used by Lake City mob in order to get men held under murder charge."

Washington had spent his whole life navigating the tricky shoals of black-white interaction, but close association with a black man was new for Rosenwald. In a letter to Gussie, who was still in Europe, he told her that, the day after the luncheon, he took Washington and a friend of his for a tour of the Sears, Roebuck plant. The friend was Dr. George Cleveland Hall, Washington's host during his stay, his personal physician, and a doctor on the staff of Chicago's Provident Hospital, whom Julius described in the letter as "a 'culled' gentleman." Of lunch at Sears, he wrote, "It was unique if nothing else to sit down in our restaurant with two darkies but I'm sure it was an object lesson which will have its effect on prejudice in many forms. I afterwards acted as guide for them through the building and could see a number of curious faces wondering how I happened to be showing 'niggers' around . . . I hear nothing but praise about my latest enterprise. The other comments are no doubt less audible in my presence but you know my views on that point, my sweetheart, don't you?" One account of Washington's visit says that Rosenwald's chauffeur balked at driving a black man in his car. But when Julius responded that he would ask someone else to drive them, the chauffeur reconsidered. He asked if Rosenwald were going to ride in the car with his black guest. When he heard that he was, the chauffeur changed his mind, telling Julius, "If you're going to ride with him, I guess I can drive him."

In a time when black-face minstrel shows were popular and literary works like the Uncle Remus stories and even newspapers invariably conveyed black speech in dialect, when Washington himself, from time to time, used it in speeches when he told jokes, Gussie and Julius used terms like *culled*, *darky*, and even *nigger* unthinkingly. Stereotypes were more familiar to them than actual black people. But Julius also noted in his letter to his wife that the YMCA dinner had been about a third "colored men" and that he was "happy to see it as it indicated that my movement was bringing the races together."

A few days later, as the Twentieth Century Limited train carried Rosenwald toward New York and a ship bound for Europe, he responded to a letter from Washington that thanked him for "the very great and helpful kindness which you showed me during my stay in Chicago" and invited him to visit Tuskegee to "see our work and hear our students sing." Julius wrote that he would like very much to come.

A week later, the Rosenwalds were all together in London, taking in the sights and sounds of the city at its most pompously festive in honor of the coronation of Queen Victoria's grandson, George V, and his wife, Queen Mary. From seats on Pall Mall, the family viewed the procession that bore the royal couple to and from Westminster Abbey. When a reporter asked what he had thought of all this, Rosenwald, an instinctively egalitarian, forward-looking man, replied, "I was greatly impressed with the manner in which the pageantry was carried out, but a far more interesting sight was the enormous crowds in London."

Rosenwald's offer to donate funds for black YMCAs drew nationwide attention. The money to match his grant was quickly raised in Chicago and work begun on the building. Members of the YMCA in Philadelphia, Indianapolis, Atlanta, and Los Angeles went to work to raise money for buildings in their cities. And Rosenwald was gratified by a letter from the president, William Howard Taft, which praised him for his patriotism and said of the black YMCA buildings that "nothing could be more useful to the race and to the country." Taft also asked Julius to meet with him in Washington, D.C., which he did. The president asked Rosenwald if he would extend his offer to help the black YMCA in Washington, D.C., which had received a $25,000 donation from John D. Rockefeller and had raised some money from its black community but had, nonetheless, run out of funds to complete its building. He agreed to the donation for the Washington YMCA.

Rosenwald was traveling so he could not be in Washington, D.C., in late May 1911, when the Twelfth Street Northwest YMCA for black men and boys opened. His good friend Judge Julian Mack, who often worked with him on Jewish fund-raising (and who was prominent as the founder of Chicago's first juvenile court and had just been appointed to the U.S. Court of Appeals), was there, though, and spoke in his stead. Reporting to Julius on the experience, he wrote, "I told them I was there really on your behalf and I caught them tremendously by saying that you were doing this thing not because they were colored or despite the fact that they were colored but simply as a man for his fellow men." This was not entirely true, of course, but Mack followed the comment with an astute observation. "They dislike as much as do we Jews to be talked about as a separate class."

At the same time, though, being Jewish was something they never forgot. At about this time Gussie was writing to Edith, who with her sister Adele was spending a year at a boarding school in Dresden, saying that she had had a letter "full of mischief about you American girls. I fear the Hessling school will have a bad impression of American girls and may not want to take them again, especially the Jewish girls. So be very careful and not go too far. You ought [sic—owe it] to yourself and to your country to uphold a certain amount of decorum." Teenaged Edith and her friend had been amused by the costume of a plump tenor and had giggled their way through a performance of the opera.

CHAPTER 7

))(

Between Chicago
and Tuskegee

More than physical distance separated Julius Rosenwald's Chicago from Booker T. Washington's Tuskegee. Tuskegee—southern, rural, and black—was a world away from bustling Chicago. Yet what Julius Rosenwald found on his first visit there captivated his interest and retained his affection for the rest of his life. Setting a pattern they would repeat many times, he and Gussie traveled there for the first time in October 1911 in a private Pullman car filled with specially invited family and friends. On their first trip the guests included Julius's good-natured brother Morris and his wife, Mae; their sister, Selma, and her husband, Sig Eisendrath; and Rabbi Emil Hirsch, whom they knew well from the Sinai congregation they all attended and whom Julius greatly admired. Three others were men prominent in Chicago and well known to Rosenwald—Dr. E. G. Cooley, a former superintendent of schools; Wilber Messer, of the YMCA; and Graham Taylor, a professor of sociology at the University of Chicago who ran a settlement house, Chicago Commons, to which Julius made regular donations. Taylor had also created the Chicago School of Civics and Philanthropy, to teach principles of social work and community building. The travelers were connected to Rosenwald and to one another by bonds of family and friendship and by their shared interest in the latest thinking about education and social welfare.

Chapter 7

After a night on the train, they got off in Nashville for visits to all-white Vanderbilt University; all-black Fisk University (the alma mater of Margaret Washington and W. E. B. Du Bois); and Meharry, the first college in the country offering medical education to blacks. They spent a night on the train in Nashville, then traveled farther south to Montgomery and then east into the Alabama countryside, through deep woods of evergreens and trees just tinged with autumnal gold. At the little station of Chehaw, Rosenwald and his guests boarded another, smaller train that took them to the station near the Tuskegee campus, where they were greeted by the school's brass band. Ranks of students in crisp blue uniforms with shiny buttons and white gloves serenaded them up the hill and along winding roads that ran past imposing buildings of Tuskegee brick. Named Carnegie, Rockefeller, Huntington, Phelps, Emery, Slater-Armstrong, the buildings commemorated men and women who had made contributions, most of them financial, to the school. At the brick guesthouse for white visitors, Dorothy Hall (named for the great-great-grandmother of the generous donors Caroline and Olivia Phelps-Stokes), right in the middle of the campus, Margaret Washington was waiting to welcome them.

Although the buildings were certainly impressive, it was the human experience that made visits to Tuskegee so powerful. Maggie Washington entertained guests with gracious receptions at the Oaks, where visitors got to know other members of the school's staff: Washington's capable young secretary Emmett Scott; the Tuskegee treasurer Warren Logan, who had been at the school almost since its founding, and his college-educated wife, Adella; Booker's brothers John and James Washington and their families; the brilliant George Washington Carver. They and many others strove to give their guests a good impression. That the situation was contrived did not make it less meaningful. The Rosenwalds' group visits to Tuskegee placed under the feet of northern whites and southern blacks common ground that they might not have found elsewhere. As they toured the campus, as they visited immaculate classrooms in well-designed and well-constructed buildings, as they were introduced to students and faculty, the visitors were favorably impressed. The young black men and women studying English and mathematics, geography, history, and science, their dress and behavior regulated by Tuskegee's strict code (which included daily inspection for neatness and grooming and did not allow them to chew gum or to go out more than two nights a week), were polite and respectful. At each stop of their campus tours—the classrooms, the model kindergarten, the farm with its "piggery," the laundry, the brick-yard, and the printing shop—Julius and Gussie talked with young men and women the ages of their own children but from backgrounds vastly different.

Just a week before his second visit to Tuskegee, in a letter describing a fancy-dress party in honor of his brother Morris's birthday, Julius wrote that one of the Hammerslough cousins had come costumed as a "Southern darkey with a dress which was made out of a coffee sack with a hole to put the head through and two others for the arms; her hair was in pig tails." This was the crude but common stereotype that the well-dressed, well-spoken men and women of Tuskegee were help-ing to banish from Rosenwald's vocabulary and from his mind.

A visit to Tuskegee always included an evening service at the cha-pel, a distinguished red brick building with sloping roof; square bell tower; and tall, narrow windows open to the evening air. Inside were whitewashed walls with shiny, dark wooden beams and the first electric lights in Macon County. The heart of these services was the sing-ing—voices of hundreds of students joined together, sending the warm harmonies and melancholy longing of songs like "Go Down, Moses," "Swing Low, Sweet Chariot," "Steal Away," and "My Lord, What a Morning" up to the rafters, filling the chapel with music black people had learned in childhood from parents and grandparents who had been slaves. Washington encouraged students to remember the songs they had grown up with and to share them at chapel time, a reminder that God had sustained their people and would continue to do so. He called spirituals "these old, sweet, slave songs," and said he hoped to make them " a source of pride and pleasure to the students." Portia had audi-tioned for her teacher in Berlin playing an arrangement of a spiritual that had special meaning for her, "Sometimes I Feel Like a Motherless Child." The Fisk University Jubilee Singers had been making fund-raising trips up north and even to Europe for twenty-five years, but in those days before the phonograph and the radio, most white visi-tors had never before heard them. What to many blacks was a painful, even embarrassing reminder of bad times was to whites a stunning revelation. The songs breathed life into their often scant knowledge of the South and of the black people who lived there. The beauty and power of the singing could move them to tears.

Under the spell of this music and of everything he had seen on his first tour of the campus, Rosenwald got up to speak. "If anyone again claims that colored men and colored women will not and cannot be as good citizens as there are in America," he told the assembled students and teachers, "I shall ask him to come down to Tuskegee and visit the places we have visited." He praised the students for the spirit of their songs. Then he concluded, "What I have seen here today has inspired me beyond words. Your principal, Mr. Washington, to my notion, has done the greatest work of any man in America. How he can be as modest as he is with what he has accomplished is something unheard of . . . if only more people knew!"

As the train that would take them back to Chehaw and then on to Chicago pulled out of the station, Rosenwald and his guests waved good-bye while students on the platform sang "Auld Lang Syne." The men and women from Chicago carried away with them not just souvenir cotton bolls and pieces of sugarcane but also powerful impressions that touched their hearts and stirred their social consciences. None of this was accidental, of course. Having entertained white visitors at Tuskegee since the school's founding, Booker T. Washington knew how to give them a powerful and positive experience. It was not for nothing that his enemies, and even occasionally Emmett Scott, his secretary, referred to him as "the Wizard."

At Tuskegee, Rosenwald had found his own optimism and energy mirrored back to him by his new friend, Booker T. Washington. "Accept our sincerest gratitude and affection," he wrote in a telegram to Washington after his first visit. "Your personal fellowship and the revelation of all you have accomplished inspire us with higher ideas and an earnest desire for more practical and brotherly service for our fellows." The *Chicago Tribune* quoted Rosenwald as saying, "I was astonished at the progressiveness of the school. I don't believe there is a white industrial school in America or anywhere else that compares with Mr. Washington's at Tuskegee." In a speech shortly after his return, Julius expressed himself more forcefully than he previously had, saying that, "a harelip is a misfortune, a club foot is a deformity but side whiskers are a man's own fault. And race prejudices are side whiskers that are a man's own fault."

He went on in language that indicated that he was beginning to see things rather more clearly than he had previously. "The horrors that are due to race prejudice come home to the Jew more forcibly than to others of the white race on account of the centuries of persecution which they [the Jews] have suffered and still suffer." He continued with an astute observation on the violence directed against Jews in Poland and Russia: "We Anglo-Saxons, of course, cry out against this as a barbarous outrage and comment superiorly on the lowness of Russian civilization, and straightway turn around and exhibit the same qualities in our treatment of the Negro, which today is little less barbarous than is the treatment of the Jew in Russia."

When he was asked to contribute to a new organization of blacks and whites that had grown out of the Niagara Movement, Julius Rosenwald responded with a small initial donation. The National Association for the Advancement of Colored People, whose founders included W. E. B. Du Bois and Ida B. Wells, but not Booker T. Washington, chose the centennial of Lincoln's birth, February 12, 1909, as its official founding day. The purpose of the NAACP was to eliminate racial prejudice and to further the interests of colored citizens with regards to suffrage, education, and employment. The following year Julius again donated, this time giving $2,000, one of the largest donations the group had received. When a Chicago branch was established, Julius contributed to that as well and agreed to serve on its board. He helped arrange for the NAACP's 1912 meeting to be held at Temple Sinai, and he made a speech at its opening session.

A month after the Rosenwald group's visit to Tuskegee, Washington wrote to the former president Theodore Roosevelt, a member of the institute's board, with important news: "I think you will be glad to know that Mr. Julius Rosenwald, head of the firm Sears, Roebuck and Company, Chicago, the Jew who has recently given so much money for YMCA work among colored people in the cities, has consented to become a member of our Board of Trustees. I think he is one of the strongest men we have ever gotten on our Board."

Four months later, Julius was back at Tuskegee for his first board meeting. This time he brought, in addition to Gussie, their twenty-one-year-old son, Lessing, and another group of family and friends that included Judge Julian Mack and his wife, Jessie. Theodore Roosevelt was not among the men who welcomed him to the group. "Teddy" (as Julius referred to him in letters, though not to his face) was getting ready to challenge the incumbent President Taft (the man he himself had chosen to succeed him when his term ended in 1908) for the Republican Party's nomination for president; he was busy, and his larger-than-life personality and the buzz that surrounded him would have been distracting. But Rosenwald met the other members of the board with whom he would be working to ensure financial stability and continued smooth operations for the school, most of them, like him, powerful white men. The board's chairman was Seth Low, the widely admired former president of Columbia University who had also served, briefly, as mayor of New York City. Robert C. Ogden was a department store owner who had been a trustee of Hampton and had, in 1901, organized the highly publicized train trip through the South with other wealthy men, to draw their attention to the sad state of schools there for both blacks and for whites, that had led to the founding of the Rockefeller-funded General Education Board; William J. Schieffelin was heir to a pharmaceutical fortune. There was Charles Hare, a white Tuskegee newspaper editor and lawyer, and Victor Tulane, a well-to-do black grocer from Birmingham who was a personal friend of Washington's. Warren Logan, the school's able administrator, was on the board, too. Despite being a new member of the board, Julius did not just sit back and listen. Right away he pledged $5,000 a year for five years, half of a special fund to alleviate an immediate financial crisis at Tuskegee. Warren Logan had written to Washington in the fall of 1911 that he had not been able to pay the teachers on time because of a lack of cash. Donations were always coming in, but the school was an enormous, expensive enterprise. Rosenwald suggested people in Chicago who might be willing to make contributions and agreed to go see them and encourage them to donate by sharing his enthusiasm for the school.

Visiting Tuskegee also introduced Rosenwald to some of the less pleasing aspects of life for blacks in the South. On one of the early visits, driving in the countryside not far from Tuskegee, Rosenwald and Washington passed a dilapidated wooden shack with just one window. That, Booker T. Washington told Rosenwald, was a typical state-run primary school for black children in Alabama. He explained that thanks to two northern donors—Anna Jeanes, a Quaker woman who had given $1 million to aid black teachers in a fund administered through the Rockefeller-funded General Education Board, and Henry Rogers, an executive of the Standard Oil Company—some new schools had been built. But Jeanes and Rogers had both recently died, and there was still a huge need throughout the state and the entire South for more and better schoolhouses for black children.

For the Rosenwalds February 1912 was memorable not just for their second trip to Tuskegee but for personal reasons as well. On February 11, Rabbi Hirsch came to their home to officiate at a small, private wedding as Julius and Gussie's twenty-year-old daughter, Adele, married Armand Deutsch, the handsome young man who had been Lessing's roommate at Cornell and whose family lived across the street from them. Whatever doubts Julius and Gussie may have had about Deutsch (who did, indeed, turn out to be more charming than dependable), newspapers reported that their wedding gift to the young couple was $1 million.

And Julius ended the month spending a night at the White House as the guest of the president of the United States. Rosenwald had always been an active Republican (unlike his friend Julian Mack, a lifelong Democrat), supporting the party and its candidates with donations and his endorsement. There had even been rumors that if Taft won reelection in 1912, he would name Julius to his cabinet as secretary of commerce. Rosenwald pooh-poohed such talk, but still, he was pleased by the invitation to come to Washington for a meeting and gratified when the president insisted that he send to his hotel for his things and stay for dinner and the night. "Just think of it," Julius wrote to Gussie from Washington. "Here I find your best fellow going to bed in the White House." He went on to describe the "simple dinner—one kind of wine, Rhine wine," and said, "I'm going to sleep under a canopy in a room twice the size of ours. When I came into it all my stuff had been unpacked and laid out." He was not too jaded to be thrilled to be a guest in the Executive Mansion.

And finally, that month, too, Rosenwald sent a brief letter confirming plans for the visit Washington would make the next month to Chicago. "We are, of course, counting on having the pleasure of your company at our home during your visit here in March. I merely mention this again so there will be no misunderstanding concerning it," he wrote. In response to an inquiry about what Washington, who suffered from digestive problems, could eat, Maggie Washington wrote to Gussie. "Poor fellow," she said. "He has always been so strong and could eat anything he wanted that it has been hard to govern him. He eats eggs soft boiled or an omelet, not rich, toast, cream of wheat, grapefruit, prunes, canned peaches, broiled steak, rare, mashed potatoes and other harmless food." As the visit drew closer, Gussie wrote to her daughter Adele, who was honeymooning in Europe, "This week we shall entertain rather simply and informally for Booker T., asking people interested in philanthropic work to be present." She also noted that, "of course, his stopping here has caused a great many comments, but we don't mind. People will get over it." Indeed, the *Chicago Examiner* newspaper deemed the visit worthy of a story, which it ran under the headline "Noted Negro Educator Will Stay at Home of Philanthropist While Here."

On March 10, 1912, Washington missed his train connection and arrived in Chicago too late to address the enormous crowd that had turned out for a planned speech at Temple Sinai. In her long letter to Adele about the visit, Gussie reported that people were disappointed not to hear Washington (but that "Dr. Hirsch gave a splendid sermon on 'Shall Women have the Vote?'"). During the week that Washington was with the Rosenwalds, Jesse Moorland, the coordinator of the program to build black YMCAs, came for dinner one evening and Julius and Gussie gave several parties. They invited the friends and relatives who had gone with them to Tuskegee to come and visit with Washington again at their home.

After her guest left, Gussie admitted in a letter to Adele that she was relieved the visit was over. Perhaps remembering the balky chauffeur on Washington's first visit, she had been worried that she might have some "unpleasantness with the help," a negative reaction from her white household staff to serving a black man. Nothing of the sort occurred, and when the visit was over, Washington wrote to Gussie from Boston to say, "How very much I enjoyed my stay at your house . . . I shall never forget my visit, and shall never cease to thank you and Mr. Rosenwald for all your kindnesses." He also said that he was enclosing with his letter the house key they had given him so that he could come and go freely while he was a guest in their home. He wrote that he had "thoughtlessly carried [it] away with me."

In April 1912 the sinking of the British ocean liner *Titanic* horrified Americans. Among the 1,500 souls who perished were William Stead, the man who had written so fervently and critically about Chicago in the 1890s and a friend of President Taft's with whom, two months earlier, Julius had dined at the White House. Edith Rosenwald's friend Edith Goodkind had planned to return home from Europe on the brand new luxury liner, too, but she had fallen ill with appendicitis and so had changed her plans. She came home safely via another boat and, two years later, would become Mrs. Lessing Rosenwald.

By midsummer 1912 Rosenwald and Washington were writing to each other regularly. Sometimes as many as two or three letters a week went between Chicago and Tuskegee as they kept each other informed about fund-raising for Tuskegee and shared the names of people they had talked to about contributions to the special fund Rosenwald had suggested. They wrote, too, about the hundreds of new and slightly used hats and pairs of shoes from Sears, Roebuck that Rosenwald shipped regularly to Tuskegee and that were sold cheaply to students. The ever-thrifty Julius wanted to be sure this was making more money for Tuskegee than the cost of sending the shoes, saying that if that were not the case, it would be better to simply donate money. Many letters were devoted to Tuskegee business, but the two men discussed other subjects as well. Rosenwald needed Washington's help to assess the many requests for money that had started coming to him as his interest in black education became widely known. One was for a loan of $50,000 to the bank in the all-black Mississippi town of Mound Bayou (which Washington approved and Rosenwald made; the bank ultimately failed and Rosenwald lost his money, which was unusual for him). Others came from small black schools all over the South, some private, some public, all underfunded and needy.

Between Rosenwald in Chicago and Washington in Tuskegee a web of relationships grew. Washington's nephew, his brother John's son, Charles Washington, a medical student at Meharry, wrote to Julius that he was having difficulty meeting his expenses. Learning from Washington that "Charlie" had been "wild" in the past but seemed to be settling down to his studies, Rosenwald agreed to give the young man $25 a month for a year. Washington wrote to Rosenwald about gifts to Tuskegee from people who had visited with him, like his good friends Judge and Mrs. Mack and his younger brother, Morris Rosenwald, who contributed $500. Julius suggested to Booker that, having met his Sears colleague Albert Loeb at the Rosenwald home, he should contact him about becoming a donor. "I make it a point never to ask him for a subscription," Julius explained, "since if I did it would place him in an embarrassing position ... but with you he would be entirely independent." The board member Victor Tulane sent Rosenwald a letter thanking him for his contributions to Tuskegee and for his "manifestation of faith and charity toward our people." And Margaret Washington wrote to Gussie, "The coming of you two into our lives here gives us new courage, more hope and greater faith. I am not alone in this. Just this afternoon a group of us met accidentally in the house and the conversation turned to you and Mr. Rosenwald. We ended up by saying Mr. Rosenwald makes you forget all of the hard things in life. His presence takes off the *chill*."

Washington wrote to Julius's sister, Sophie Adler, thanking her for a newly published book she had sent him, Mary Antin's *The Promised Land*, a memoir of life in Poland, of fleeing anti-Jewish pogroms there and settling in America. Washington wrote that it was "a wonderful book, inspiring and helpful," although he obviously resented the emphasis it placed on the suffering of immigrants while ignoring the plight of blacks. "I was a little disappointed," he wrote, that the author "referred to the Negro in about the same careless and rather indifferent way that the average white American refers to my race. I was especially interested in how she would refer to the Negro in view of her own suffering." Still, he concluded by saying he had found the book valuable and had sent the book to his older son at college with instructions that he read it.

In June, Washington wrote a long letter to Rosenwald on a subject the two men had obviously been discussing. "I have considered

carefully the suggestion which you made regarding the method of helping the colored schools of the South," he said. If a special fund were
available for southern schools, he wrote, "a good, strong man" would
have to be hired to run it and to work with the state and county officials responsible for public education. Washington explained that state
governments, maintaining two separate school systems, white and
black, generally favored white schools, dividing the funds unevenly
so that the black schools received very little. In Alabama, for example, where about half the children were black, white schools received
more than $2 million a year, whereas black schools received only about
$350,000. If Rosenwald were to donate money for black schools, it
would be important to work in collaboration with local officials but
also to see that the county and state not fall back on the fund and
end up using it as an excuse to do even less than they currently were
for black children. But the need was great. "Many of the places in
the South where the schools are now taught are as bad as stables,"
Washington wrote. "And it is impossible for the teacher to do efficient
work in such places."

Another point Washington made was that any person whom they
might hire would have to spend time speaking with white southerners
"and convincing them that it is to their interest to help educate the
Negro." The southern white man, he continued, "likes to be talked to,
but does not like to be talked about. Great care should be exercised
to let the county officials feel as far as possible that they are doing the
work—in a word, to place the responsibility on them." Washington's
crucial insight was that the problem for black schools in the South
was not simply that they lacked funding; it was the attitude that lay
behind that lack. Some whites in the southern states weren't sure they
wanted schools for blacks at all, and they certainly did not want aid
to black schools to divert resources from their own children's education. Any effort to build better schools for blacks had to provide more
than money; it had both to convince white people that schools for
blacks were important and to persuade blacks that they themselves
could be part of bringing about something better. It had to help change
attitudes.

The following month Rosenwald responded to Washington with a
letter labeled "Personal." Sandwiched between details of their work

raising money for Tuskegee, Julius placed a question. "If you had $25,000 to distribute among institutions which are offshoots from Tuskegee or doing similar work to Tuskegee," he wrote, "how would you divide it?" Immediately, Booker replied that such an infusion of money for Negro schools would be a "Godsend . . . and can be made to accomplish more good just now than any one realizes. I think I am not stating it too strongly when I say that a wise expenditure of such a sum of money will enable these schools to do fifty or one hundred percent better work than they are now doing."

"Rosenwald Gives $687,000 to Public on 50th Birthday" announced a front-page headline in the *Chicago Tribune* in August 1912. Privately, Julius had marked his half century by making generous gifts to his mother (to whom he gave a house a block from his own as well as Sears, Roebuck stock); his five children; and his and Gussie's many siblings, nieces, and nephews. His public donations included $250,000 each to the University of Chicago and the city's Associated Jewish Charities (of which he was board president); $50,000 to Jane Addams for a country retreat for Chicago social workers; $50,000 to the Chicago Hebrew Institute, which assisted recent Jewish immigrants, for a new gymnasium; $12,500 to a Chicago-area manual training school for boys; and $25,000 each to a Chicago home for Jewish orphans, a tuberculosis sanatorium, and to "Booker T. Washington as trustee for improvement and establishment of Negro schools such as Tuskegee Institute."

Rosenwald used his fiftieth birthday as an opportunity to seriously focus on the philanthropy that, increasingly, was absorbing his time and attention. He decided to hire a secretary whose sole job would be to help him keep track of the requests for money that regularly piled up on his desk, requests that came from schools and individuals as well as from organizations large and small that thought their goals might appeal to him. In 1912, for example, he responded for the first time to a request for a donation from the Anti-Cigarette League's Save the Boy campaign with a $500 contribution. To help him deal with results like this, William Graves, who had worked at the Illinois Board of Charities, came to work for Julius out of an office next to his at Sears.

The relationship between Julius Rosenwald and Booker T. Washington became a double one, as their two assistants, William Graves and Emmett Scott, took over part of the copious correspondence involved in putting their plans to work. Between Chicago and Tuskegee, articles, books, reports, and letters went continuously back and forth. Rosenwald became fond of Emmett Scott; he invited him to his home and gave him and his son a personal tour of the Sears, Roebuck plant, a visit Scott, in his thank-you letter, called a "perfectly delightful, helpful and instructive day." In the fall of 1912 Graves wrote to Washington saying that Rosenwald was collecting a library and wanted to include "all the works of real value touching upon colored people, their development etc., etc.," and asking advice on which ones to buy. Washington responded right away with a long annotated bibliography, recommending books of history and sociology as well as his own writings. He named W. E. B. Du Bois's *The Souls of Black Folk* (which had been quite critical of him) and *The Quest of the Silver Fleece;* books on the Underground Railroad and black folk music; and a work called *Present Officers in Negro Progress,* by W. D. Weatherford, of which he wrote that it was "valuable . . . as showing the sentiment of the people who are in the South who are beginning to turn their attention to the necessity of doing something to improve the conditions of the Negro." After one visit to Tuskegee, Graves wrote to Washington, "Didn't we have a lovely ride together yesterday? I shall long remember it with pleasure."

Booker and Maggie Washington visited Chicago at the end of August 1912, and all that is known about their visit is from a letter that Booker wrote to Julius saying that "all of us are at home again, and we shall always feel grateful to you for the good time which you gave us while we were at Chicago." Booker and Maggie may have visited the Rosenwalds at their new summer home in Ravinia (now Highland Park) on the elegant North Shore of Lake Michigan or dined with the Rosenwalds at their house in town. Certainly, as always when Rosenwald and Washington got together, the visit included a lot of talk. Many years later, William Rosenwald would remember that he wondered what his father found so fascinating about his guest that he spent so much time talking with him. Washington wrote to Rosenwald, "bearing upon our conversation in reference to the need of schoolhouses in the South for our people," he was sending Julius an article he had written on the subject. Their conversation had moved on from the needs of already-established institutions like Tuskegee to the glaring need of many rural communities simply to have a schoolhouse. He wrote that he was working on a plan "for providing school buildings and I shall have something to submit to you pretty soon."

Julius and Booker were formal men living in a formal time. In writing, and presumably in person, they never addressed each other by their first names. But as the summer of 1912 gave way to the fall, Booker began writing to "My dear Mr. Rosenwald"; Julius responded with letters to "My dear Dr. Washington." Although this less guarded, more affectionate form of address did not last long in their letters, it was the beginning of their collaboration on a project that both men clearly found exciting.

On September 12, Washington formally proposed "a plan for the helping of colored people in the direction of small country schools." Reminding Rosenwald that $2,800 remained from the grant he had made to Tuskegee in honor of his birthday, Washington suggested "an experiment in the direction of building six school-houses at various points, preferably near here, so that we can watch the experiment closely." Each small school building would receive $350 from the funds Julius had already donated on the condition that the people in the community or the public school authority raise an equal amount. Traveling expenses of $50 per school would be spent for someone from Tuskegee "to get people stirred up and keep them stirred up until the school-houses have been built. I really think," Washington wrote, "the experiment is worth trying."

Then he added, almost as an aside, a thought that was, in fact, central to the program he was proposing: "One thing I am convinced of and that is that it is the best thing to have the people themselves build houses in their own community. I have found by investigation that many people who cannot give money, would give a half day or a day's work and others would give material in the way of nails, brick, lime, etc. I feel that there is nothing just now more needed in the education of the colored people than the matter of small school-houses and

I am very anxious that the matter be thoroughly planned for and well worked out and no mistake made."

A few days later Rosenwald replied approving the plan.

In the fall of 1912, Lessing did not return to Cornell. As the result of a childhood injury he had trouble with one of his eyes, which made it hard for him to study for long periods. Also, he was anxious to get to work. Typical of Rosenwald, he insisted that his son start at the bottom and thoroughly learn the family business from the ground up. In September, Lessing began what would be a long career at Sears, earning $12.50 a week and rotating through the departments in search of the place that would suit him best.

By then Washington's sons were both college students; Booker Jr. was at Fisk, and Davidson attended Talladega College, then transferred to Shaw University in North Carolina. He, too, had vision problems; he was blind in one eye. But he worked hard and was well liked by other students. From his older son, Booker Jr., Washington received the kind of letter familiar to most parents of children in college. "My dear Papa," he wrote in June 1912 on letterhead paper of the *Fisk Herald*, of which he was the editor. "I hate to bother you about money matters, but I must have some as it requires more in my senior year than it did when I was not a senior. Trusting that you will give this matter your immediate attention, Your son, Booker."

Portia Washington had studied piano for two years in Berlin, working with a well-known teacher, Martin Krause, and living in a boarding house, but she had returned home in October 1907 to marry. The groom was Sidney Pittman, an Alabaman who had attended Tuskegee, then gone on to get a degree in architecture from Drexel Institute before returning to teach at Tuskegee. He had been taken with Portia after hearing her practice the piano while he was repairing a mantelpiece at the Oaks. "You got some talent, girl," he had told her and had pursued her ever since with letters urging her to come home and marry him. With some slight misgivings, she accepted. The wedding took place at the Oaks, which had been decorated on the outside with colored lights and inside with "grasses, ferns, wild Southern smilax, white roses with multi-colored lights which made the interior most beautiful." A "particularly dainty" wedding feast featured chicken salad, rolls, cheese, and olives, followed by "ice cream in the form of red apples, lilies, white and green colored pears, busts of famous characters, roses and many others of similar kind." The young couple moved to Washington, D.C., where Sidney had several commissions including the design of the Twelfth Street YMCA building for blacks there. They soon had three children.

About the time their children all went off to boarding schools, the Washingtons became parents again when Maggie's orphaned niece and nephew, Laura and Thomas Murray, came to live with them. Thomas was soon grown and moved out after he found a job at a bank in Tuskegee, but Maggie and Booker adopted Laura. She became another daughter. Washington wrote to her and signed his letters "Papa."

Booker stayed in touch with his sister, Amanda, who was married and still lived in Malden. Unlike her brothers, she had not gone to Hampton. Her education was minimal. "My dear brother," she wrote in one letter. "I recived the three boxes of things yu sent me they were all the things I needed. I thank yu so much for them." Discussing some land she had wanted to buy, she wrote, "Brother the ground on the Hill is $50.00 & acker I am saveing peach stones to plant I'll Have & Orchard tell me how much to get." A conscientious brother, Washington sent her money and gifts and visited her when he could. To him Amanda was a reminder of the ignorance that he had left behind but in which, he knew, so many blacks all over the South still lived.

Always thrifty, Rosenwald thought that perhaps the new schools could be built most inexpensively if the construction materials came from Sears, Roebuck. He even thought they might be made out of the pre-fabricated houses that Sears sold. Washington wrote to Rosenwald at the end of September that each schoolhouse must be big enough for forty or fifty children. "It is often true," he wrote, "that children have to walk three, four and five miles to school . . . After you have gotten the plans and specifications from us, then it seems to me you will have the information which will enable you to determine which will be best—to have the houses gotten up by your firm & shipped to us, or whether it will be best to have them wholly built here." But the Tuskegee architect Robert R. Taylor had already begun thinking about what the design of the new schools should be. Clinton Calloway, another Tuskegee employee, was working to find communities ready to sponsor schools, and he realized that part of the enthusiasm he found in small towns was because the schools were to be community projects. The business generated for local enterprises was part of the project's appeal. Calloway wrote to Washington that "there seems to be a feeling in most cases that some local sawmill and local business house shall get some of the benefit of the money spent in putting up the building." So Washington diplomatically suggested to Rosenwald that the heavy building materials would best be acquired locally but that other materials such as hardware, paint, and furnishings for the schools come from Sears at a good price. This Rosenwald understood. At the end of the year he wrote to Washington, "I do not want Sears, Roebuck & Co. to be considered in the purchasing except as a factor toward reducing cost."

Julius and Gussie's trip to Tuskegee in February 1913 was their biggest yet. They took forty people, including their daughter, Edith; their relatives Joseph Eisendrath and his wife; and longtime friends Jacob Loeb (the brother of Rosenwald's Sears colleague, Albert, and a fellow fundraiser for the Chicago Hebrew Institute) and Lessing Rosenthal and their wives. Julius had wanted to visit an existing rural school near Tuskegee, and Washington suggested Mt. Meigs Institute, fourteen miles from Montgomery, as a "good and interesting" school located on an "old typical Southern plantation." The principal was a graduate of Tuskegee. There was much back-and-forth between the two men about how the group would travel from the train to the school, with Washington suggesting "the novelty of riding three miles through the country in . . . ordinary farm vehicles." Rosenwald finally rejected this idea in favor of automobiles, which, Washington wrote, would cost $70 but, he said he would "try to get it down cheaper." The group spent just enough time at Mt. Meigs for Rosenwald to see the students and note their excitement at his visit.

Afterward, Washington wrote to Rosenwald, "I cannot find words with which to describe the help which you have given us. You cannot realize how much the bringing of these important people into our school and into this part of the South means to us as a race and how much it means in the direction of bringing about happier relations between white people and black people."

A week later, Washington wrote to Rosenwald that one of his guests, Mr. Eisendrath, had donated $1,200 to Tuskegee for a scholarship. He also noted that "Mr. Eisendrath said he has talked Tuskegee so much to his business partners since his return that they have employed two colored men to do certain kinds of works in the firm."

That spring Washington wrote Rosenwald that three schoolhouses were almost complete. "You do not know what joy and encouragement the building of these schoolhouses has brought to the people of both races in the communities where they are being erected," he had written earlier. It was a statement designed to make Rosenwald feel good about the school building project. It was also, undoubtedly, true.

CHAPTER 8

X

Swing Low, Sweet Chariot

The carnage of the war to come—the Great War, the "war to end all wars"—was impossible to imagine in the hopeful spring of 1914, when Washington was traveling around the country making speeches, and Rosenwald was returning from an exotic overseas trip. In February, he had telegraphed the Tuskegee board that he was sorry to miss his usual visit, but in the words of his favorite of the spirituals he loved hearing there, he was "Walking in Jerusalem, Just Like John." He and Gussie were on an extended trip that took them to Europe, Egypt, and Palestine.

In November of the previous year, Julius and Gussie had seen two more of their children marry. They were delighted when Lessing married his sister Edith's lovely friend Edith Goodkind at the bride's home in St. Paul, Minnesota. Six days later they watched, less enthusiastically, in their own living room as their eighteen-year-old Edith married Germon Sulzberger, the son of a Chicago meatpacking family rumored to be in financial trouble. Lessing's marriage was to be a long and happy one; Edith's, brief and miserable. Nonetheless, at the end of December, the three couples sailed for Venice, then on across the Mediterranean to Egypt for sightseeing around Cairo and a trip up the Nile to Luxor.

The University of Chicago was a leader in the burgeoning field of Egyptology, and at Luxor, Gussie and Julius were treated to VIP tours of the excavations of the ancient city of Thebes and, across the Nile, of the Valley of the Kings. Walking through the rubble of excavations there, Julius kicked something that, when he looked at it closely, turned out to be the arm of a mummy. "Well," he told his companion, "we are going to be dead an awfully long time so we might as well enjoy this life while we can." Fascinated by what he saw, Julius donated $30,000 to the University of Chicago's Egyptian work. Then he and Gussie set off on a weeklong desert excursion with their new friend Aaron Aaronsohn.

Aaronsohn's parents had migrated to Palestine from Romania after his grandfather had been killed by an anti-Jewish mob. In 1909, Aaronsohn, an agronomist, came to the United States to raise money for his experiments in modern farming methods and the cultivation of the wild wheat that he thought held a key to future self-sufficiency for Jewish settlers in Palestine. Julius and Gussie had liked him right away, and his descriptions of Palestine and of his work there fascinated them. They invited him to visit whenever he was in Chicago. When Aaronsohn founded a Jewish technical college in Haifa, Julius, along with other prominent Jews in Chicago, including Julian Mack, agreed to contribute to it and to serve on its board. On one occasion, Aaronsohn was in town at the same time as Booker T. Washington, and the Rosenwalds introduced the two men. Washington was impressed and wondered whether Aaronsohn's ideas about farming in the hot, dry climate of the Middle East might have some application in the South. But he never managed to get Aaronsohn down to Tuskegee.

After nine days of desert exploration via camel, the Rosenwalds and Aaronsohn traveled from Egypt to Palestine, where they saw the Haifa technical college; visited the Agricultural Experiment Station at Athlit, near Mt. Carmel; went rowing on the river Jordan; saw Jericho and Jerusalem; and then drove via Nazareth to the ancient city of Damascus.

Although he had agreed to donate to the technical college and was personally very fond of Aaronsohn, Rosenwald had doubts about whether the new settlements could ever become genuinely self-sufficient. Unlike many of his friends, he was not a Zionist: he totally rejected the idea that the biblical account of God's gift of the land to Abraham meant that there was or should be a Jewish "homeland" in Palestine. The migration to Palestine of Jews from Europe and, to a lesser extent, from America, was a subject on which American Jews disagreed. The movement had begun in the nineteenth century and had gained momentum as European and Russian Jews fled repeated state-sanctioned violence against them. Some Zionists, as they were beginning to be called, were even considering the possibility of a Jewish state in Palestine. At the same time, though, Palestinians were expressing reservations about the settlements, and by 1914 there was organized resistance to them. Julius's friend Julian Mack, like many American Jews, was enthusiastic about the settlements and the new institutions the colonists were creating in Palestine. Reflecting views he had discussed with his friend and mentor Rabbi Hirsch, Rosenwald saw no need for American Jews to support a new Jewish state there. Hirsch felt, and Rosenwald agreed, that Jews had already found a secure place to live and thrive. In their view the promised land for Jews, as Mary Antin had hinted with the name of her memoir, was not and would never be in Palestine. It was America.

Washington did not travel for pleasure as much as Rosenwald did, but in the fall of 1913, he had a rare real vacation. Concerned about his high blood pressure, stomach problems, and general exhaustion, Emmett Scott had urged Washington to take a break. With some close friends, he went on a two-week fishing trip to a small town called Coden on the Alabama coast at Mobile Bay. There, the refreshing nighttime breezes chased away the mosquitoes and the water of the bayous teemed with fish and oysters. The vacationers, who included Victor Tulane, the black Birmingham grocer who was a friend of Washington's and a longtime member of the Tuskegee board, stayed at a fishing camp run by a member of the National Negro Business League (of which Washington was the founder and guiding spirit), a local undertaker whom everyone called "the Admiral." In a postcard home Washington wrote, "Got up at five this morning. Caught fifty fish yesterday." He wrote that he liked "fishing with the old-time pole and line. The new fangled fishing apparatus I have never had any use for or success with." Never able to completely let go of his responsibilities, he added, "Look after the garden and chickens." Each day, the friends went out on the water to fish, and at night they feasted on the shrimp, trout, and diamondback terrapins they caught. Ironically, one of the landmarks near Coden, mentioned by Washington in one of his last speeches, was the wrecked remains of the *Clotilda*, the ship that in 1860 had illicitly brought Africans to America to be sold as slaves. The shipowner's attempt to scuttle the ship was only partially successful, and its hull could be seen at low tide.

While Rosenwald was on his Middle Eastern trip, Washington was making the rounds of the conventions and meetings that were always inviting him to speak. In January, at the invitation of Tuskegee supporter John Harvey Kellogg (the inventor of cornflakes), he addressed the first National Conference on Race Betterment in Battle Creek, Michigan; then he went on to give speeches in Boston and Hartford. In February, back in Tuskegee, Washington issued a press release urging better treatment on railroads for Negroes (Washington preferred that the word be capitalized, and his files contain a letter from editors at the *Atlantic Monthly* assuring him that it would be in that publication, but even Washington's own writings are inconsistent). Later in the spring, his travels took him to Kansas and California (where he sent a crate of oranges to his sister, Amanda, in Malden). His travel was frenetic, but he kept up his correspondence as well. To a man named Tom Johnson who wrote asking his advice about immigrating to Africa, he wrote, "I am not in favor of such a movement for the reason that there are better opportunities offered Negroes in this country than in any other country in the world; and my advice has always been that they remain in this country, and as far as possible, in the South." With much more reason for reservations than Rosenwald, Washington, too, had faith in the promise of American democracy.

In June 1914, shortly before the assassination of Archduke Franz Ferdinand of Austria-Hungary unleashed the fury of war, Washington sent Rosenwald an enthusiastic account of a visit to the schools:

> Yesterday I spent one of the most interesting days in all my
> work in the South. Through our extension department under
> Mr. Calloway, a trip was planned that enabled us to visit four of
> these communities where schoolhouses have been completed.
> We traveled all told about 135 miles. At each one of the points
> visited there was a very large gathering averaging I should say

about a thousand people of both white and black people. It may
interest you further to know that two of the state officers from
the agricultural department accompanied me on the entire trip.
It was a most intense and interesting day and the people showed
in a very acceptable way their gratitude to you for what you are
helping them to do . . . I have never met a set of people who have
changed . . . from a feeling of almost despair and hopelessness to
one of encouragement and anticipation.

Later that month he visited Chicago, bringing photographs of newly
completed schoolhouses. By the end of their meeting Rosenwald had
told Washington that he would give $30,000 to help build one hun-
dred more schools.

When this plan was made public, an extraordinary avalanche of
letters cascaded onto the desks of each man. Teachers, ministers,
shopkeepers, and other local leaders from across the South wrote to
both Rosenwald and Washington asking how they could get schools
for their communities. From a white teacher in Virginia came a letter
telling Rosenwald that "the surrender of Gen. Lee has been 49 years
ago last April 9th, and it is both a pity and a shame to know that we
have Rural Districts in the County, thickly settled with Colored people, without any school houses whatever for the instruction of their
children." The author added in a postscript that "there are mountains of Race Prejudice yet against the education of Negroes in many
of these back corners." Washington heard from a white merchant in
Mississippi that "the white school has a good neat school house. The
colored school with four or five times the scholars has a much smaller
house and a dilapidated shack at that." A black teacher wrote that he
was "building a schoolhouse fifteen miles East of Greenville, Alabama
and will indeed be glad of any help possible." The superintendent of
schools for the state of Kentucky, a white man, wrote to say, "I am very
much interested in the negro schools, and especially the negro rural
schools." A white Virginia lawyer wrote that he and "a good colored
friend" had already built a school with contributions from both blacks
and whites, but they had not yet fully paid for it and wanted help.
W. E. B. Du Bois wrote to Rosenwald asking for a statement on the
offer for the *Crisis* (the NAACP publication of which he was editor).

William Graves referred Du Bois to Tuskegee for information. A black school principal from North Carolina wrote to Washington, "I have been preaching to our people here the Gospel of Self Help. I have told them that the very best way in which to secure all the help needed is to help ourselves all we can. This Rosenwald proposition is a loud and most eloquent confirmation of that fact."

One thing the letters made clear was that many people across the South were already at work creating schools for black children. Another was that they were under the impression that Rosenwald's offer was for unlimited aid, a dollar-for-dollar match of any amount raised anywhere, so long as it was for a school. In some communities where classes were being held in churches, homes, and shacks, people had already started raising money and were looking for donations of land and materials so they could build decent school buildings. Many things went into improving education, of course—better teachers, longer school terms, and improved curricula and teaching methods. But a new schoolhouse was a visible sign for all to see of a community's determination that its children were going to have more opportunities to learn than their parents had had.

By the fall, Washington had released the one-page "Plan for Erection of Rural Schoolhouses," a statement that carefully defined the program and Rosenwald's commitment to it. The amount the public raised had to be as much as or more than the $350 maximum Julius promised to donate for each new school. Rosenwald's money was "to be used in a way to encourage public school officers and the people in the community in erecting schoolhouses in rural and village districts by supplementing what the public school officers or the people themselves may do." This emphasis on involving public school officials was new, a result, in part, of the interest in several states of agents for black schools. These were white state officials charged with supervising black education, working in a role that had been created at the urging of the General Education Board and with salaries the board paid. Tuskegee would administer the program through what it called its Extension Department, approving architectural plans and providing all administration, including sending agents out into local communities to encourage work there toward getting a school. The offer was good for five years and was expected to partially fund about one hundred rural schoolhouses.

President Woodrow Wilson had declared America's neutrality in what many assumed would be a short war of limited importance to the United States. But by late summer, the Central powers of Austria-Hungary, Germany, and the Ottoman Empire were at war on two fronts with the Allies—England, France, Russia, and Japan. The war raised issues that set Rosenwald at odds with his friends on the American Jewish Committee (which had been founded after the pogroms of 1903 to help European victims of anti-Semitic violence). He feared that for American Jews to generate too much war relief aimed specifically at Jews overseas would stir up ill will against them. But when Rabbi Hirsch called a special meeting at Temple Sinai to discuss the dire situation of the Jewish settlers in Palestine, cut off by the war from foreign support and isolated among increasingly hostile neighbors, Rosenwald was there and reacted in a typically generous way. He agreed that as long as the war went on, he would donate $1,000 a month for relief work to help Jews in Palestine.

Indeed, the war created so many needs that Rosenwald was soon donating to a variety of funds for its victims. He gave money for displaced and targeted Armenians, for German war widows, and to Jews in Europe affected by the war. Hearing reports of the numbers of Jews made homeless by the chaos of revolution and war—the American Jewish Committee estimated that there were 750,000 in Russia alone—helped change Julius's mind about war relief specifically for Jews. The Jews of America, safe from war, safe from violent hostility, were the keepers of their brothers and sisters in Europe. Julius would soon make an extraordinary contribution to the efforts of American Jews to help them.

"Our Tuskegee trip was, if possible, even better than any previous one," Rosenwald wrote to Julian Mack in February 1915. The six Pullman cars that left Chicago on February 12 carried Julius and Gussie, Gussie's sister Lena, Julius's sister Sophie Adler, his cousin Julius Weil and his wife, and a group of particularly prominent guests. Among them was the Rosenwalds' good friend Jane Addams, increasingly a figure of national and even international stature for her valiant work with Chicago's poor but also for her emerging roles advocating for women's rights and against American involvement in the European war. Jacob Billikopf was a new friend, a young man prominent in Jewish fund-raising circles and president of the National Conference of Jewish Social Workers. Grace and Edith Abbott were sisters, social workers who served on the faculty of Chicago's School of Civics and Philanthropy. William Parker had come to know Julius through the YMCA. It was not just this stimulating group of people, though, that made the trip so memorable. To Julian Mack, Julius wrote, "We had some exceptionally novel experiences."

The train from Chicago reached Montgomery at about nine o'clock on a Sunday morning, and the Alabama state agent for black schools, a white man named James Sibley, met it there with eighteen automobiles to take the visitors out into the countryside to visit four new schools: Big Zion, Davenport, Pleasant Hills, and Madison Park. "At each place," wrote one of Julius's guests, "not only the children, but all the colored community in the vicinity, and many whites, were there to greet the party. They were lined along the road several tiers deep, waving evergreen branches and singing the old plantation refrains of their fore-elders." Another account said that as the guests gathered in front of the schools, children called out Julius's name.

The welcoming programs included reports on the amount of money the residents had raised for their school, how long the school term was, and how many students were enrolled at each school. They even mentioned the number of houses that had been repainted or whitewashed to help convince the building agents from Tuskegee that the community was worthy of a new schoolhouse. At each stop Rosenwald spoke to the crowd, telling the people how impressed he was by what they had accomplished. Near the close of one of these programs, a teacher asked if it was all right for a student to give something to Julius. He said it was, and a girl came forward, shyly clutching a scraggly bunch of wildflowers tied with a calico string. She said a few words of thanks and handed the bouquet to Rosenwald, who, for a moment, lost his usual composure. He took them with tears running down his face. Years later he remembered the incident and told a companion that this was one of the most beautiful experiences he had ever had.

By evening, the travelers were in Tuskegee, attending the weekly chapel service. The next day they began a three-day tour of the institute. The schedule was packed full of meetings for the trustees and special visits for their guests. One presentation featured a student explaining the nutritional value of the foods as she prepared a meal. Another was a demonstration of building techniques. One of Rosenwald's guests, Albert Pond, a prominent Chicago architect, talked to the students in the Division of Carpentry, Brick and Masonry, and Architectural Drawing. S. L. Rosenfels, head of the Sears advertising department, spoke to the printing division about his work and about the importance of what the students there were learning. And everyone, Rosenwald's guests and another trainload of visitors that had come with Seth Low from New York that included Ruth Baldwin, the widow of William Baldwin, visited the newly created farming community twelve miles from Tuskegee, dedicated to Baldwin's memory. Baldwin Farms was a two-thousand-acre tract of land, purchased with funds raised up north, and being sold in small lots with financial assistance to help black farmers to get started.

It was the new country schools, though, that generated the most buzz of the visit. Booker T. Washington's son Booker Jr. had begun working with Clinton Calloway, the longtime Tuskegee administrator who ran the school-building program, and he gave the visitors a slide show contrasting images of old school buildings with the new ones. An elderly black woman named Mary Johnson was there to tell her story. She had worked for nine years in nearby Notasulga, holding bake sales and even hosting a minstrel show to raise money so "those poor little children wouldn't have to freeze in that old schoolhouse." Once the building began, she was there herself, day after day handing planks to the carpenters. Her earnestness and satisfaction were even more powerful than the testimony of the slides.

A week later, Washington sent Rosenwald a copy of the *Montgomery Advertiser* marked up to show its coverage of the Chicago group's visit. "Unless you have lived in the South, as I have," Washington wrote, "you cannot know what this recognition on the part of the people in Montgomery means. The mere fact that a newspaper of the character of the *Advertiser* would give such wide publicity to a Northern party that came South, primarily to visit Negro schools, indicates more in the way of growth and tolerance than you can imagine."

Rosenwald returned to Chicago feeling good about Tuskegee and convinced that the program to assist in the building of rural schoolhouses would have a significant impact on southern communities. Letters he received from his guests expressed what the trip had meant to them. William Parker, of the Chicago YMCA, wrote, "The good fellowship, the earnest conversations, the revelations of prejudice gradually giving way before worth and mutual acquaintance, the spectacle of a race finally finding itself, these and many other experiences combined to make the visit memorable."

That spring, Julius Rosenwald donated $10,000 to Tuskegee Institute for improvements that included the school's first central heating system. He agreed, as well, to pay $125 a month to formally establish Booker T. Washington Jr.'s job as an assistant with the school-building program. Gussie made a few gifts of her own, underwriting the purchase from Sears of new rugs and window shades for Dorothy Hall. And, to mark their twenty-fifth wedding anniversary in April, Julius and Gussie made a gift of $5,000 to be divided as personal gifts to longtime members of the Tuskegee staff and faculty. Thirty-four members of the staff received gifts of between $25 and $275. Julius and Gussie gathered the many letters of thanks they received into a scrapbook. "In accepting this gift, my heart glows with renewed joy in your service," wrote one teacher, "for it assures me that your friendship is not for an hour or a day but for all time." Another said, "Your gift lifted a mighty burden off my heart and sent me on my way rejoicing. I love this work."

In the summer of 1915, the Tuskegee Extension Department published a booklet telling communities in great detail how to get a schoolhouse through the Rosenwald program. *The Negro Rural School and Its Relation to the Community* gave architectural plans and other guidance for creating a one-teacher elementary school, a central school drawing students from a four- or five-mile radius, and a county training school, designed to train older students in farming, home economics, and other trades. The booklet assured readers that "the designs for the buildings and grounds have been approved by the State Department of Education of Alabama. Communities in Alabama erecting buildings according to these plans may feel therefore assured that they will be accepted by the State." James L. Sibley, the state agent for Negro schools of Alabama, was one of the authors, as were three men on the Tuskegee staff—Clinton Calloway; George Washington Carver; and R. R. Taylor, the architect and director of the Department of Mechanical Industries.

"The first thing to do when a community desires to erect a new schoolhouse is to see the school authorities of the district and confer with the county superintendent in regard to the location of the new school building." Beginning thus, the book took the reader through every aspect of selecting a site (a school should, it said, "never be located within 200 yards of a railroad," nor should it be placed on "wet or swampy land"), emphasizing that "the title should be vested in the district, county or state authorities." There were instructions on how to situate the building, preferably with an east or west orientation so as to maximize natural lighting and at least two acres of land for gardens and playgrounds. Cloakrooms separate from the classroom should be provided and, if possible, a library and a workroom. Desks should be simple, and "wherever funds will permit," there should be one per pupil. The "indiscriminate tacking of small pictures around the walls should be avoided," but "one or two pictures of Negro leaders" and flags of the United States and the state should be displayed. There should be a school pig, "kept near the school if the teacher does not reside nearby, which should be cared for and fed by the children. Besides the educational value, the money value is not to be overlooked. The pig can be butchered in the fall or used for breeding purposes." Where there was no septic tank, a sanitary outhouse should be built. There were instructions on how to build a urinal and how to make a pad of toilet paper from old newspaper (although the book specified that commercial toilet paper could also be purchased "from local stores at very low cost").

The booklet also addressed how to raise money for the schools:

> Through the pastors and other leaders, work up a big meeting
> at which some good speaker will preach the doctrine of good
> school houses from his heart—a man or woman who can stir up
> and put new life into a dead community . . . When the women
> want to raise money they often cook good food at their homes
> and each takes a basket of theirs to a community place where the
> men and others are served but charged a good price for what they
> eat. Singing, speaking and harmless games can be put into the

131

program for the basket supper . . . Special educational rally days,
basket suppers, evening socials, concerts, opossum and rabbit
suppers and a canvass for help among the white people of the
community are some of the ways local funds can be raised.

Suggested games were pin the tail on the donkey, tug-of-war, walking
to Jerusalem, and the fishing pond. Another tip provided was that a
white landowner asked to donate for a school "can readily understand
how a dollar put into a school house will enhance land values by bringing a better class of renters to the community."

Part of the appeal of the schools, as an article in *Southern Workman*
pointed out in 1916, was that the buildings became not just schools but
community centers as well:

The black man has few public buildings which stand open to
him. Libraries, museums, city halls, theaters, lyceum buildings
are in general closed to him, especially in the South. Only the
court house and the jails among the public buildings stand with
their gates ajar to him . . . The Rosenwald School . . . is serving
as an assembly hall for all these people. Here are to meet mother's
clubs, boys and girls canning clubs, farmers conferences and
community improvement gatherings. Here on the school grounds
the colored boys whether students or not have their baseball
games, here they gather for their basket picnics, their suppers
and their socials.

Near the tiny town of Boligee in western Alabama, where the rav-
ages inflicted by the boll weevil had left black cotton farmers even
poorer than they had been before, a local black pastor named Reverend
M. D. Wallace rode a mule around the county to invite people to come
to an "arousement" about a new school. An observer (whose name has
not survived) described one of the people who came forward: "One old
man, who had seen slavery days, with all of his life's earnings in an old
greasy sack, slowly drew it from his pocket and emptied it on the table.
I have never seen such a pile of nickels, pennies, dimes, and dollars,
etc., in my life. He put thirty-eight dollars on the table, which was his
entire savings."

In the fall of 1915, Washington, as always, was busy attending to family matters, dealing with Tuskegee business and traveling. To Booker Jr., newly married and the father of his grandson and namesake, Booker T. Washington III, he wrote that he could not lend any money to repair his barn, but he did say how pleased he was "to see how nicely you are fixing up your front yard." To his and Maggie's adopted daughter, Laura, who had just entered Spelman College in Atlanta, Washington wrote that he had sent her a book "which I hope you will read and enjoy" and asked her to let him know "if you need any pictures or anything like that for your room." He closed by hoping that she had "good agreeable roommates" and assuring her that "we think of you constantly." He wrote an article that appeared later that year in the *New Republic* titled "My View of Segregation Laws," which he introduced with a typical bit of common sense. "It is probably useless to discuss the legality of segregation; that is a matter which the courts will finally pass upon. It is reasonably certain, however, that the courts in no section of the country would uphold a case where Negroes sought to segregate white citizens. That is the most convincing argument that segregation is regarded as illegal, when viewed on its merits by the whole body of our white citizens."

His article ended with a summary of why segregation "is ill-advised," which began with "it is unjust" and ended with a revealing observation: "There has been no case of segregation of Negroes in the United States that has not widened the breach between the two races. Wherever a form of segregation exists it will be found that it has been administered in such a way as to embitter the Negro and harm more or less the moral fibre of the white mass. That the Negro does not express this constant sense of wrong is no proof that he does not feel it."

Traveling up north, Washington's speeches were as forceful as ever. "There is sometimes much talk about the inferiority of the Negro," he said in one address. "In practice, however, the idea appears to be that he is a sort of superman. He is expected, with about one-fifth of what the whites receive for their education, to make as much progress as they are making." To Maggie he wrote, from his speaking tour, that he was "getting on very well."

In truth, though, this frenetic activity was deceptive. Washington was dying. His friend George C. Hall, the Chicago physician who had been part of the fishing trip to Mobile Bay in September, wrote to Rosenwald that fall saying that Washington's two weeks of rest had not improved his health; in fact, his blood pressure was dangerously high, and he was suffering from arteriosclerosis. Washington wrote to Rosenwald expressing regret that he had to be in New York for medical tests in November and so would not see him when he came south for the inauguration of the new president of Fisk University. From Nashville, Rosenwald wrote to Gussie that he had seen Washington's secretary, Emmett Scott. "He is a fine chap and a wonderful mind," he wrote. "Of course, they are all much saddened by Mr. W. illness but they are not apprehensive."

From Nashville, Rosenwald journeyed on, leaving the train at Montgomery to continue by car with another Tuskegee representative, Ernest Attwell, for quick visits to four new schools. Writing to Gussie, he mentioned having heard a concert by the Fisk Jubilee singers in Nashville. "When I came forward, everyone in the audience rose and waved, a most unexpected thing there. I was quite touched." At the schools, he said, there were great crowds with "signs—Welcome Mr. R—to school. I just stopped long enough to go inside and to thank them for the reception. Such enthusiasm as they evidenced. I am greatly pleased with this work." At Tuskegee, Julius enjoyed "the loveliest meals" at Dorothy Hall and conversation with Emmett Scott, Warren Logan, Ernest Attwell, and other teachers and administrators. "The more I see of the staff," he wrote, continuing his long letter to Gussie, "the happier I am to be connected with the school." As he was leaving Tuskegee, in the little train station town of Chehaw, Rosenwald visited another new schoolhouse that had been built with funds he had provided. "The usual yelling and singing" greeted him, he wrote, and bonfires lit up the November evening.

But even as Rosenwald headed for New York, Margaret Washington was writing to him that it would not be possible for him to see her husband. "The doctors all agree," she wrote, "that I should go South at once. We wanted to see you but think we must go on. Every day he is weaker and weaker . . . It is terrible, Mr. Rosenwald, to see him so broken all at once it seems and yet he had not been well for some time." Then she added a hasty postscript: "Thank you again and again for what you are to us all."

Mrs. Washington was taking her husband home to die. In a statement released to the Associated Press as he boarded a train at Pennsylvania Station, Washington explained, "I was born in the South, I have lived and labored in the South and I expect to die in the South." It was nine o'clock Saturday evening when he and Maggie reached Chehaw station, where Booker Jr. met them with an ambulance. It carried Washington up the hill to Tuskegee and home to the Oaks. There he was laid in his own bed, and very early Sunday morning, with his wife and children near him, he died.

Just a few weeks before his death Washington received a letter from a man who had heard him speak in New Haven. William H. Jackson wrote of approaching and asking to "shake the hand of the man whom he had been reading so much of and trying to follow the examples and teaching of him and remember also how readily you extended your hand and gave him that sincere grip which he will long remember and honor." Booker T. Washington's role as mentor and champion of black people emerging from the degradation of slavery had been unique. The thousands of students and teachers, powerful men and simple working folk, blacks and whites, who packed his funeral service in the Tuskegee chapel were tribute to that. They filed silently past his coffin and wept as they sang the words of the spirituals that he had made such a part of Tuskegee's life. "Swing low, sweet chariot," they sang, "coming for to carry me home . . . Swing low, sweet chariot."

Having just returned to Chicago from Tuskegee, Julius did not attend the funeral. But he wrote Margaret Washington, "My heart is too sad to attempt words of consolation for you in our country's great loss. One of our noblest and foremost citizens has passed to his reward."

The board moved quickly to name a successor to Washington at Tuskegee. Rosenwald thought leadership should pass to Emmett Scott, who had been so close to Washington over many years and of whom he was very fond. Others, though, including Margaret Washington, favored a new beginning with someone a little removed from the insular world of Tuskegee. Robert Russa Moton, a vice principal at Hampton, had been a close friend of Washington. Indeed, he had visited Washington in the hospital a few days before his death (at which time Booker had told him how much he appreciated Julius's "personal kindness" to him). Rosenwald reluctantly agreed to support him after receiving a strong letter from Theodore Roosevelt expressing admiration for Moton (and assuring him that Moton "has great strength, and yet he is absolutely free from the bumptiousness or self-assertiveness which would at once ensure failure in his position"). The institute would go forward, he knew, much as it had before, under this new leadership.

But what of the plan to build small rural schoolhouses? What could replace the extraordinary attention and care that Booker T. Washington had personally focused on them? With Washington gone, Rosenwald was the guardian of their shared vision of a partnership with rural southern communities to build modern schoolhouses for their black children.

CHAPTER 9

X

A School in Every County

"Inadequacy and poverty are the outstanding characteristics of every type and grade of education for Negroes"—this was the conclusion of the 1917 Jones report, a major study of black education that the federal government conducted over a period of several years (aided by a grant from a charitable foundation, the Phelps-Stokes Fund). Although the details of the report's findings were controversial, no one disputed this essential finding. Educators could argue about some of Jones's specific recommendations and comments on particular institutions, but no one could deny his assertion that for southern blacks, despite all the contributions the General Education Board and individual philanthropists had made, opportunities for education, from primary school through college, were still much too limited. Despite the beginnings that the Rosenwald building program had made in providing schoolhouses in one Alabama county, the work of educating the mass of black children in America, and especially in the rural South, was just beginning.

The same year the report was published, 1917, Rosenwald approved funding for three hundred more schools to be built under the supervision of Tuskegee in response to requests from states across the South. The new agreement added more staff to assist Clinton Calloway, including Booker T. Washington Jr. and assistant rural school agents in nine states who would get half their salaries from the states and half from Rosenwald. He added, as well, a small amount of extra financial assistance to jurisdictions that agreed to keep their schools open for at least five months a year. As Booker T. Washington had often pointed out in his speeches, black children can't learn as much as white children if they only go to school half as much.

For the next year and a half, though, Rosenwald's attention would move elsewhere. In April 1917, the United States entered the European war, and he was recruited to go to Washington as part of a group of prominent businessmen serving on the Advisory Commission to the Council of National Defense. Leaving his trusted secretary, William Graves, in charge of his charitable work and Sears under the care of Albert Loeb, and canceling his own salary, Julius moved to Washington and became a dollar-a-year man, serving the government without compensation. He and Gussie rented a mansion on Sixteenth Street Northwest and plunged into the frenetic social and political life of the patriotic, energized wartime capital.

Government bureaucracy was an unfamiliar milieu for Rosenwald. As chairman of the Committee on Supplies, assigned to advise the government on the procurement of materials needed to ready the military for war, he worked to cut prices by, among other things, eliminating intermediary suppliers as he had at Sears. But the mandate of his committee was unclear, and some people questioned Julius's motives and methods. Awkward in responding to criticism of him from Congress and furious at any suggestion that his leadership would inappropriately benefit Sears, Rosenwald became increasingly frustrated with the work and unhappy in Washington. In the summer of 1918, when a representative of the YMCA asked him to suggest someone from Sears who might go to Europe and make speeches about business and the opportunities it offered as part of the YMCA's programs to care for the troops, he did suggest someone—himself.

The trip got him away from the frustrations of the capital city and perfectly suited Rosenwald's gregarious personality. In August, he and six thousand young soldiers sailed for France on the liner *Aquitania*. Once there, he toured battlefields, rode in a tank, tramped around the trenches in the mud, and observed the enemy's lines through a telescope. He donated Sears, Roebuck catalogs to military hospitals so the wounded could read something that would remind them of home. He visited Paris where he ran into Edwin Embree, an employee of the

Rockefeller Foundation of which he was a trustee, and the two had several convivial dinners. And, always fond of word play and humor, Rosenwald was ready with a witty rejoinder when, along with a group of military officers, he was invited to meet Secretary of State Newton Baker. Dressed in military fatigues but without any sign of rank, Julius stepped briskly forward and introduced himself to the secretary as "General Merchandise!"

One person who met Julius in France found him "very friendly and democratic, stopping soldiers on [the] street to introduce himself and get their names so he could write home about them." In tents and bivouacs, Julius gave dozens of talks to American troops. In a letter home he said that he made a point of shaking hands with everyone and always, as he said, "made a fuss over the Chicago boys." He thanked the soldiers for their service and emphasized the wealth of opportunities that awaited them when they returned home.

He also followed up on a letter he had received before his trip from Emmett Scott who had left Tuskegee and was working as a special assistant to the secretary of war with responsibility for Negro troops. Scott suggested that Rosenwald remember them especially, and he did. "I speak of civic matters and politics," he wrote in one letter home describing one of his speeches. "I often show them what a disgrace it is to our country to treat the Negro as we do, and not give him a square deal, such as they like to have." One observer recalled having the impression that not everyone liked Julius's message of racial fairness, but another said his talk was the first one he had ever heard the troops cheer. "All my speeches were on the subject of making America a better place to live," Julius told a reporter when he returned home. "The Negro soldiers were willing to fight and willing to do any menial task asked of them. Every officer with whom I talked on the subject frequently praised their willingness to do their part in the war. I never heard any opposition to my sentiments."

During the summer of 1919 there were race riots in many American cities; the most devastating was in Chicago. By 1910 blacks had begun leaving the South in large numbers, seeking escape from sharecropping and the boll-weevil infestation and wanting better education for their children and relief from the oppressive segregation of southern life.

Leaving the countryside and small towns of the South, they headed north—to New York, Philadelphia, Detroit, Cleveland, St. Louis, Chicago. But a year after Julius's encouraging words to black troops in France, what many blacks were finding in the North was not the fair treatment they longed for.

Exactly how the Chicago riot started is not clear. In the middle of a midsummer heat wave, a black teenager cooling off in Lake Michigan near a city beach drifted over to what was considered the white side. He drowned, possibly after being hit by a rock thrown from the beach. No one is quite sure. Furious crowds gathered, and for four days mobs battled each other throughout the city. Before order was restored, twenty-three blacks and fifteen whites had died, and hundreds of black homes had been destroyed. When the governor of Illinois set up a commission to study the riot, one of the first people he asked to serve on it was Julius Rosenwald. He accepted and suggested that Booker T. Washington's friend, Dr. George Hall, be appointed as well, which he was.

Just a month before the Chicago riot, the war officially ended with the signing of the Treaty of Versailles. Despite casualties that some counts put as high as ten million, the war did not lead to the lasting peace it was supposed to achieve. Similarly, the admirable combat service in France of more than forty thousand black soldiers did not end discrimination against them in the armed forces or anywhere else in American life. A month after the Chicago riot, Omaha exploded into racial violence that ended only with the arrival of federal troops. Across the South, in the year after U.S. soldiers returned from France, seventy-six black men were lynched, some of them soldiers in uniform. Six years after the welcome home of the Harlem Hellfighters, the black 369th Infantry, which had served longer in uninterrupted combat than any other division (and whose regimental music had given Europeans their first exciting taste of jazz), another army would parade on Pennsylvania Avenue in Washington, D.C.: thirty-five thousand white-robed members of the resurgent, viciously racist Ku Klux Klan.

By then, the report of the Chicago Race Commission had been issued, detailing the circumstances of the 1919 riot, identifying discrimination against blacks and segregation as contributing factors to it, and making a number of specific suggestions to improve the racial climate in Chicago. One was to allow blacks to join labor unions on an equal footing with whites. Another was encouragement of "race contacts in cultural and co-operative efforts as tending strongly to mutual understanding and promotion of good race relations." One senses Rosenwald's influence in the suggestion that getting to know people of the other race by working with them would improve relations. That had always been one of his assumptions. And the report stressed that riots could not be dismissed, as they often were, as having simply been caused by "hoodlums" or a disruptive "element." The riots were the result of prejudice and unjust, impractical, all-pervasive social structures.

During the war, Julius made a dramatic pledge in support of overseas Jewish war relief. In 1917, his young friend Jacob Billikopf had asked him for an enormous donation—$1 million, the lead gift in a $10 million campaign for the European relief work of the American Jewish Committee. Julius had agreed, although as usual for him, he insisted that others match his gift. "Be the Julius Rosenwald of Your City!" suggested the literature for the successful fund-raising campaign that followed. "We have had the good luck to live in this free country, the United States," Julius wrote in one of the campaign's brochures. "And it is our duty to help those whose cradles happened to be rocked in Russia instead of here. They are no more to blame for their condition than our children would be if they were similarly situated. What we must do is bring it home to the Jews of this country that it is our duty to aid the Jews of Europe." Julius made personal visits to request gifts from wealthy friends and acquaintances, and he attended several high-profile fund-raising dinners. At one in Chicago in May 1917, Julius announced that he had a new grandson, Richard Deutsch, and that he was making a donation to the cause of $500 in the young man's name. Julius also said that he and Gussie were adding $150,000 to what they had already given.

In April 1918, the American Jewish Committee honored Julius and Gussie for their extraordinary generosity and leadership of this campaign with a surprise banquet, affectionate speeches, and the gift of an antique gold loving cup from England. It was inscribed to "the Honorable Julius Rosenwald—Patriotic American, Faithful Jew, Far-seeing Philanthropist."

In 1919 Rosenwald hired Fletcher B. Dresslar, a professor of educational architecture at George Peabody College for Teachers in Nashville, who had written extensively on school design, to conduct a study of the more than six hundred school buildings to which he had contributed. The work of evaluating the buildings was challenging because the schools were spread out over a large distance and in rural areas where roads were often rough and unpaved. But Dresslar persevered in evaluating them, and what he found was disturbing. Not all of the schools met the high standards for design and construction that had been crucial to Rosenwald's original concept. Local builders were making changes to the plans without approval from anyone in charge. The very strength of the program—its reach into the local community—had become in some places a liability. Efforts to save money were resulting in shoddy workmanship or the use of second-rate materials. Tuskegee, finding it hard to supervise work going on in many different places at once, had scrimped on administrative expenses, and as a result the program's financial records there were in disarray.

Rosenwald digested the Dresslar report and swiftly made a dramatic decision. Over the strong objections of both Margaret Washington and the new Tuskegee president, Robert Moton, he took the program for rural schools away from Tuskegee. He decided, rather, to retain control of it himself via the newly established Rosenwald Fund, a charitable foundation he had set up to handle his donations and to promote "the well-being of mankind," a rather vague formulation that could mean anything he wanted it to. For those associated with Tuskegee this felt like betrayal; they saw it as resulting from mistrust of black leadership. To Rosenwald it was a practical question, a matter of sound business policy, and it was the kind of decision about which he was unsentimental. If he hired the staff himself and they answered to him, he would have more control, and he could insist on the efficiency, thoroughness, and excellence he so valued even as the program continued to grow. To open an office for the fund in Nashville, he chose S. L. Smith, a white agent for Negro schools who had been employed by the state of Tennessee. Smith was southern but had studied sociology at the University of Chicago. A class there taught by Graham Taylor had taken a field trip to Sears, and Rosenwald's remarks about his philanthropic work had deeply impressed Smith. As general field agent for the Rosenwald Fund, Smith would run the rapidly expanding school-building program.

Rosenwald had earlier announced that he would provide one half of the salaries for black men to work as assistants to the white state agents for black schools employed by the various states (whose salaries, in turn, the General Education Board supported) if the states would provide the other half. Soon, eight southern states had what they were calling "Rosenwald Building Agents," often former teachers or principals, some of them employed at black colleges or part of statewide education associations, working with people out in rural communities, encouraging them to think that a modern school building for their children was something for which they could realistically hope. They communicated these hopes to the county school superintendents and other state officials and then acted as intermediary between the state officials and the fund. The creation of this position was one of the factors that allowed the Rosenwald school-building program to flourish as it did in the 1920s. Edwin Embree, who took over as president of the Rosenwald fund in 1928, described the way the program actually worked:

> Slowly, doubt and antagonism were overcome. The State agents for Negro schools and the Negro building agents went from one county to another, seeking to interest officials in the program. The county superintendents, when their support was enlisted, went into communities even offering to arrange the sale of farm products to enable them to meet their share of the cost . . . Sometimes Negro preachers or other community leaders, having heard of the Rosenwald offer, themselves took the initiative and called meetings at which they held before the people the splendid vision of schooling for their children. And the vision, made concrete by a new and beautiful building going up here and there, caught the imagination of rural Negroes and support of white friends . . . Always, the Negroes gave more than they could afford.

Even as he was distancing the school-building program from Tuskegee, though, Rosenwald was maintaining his bond with the institute. In the summer of 1919, he visited the summer program for teachers there, and Ezra Roberts, one of the administrators, wrote to the new Tuskegee principal Robert Moton, "I know of nothing in connection with the summer school that has been a source of more genuine feeling and inspiration than the visit of Mr. Rosenwald." He said that some teachers had wondered whether such a person really existed; "they looked upon him as some sort of mythical person conjured up in order to get money out of colored people . . . There was so much of genuine admiration, respect and affection manifested for Mr. Rosenwald, together with the satisfaction, they felt in really knowing that such a person really existed and they had shaken hand [sic] with him . . . It seems to me that Mr. Rosenwald should know about the feeling of these teachers for him, and he should know something of the gratitude all them felt for him in their hearts."

In late 1921, Julius had to deal with a financial crisis at Sears, as prices fell after the war, and cost-cutting measures failed to slow the company's downward slide. At the suggestion of Albert Loeb, Julius made the decision to donate $5 million of his own money to Sears, Roebuck and to purchase the land on which the plant stood, which amounted to another gift of $4 million. What many contemporary commentators considered an extraordinary act of personal generosity and visionary leadership saved the company from failure. Many people wrote praising his action. One was his old friend Harry Goldman; another was Bernard Baruch, who had served with Rosenwald on the Council of National Defense and who told him, "Truly, you are a noble chap."

Despite an improving business climate, 1924 was a sad time for Julius Rosenwald. Early in the year, his younger brother Morris, of whom he was very fond, died after a mysterious illness. Then that spring a gruesome crime shook his Hyde Park neighborhood when a twelve-year-old boy, Bobby Franks, the son of neighbors, was abducted from the street almost in front of the Rosenwalds' home and was later found murdered. The shock was compounded when the son of Julius's close friend and Sears colleague Albert Loeb was arrested for the crime along with another young man they all knew. Richard Loeb and Nathan Leopold confessed to the murder and later revealed that the child they had originally planned to take was the Rosenwalds' eldest grandchild, eleven-year-old Ardie Deutsch. He had inadvertently disrupted the plan by going to the dentist rather than home from school on the afternoon in question. Julius and Gussie, who had known "Dickie" Loeb all his life, were, of course, horrified. The murder trial was sensational, lasting through the summer and revealing an essentially motiveless crime, a murder committed by two highly intelligent but nihilistic young men. They were convicted, although Clarence Darrow's brilliant defense saved them from the death penalty. That fall, Albert Loeb, who had been Julius's close friend and colleague for twenty-five years and the architect of the generous profit-sharing program for employees Sears had instituted in 1916, died of a heart attack.

Even before Albert Loeb's death, Julius had begun thinking about retiring from Sears. He had been ill when he returned from France, with pneumonia and an infected foot. He had recovered, but he was over sixty and had many interests he wanted to pursue beyond business. By the end of 1924, Rosenwald had hired Charles Kittle, a successful railroad vice president, to take over as head of Sears, and Robert E. Wood, whom he had met in Washington during the war and who had recently left Montgomery Ward, to join the company as vice president. Rosenwald did not give the job to someone within the Sears management; he felt fresh ideas from outside the company would revitalize it, and he generally opposed nepotism. His son, Lessing, was still young and, in any case, had moved to Philadelphia to run the branch office there. He himself remained chairman of the board of Sears.

Early in 1928, though, the issue of Sears leadership came up again when Kittle died unexpectedly. This time Lessing did want the job; so did two other longtime Sears executives, one of them Julius's brother-in-law, Max Adler, the husband of his sister Sophie. It was Gussie who encouraged Lessing not to resign if passed over, as he had threatened, but to see the advantages for him and his large family of remaining in Philadelphia, of not being overshadowed by his father's enormous reputation in Chicago, and of allowing himself more time for the art collecting that was becoming his passion. Julius himself felt no sentimental attachment to keeping management of Sears in the family and chose, rather than hiring Lessing, to promote Robert Wood, the gifted young vice president, who was already looking ahead to expanding Sears with a chain of retail stores. Max Adler, disappointed, resigned. Although in the years to come there would be criticism of

145

Wood as an anti-Semite and isolationist, in business terms the choice was a sound one.

The following year, when the stock market crashed, Lessing took the lead in wiring all the Sears stores to say that the company would protect its employees by guaranteeing the value of their Sears stock. Julius immediately backed up his son's initiative and pledged his own fortune for that purpose. According to an account of his transactions on that day written by Edwin Embree, Julius "saved hundreds of persons from immediate bankruptcy. He saw his own fortune in the collapse which culminated this day reduced by a hundred million dollars. He saw his business and his personal affairs plunging inevitably into the most troubled waters. It was one of the happiest days of his life." The press widely covered the Sears action, and Julius was embarrassed by all the mail he got praising him for what he had done. If his action was laudable, he suggested in a letter to the editor of one of the Chicago newspapers, it was because it had, perhaps, helped create confidence in the economy and keep panic at bay. On the last day of 1929, Julius wrote a letter instructing all Sears department heads to let their employees know that, in fact, the credit for this generous action belonged not to him but to Lessing.

As he freed himself from day-to-day management responsibility at Sears, Rosenwald became more deeply involved in philanthropy and launched some new ventures. One was a science museum for Chicago. Years earlier, he had visited the German Museum of Masterpieces of Science and Technology (usually called simply the Deutsches Museum) in Munich with his son, William, who had been fascinated by the place and had asked to visit it again and again. In 1926, Julius offered to donate $3 million for the establishment of a similar museum in Chicago and suggested that it be located in the old Palace of Fine Arts, the only building that remained standing from the 1893 World's Columbian Exposition. The project moved slowly forward. Originally it was named the Rosenwald Industrial Museum, but Julius pushed for several years to have his name removed from it, insisting that his motivation was less modesty than concern for future fund-raising— if the museum bore his name, people would assume that he or his family members were permanently subsidizing it. Today, it is called the Museum of Science and Industry, and it is one of the jewels of Chicago.

And Rosenwald embraced an experiment in collaboration with the young Soviet government of Russia. From the financier Felix Warburg, who was chairman of the Joint Distribution Committee, he learned about a project to finance Jews in the Soviet Union to move from cities to rural colonies in the Ukraine and the Crimea. To Rosenwald this seemed like a hopeful endeavor, an opportunity for Russian Jews to help themselves achieve stability and prosperity and infinitely preferable for them to moving to Palestine, as some European Jews were doing. In 1925, Julius agreed to donate $1 million to the colonies if $9 million could be raised for the same purpose from other sources. The following year he was not well enough to travel to the Soviet Union for a visit, but twenty-two-year-old William Rosenwald, who was then studying in London, did join Jacob Billikopf on a tour of the colonies. It was an emotionally gratifying experience for William—the colonists were spirited and wildly grateful to their American benefactors, greeting them with words he remembered sixty years later. "Nashi! Nashi!" (Ours! Ours!). No one foresaw the way the collectivized Soviet economy would absorb the colonies, essentially obliterating them in the misery and increasing anti-Semitism of the 1930s. Rosenwald was not the only American progressive to be taken in by Soviet promises. The Russian colonies were his one major investment that simply did not pay off.

Rosenwald remained on the board of Tuskegee until the end of his life. He commemorated Booker T. Washington with a donation of $100,000, part of which was used to build up the school's endowment, and he stayed in touch with Margaret Washington until her death in 1925. But Rosenwald was never personally as close to Robert Moton as he had been to Washington. As the years went by, he increasingly raised questions about Tuskegee's financial management and the efficiency of its board while supporting changes to the curriculum that included the introduction of the first college-level courses. Moton wrote regularly to the Rosenwalds, sending them sweet potatoes, beets, turkeys at Thanksgiving, and, in the summer, peaches and flowers from the Tuskegee farms. In a letter to Julius's assistant, William Graves, Moton said that "what Mr. and Mrs. Rosenwald have meant to me personally in the way of encouragement and frank, wholesome suggestions and counsel, means as much to me as any single thing that has come to me during my service here." In one note of thanks, Gussie wrote to Moton that the Alabama peaches he had sent "taste like the real thing," and in another that the flowers were "a breath of springtime" and made her "homesick for Tuskegee."

Tuskegee weathered a severe storm in 1923 when a new Veterans' Administration hospital opened near the school. Moton had pushed hard to have it placed there, and so he was disappointed when it became clear that the local administrators of the hospital planned to hire only whites as senior staff. The situation was absurd—by law in Alabama white nurses could not care for black patients. The plan was to have poorly paid black nurses' aides do the actual work of caring for the hospital's black patients while white nurses took home the high salaries. Moton held firm in his insistence that the professional staff be black. The situation became extremely tense when Ku Klux Klan members paraded through town and even into the hospital itself. The NAACP and local church groups and lawyers pressed hard for a resolution to the case, and after a tense summer, supported by the Veterans' Administration in Washington, they prevailed. From the following summer on the staff was entirely black.

When Julius, in his late sixties, could no longer travel to Tuskegee because of Gussie's and his health, his children maintained the family's connection to the school. In 1929, Lessing's fourteen-year-old son, Julius Rosenwald II, accompanied the annual party that traveled there and, according to Robert Moton, "brought down the house" with his "gracious and attractive speech" in the chapel. In the spring of 1931, when Tuskegee celebrated its fiftieth anniversary, nine members of the Rosenwald family were present. William Rosenwald joined the board in 1935 and served for forty-one years.

During the 1920s the school-building program was extraordinarily productive, producing more than four hundred schoolhouses a year. A report written for the fund in 1927 by O. H. Bernard, state agent of rural schools in Tennessee, offers a view of how it worked. He writes that in 1917, as superintendent of schools for Robertson County, he was trying to improve educational facilities for black students and that the most important need was "better buildings and equipment." He goes on:

We had neither funds nor sentiment sufficient with which to
erect the much needed new buildings. Through the agency and
co-operation of Mr. S.L. Smith . . . I learned for the first time
of the Julius Rosenwald Fund and its application. With the
assurance of $400.00 from this Fund, I personally undertook the
building of the first Rosenwald school in Robertson County,
and one among the first in the State. After holding a number
of public meetings with the colored people of one of our school
communities an old colored woman agreed to deed to the county
a desirable building site consisting of two acres of ground. Other
colored people in the community gave building material and
labor. With this as a beginning a small cash appropriation was
secured from the Board of Education, which, with the Rosenwald
Fund, was sufficient to complete a one-teacher modern school
building, the best and most attractive of its type in the county for
either white or colored children, and even compares favorably
with the best buildings today.

In 1928 Julius reorganized the Rosenwald Fund with the goal of
making it more efficient and professional and hired Edwin Embree to
run it. A Yale graduate, Embree had grown up at Berea College, which
his grandfather had founded as a racially mixed school. Embree once
said he grew up thinking that *coeducational* meant blacks and whites
together. He and Rosenwald had met when they worked together as
trustees of the Rockefeller Foundation. The two men shared an optimistic outlook and an imaginative approach to philanthropy. At the
same time that he reorganized the fund, Julius made a major donation
of Sears stock, which placed the Rosenwald Fund among the ten richest American foundations. He formalized his long-standing opposition
to turning charitable funds into perpetual endowments, which he felt
could easily become bogged down in bureaucracy and lose sight of the
donor's goals for his giving, with the announcement that the Julius
Rosenwald Fund would expend all its money within twenty-five years
of his own death, putting itself out of business. To guide the fund, he
appointed a board of directors that included family members (Lessing
Rosenwald; Adele, then divorced from Armand Deutsch and the wife
of the prominent New York psychiatrist David Levy; and Edith's second

husband, Edgar Stern, of New Orleans) who would serve alongside several men he knew from his other charitable work. Julius decided that, with the exception of himself and Embree, no one would serve on the board for more than six consecutive years.

In the reorganization of 1928 the decision was made to move away from isolated, small schoolhouses and to build the larger schools that would attract higher-caliber faculty and to branch out with high schools, some of them in urban areas. The program was expanded so that in some places it paid for houses for teachers, libraries, shops, and school buses, as well. A report to the fund from Mississippi reflects these changes:

> Forrest County has a very unique system of education for
> the Negroes as a result of the Rosenwald building fund. This
> county has 977 Negro children . . . A complete consolidation
> with transportation has been put into effect in this county and
> instead of having eighteen or twenty small schools scattered
> over the county, they now have seven schools, all assisted by the
> Rosenwald fund, most of them with good teachers' homes, with
> 360 children being transported to and from these schools daily, at
> the expense of the county public fund. I am free to say that this
> would not have been done for a long time to come, if ever, if it
> had not been for the stimulus from the Rosenwald fund.

The writer concluded, in a perhaps overly optimistic vein, "With the interest now manifested on the part of the white people of this state every Negro child in the state will ultimately have an educational opportunity as good as any other child in the state."

Julius attended the dedication of the four-thousandth Rosenwald school in Method, North Carolina, in 1928. By 1932 there was, as Embree had intended, a Rosenwald school in every county with significant black population in the South. By Embree's estimate a third of all black children in the South were attending Rosenwald schools.

When Julius traveled, as he often did, Embree stayed in close touch, sending him long, thoughtful letters about the fund and the issues associated with it, including the cutbacks they had to make in fund staffing and in new grants after the stock market crash. Embree was always full

of ideas. One that came to nothing but that he and Rosenwald discussed in letters was the creation of rural schools in Mexico on the
model of the Rosenwald schools. Together, they took the fund's philanthropy into new areas—among them programs designed to improve
the health of black people in the South, including work to eliminate
hookworm and an important study of the prevalence and treatment of
syphilis (the Rosenwald Fund was no longer involved in 1932 when
the U.S. Public Health Service began the study that, by withholding treatment from 399 participants, became a notorious example of
exploitation of the black community and disregard of ethical standards
in medical research—the U.S. government issued a formal apology
to surviving study participants in 1997.) The fund made significant
grants to higher education, especially to black institutions—Howard
University in Washington, D.C.; the newly created Dillard University
in New Orleans; Fisk University in Nashville; Morehouse and
Spelman colleges in Atlanta; and Meharry Medical School—and it
gave $50,000 to the Commission on Interracial Cooperation which
was studying ways to improve American race relations.

The most dramatic new program undertaken by the fund began in
1928 and gave fellowships to several hundred individuals of promise,
most of them black. Many of the recipients went on to exceptional
careers educating in the arts and public service—among them the
diplomat and 1950 Nobel Peace Prize winner Ralph Bunche; the sociologist Charles Johnson; James Weldon Johnson (author of "Lift Every
Voice and Sing," often called the black national anthem); the educator Horace Mann Bond (father of the former NAACP chairman Julian
Bond); the sociologist Frazier E. Franklin; the medical researcher
Charles Drew; the biologist E. E. Just; the singer Marian Anderson; the
dancer Katherine Dunham; the photographer Gordon Parks; the paint-
ers Jacob Lawrence and Aaron Douglas; the sculptor Augusta Savage;
the musician William Grant Still; and the writers Ralph Ellison, Zora
Neale Hurston, Claude McKay, Langston Hughes, Arna Bontemps,
Sterling Brown, Robert Hayden, W. E. B. Du Bois, and James Baldwin.
Among the whites who received Rosenwald fellowships were the historian C. Vann Woodward and the folksinger Woody Guthrie.

Ralph McGill was a white journalist whose career benefited from a
Rosenwald fellowship that allowed him to travel to and report from

Europe in the late 1930s. He later won a Pulitzer Prize for editorials in the *Atlanta Constitution* condemning racist policies and attitudes in the South. McGill credited the "human and spiritual values created by the Fund" with allowing many southerners to "begin acceptance of the United States Supreme Court's school desegregation decision without violence." It was, McGill wrote, one of the reasons that "when defiance did appear, there were Southerners ready and willing to combat and help defeat it."

In May 1929, after a long illness, Gussie died. At a family funeral service for her in their home, Julius eulogized his wife. "Without her inspiration and encouragement, which was constant," he said, "my own life would have lacked much of the joy which has come to me." There is no doubt that theirs had been an unusually loving and mutually supportive marriage, but Julius was not one to dwell on the past. Eight months after Gussie died, he remarried. The new Mrs. Rosenwald was his son Lessing's widowed mother-in-law, Adelaide Goodkind. The newlyweds traveled to Egypt for their honeymoon. On their return, they moved out of the Ellis Avenue house that had been Julius's home for almost thirty years and into an apartment in the Drake Hotel. The house on Ellis Avenue later became the headquarters for the Rosenwald Fund.

Julius suffered from heart disease and was secluded and bedridden for much of his final year. He and Addie spent several months in Hawaii, where he rested and they played cards; received a few visitors; and made occasional excursions like the one they took to the Royal Hawaiian School for students of mixed races, which Julius described as "a glorified Tuskegee." When they returned, his health had not improved, and his activity was very restricted. His longtime chauffeur, Harry Kersey, described in a memoir how he used to wait outside the sickroom door at the family's country home in Ravinia in case anything was needed. On the morning of January 6, 1932, he got the nurse on duty to let him go in. "I walked to Mr. Rosenwald's bedside," he wrote. "He was in a coma. I took his hand and rubbed it, calling his name; he made no move but was breathing hard. I stood there and watched my friend and employer slowly passing away." A few hours later, Rosenwald died. Of the man he had seen almost daily since 1914, Kersey, a black man who remembered driving Booker T. Washington and Rosenwald, wrote, "If there was ever a person who did not suffer from racial prejudices, he was that person."

Julius's funeral in Chicago was, as Gussie's had been, a small, private affair. But a month after his death, there was an emotional memorial service for him in the Tuskegee chapel. Students sang "Oh God, Our Help in Ages Past" and his favorite spiritual, "Walking in Jerusalem, Just Like John." Robert Moton praised Julius for his generosity, for his personal dedication to Tuskegee and for the serious approach he brought to giving away his money. He said that John D. Rockefeller Jr. had told him he would donate to anything Rosenwald did because he trusted his philanthropy. Moton also told the story of Julius receiving flowers from the little girl at one of the first Rosenwald schools. And he recounted a conversation he had with him in his office at Tuskegee one rainy afternoon when, he said, Rosenwald told him that "the greatest joy I have ever gotten out of life has been through my contact with Tuskegee Institute and colored people."

In an article for the Associated Negro Press, Moton wrote an apt assessment of the relationship between Julius Rosenwald and Booker T. Washington. "It was the hard common sense in each that appealed to the other," he said. "It was a fortunate day for black people" when the two men "met and trusted each other."

CHAPTER 10

X

Rosenwald and Main:
Sweet Home

They varied a good deal, the schoolhouses that were born of the collaboration between Booker T. Washington and Julius Rosenwald. Many were small, white clapboard structures with distinctive rows of tall windows facing east or west to maximize the natural light inside. Like Second Union School in Goochland, Virginia; Castalia School near Rocky Mount, North Carolina; and "Little Red," in the Mississippi Delta town of Drew, they sat on leafy country roads, schoolhouses just big enough for one or two teachers, with a potbellied stove, a large classroom with a partition that could divide it into two spaces, a cloakroom, and an outhouse. Some had kitchens so they could offer classes in cooking, shops for vocational training, raised platforms for performances, and gardens where students learned to raise small crops. Many, like the Shiloh and Tankersley schools in Alabama, were two- or three-teacher schools, low buildings with gently sloping roofs, small front porches, blackboards on green bead-board walls, and windows opening onto vistas of woods and fields. Orange County Training School in North Carolina; central Oklahoma's Rosenwald Hall; and Peake High school in Arkadelphia, Arkansas, were bigger, sturdy brick structures. Dunbar High School in Little Rock was a rare urban school, a grand, three-story art-deco-style building. It still stands with its industrial training rooms, a gymnasium, and ball fields.

When the Rosenwald program ended in 1932, it had built 4,977 schools, 217 homes for teachers ("teacherages," as they were called), and 163 separate shops. These buildings were located in every state of the American South, from Maryland to Texas (and there were also three in Missouri). With 813 schools, North Carolina had the most, but Texas and South Carolina were close behind, with 500 buildings each. The schools had their own wonderfully individual names, some of them inspiring, like Peace and Good Will, Utopia, God Send, Friendly, and Sweet Home. Others were colorful—Basic, Short Journey, Mud Hall, Alligator, Alamo (in Crockett, Tennessee). Some were patriotic, like Independence and Jefferson, and others biblical, like Beulah, Galilee, Antioch, Bethlehem, and Shiloh. In Okfuskee, Oklahoma, the school was called Booker Tee, one of the many named for Washington, and in Shelby, Tennessee, the name was Augusta Rosenwald, for Julius's wife. Many were simply "County Training School." Local names notwithstanding, as a group they were referred to as Rosenwald schools.

In fact, this is a misnomer. The $4.3 million that Julius Rosenwald contributed to the construction of these schoolhouses provided only 15 percent of their total price. In 1922, for example, the school near Woodville, Virginia, cost a total of $3,225; of that $1,100 was raised by blacks in the community the school would serve, $125 from whites, $1,200 from public coffers, and $800 from Rosenwald. The bulk of the money that built the five thousand Rosenwald schools—more than $18 million—came from the state governments that became their proprietors and administrators. Almost $6 million—a sum greater than Rosenwald's financial donation—came from local people, most of them black, most of them poor. Despite the fact that they had already contributed to the tax revenues that went toward the government contribution to the schools, they gave again. They donated not just money but also land, building materials, labor, food for workdays, and—most important—the energy and persistence to insist the schools be built. Theirs was the crucial ingredient; theirs was the contribution without which the schools would not have existed, without which they would not have been the significant elements in their communities that they became.

Today, all across the South, the spirit that built the Rosenwald schools is resurgent in the movement to preserve them and the history they represent. On the day in May 1954 when the Supreme Court ruled in *Brown v. Board of Education* that separate education for black children was inherently unequal and, therefore, unconstitutional, the Rosenwald schoolhouses that communities had been so eager to acquire became in theory, if not immediately in practice, obsolete. Over the following few years, as school districts moved to consolidate their facilities, they generally passed over the black schools and placed newly integrated classes in formerly all-white school buildings. The schoolhouses that, in the early decades of the twentieth century, had been a source of pride for black communities suddenly became redundant. They were no longer needed. Some schools simply vanished—the buildings fell apart or were demolished without fanfare or notice. Some stood empty for decades.

Others have come back to life. Thanks in part to pressure from former students, the National Trust for Historic Preservation in 2002 placed the Rosenwald schools as a group on that year's list of most endangered historic sites in America and, since then, has offered the steady encouragement of publicity, conferences, and financial assistance to local groups seeking to document, preserve, and renovate individual Rosenwald schools, "iconic landmarks of African American history" in the words of the former trust president Richard Moe. In 2008, the Lowe's Charitable and Educational Foundation, an offshoot of the home improvement stores, donated $1 million toward the renovation of seventeen Rosenwald schools. In 2009, a second $1 million grant underwrote another sixteen projects, and in 2010 a third, slightly smaller grant, was distributed to eight schools in seven states.

Encouragement and financial aid has come, too, from Alice Rosenwald, the youngest daughter of Julius's son, William, whose Flexible Fund for Rosenwald Schools, administered by the National Trust for Historic Preservation, offers matching grants for amounts up to $5,000 for nonprofit organizations and government agencies working to preserve individual schools. Alice grew up in, as she puts it, a "philanthropically oriented household." In 1964, when her father was given an honorary degree in recognition of his long service on the board, Alice, then sixteen, went with him to Tuskegee. They took the train, just as Julius Rosenwald and his guests had done so many times. Alice remembers waking up when the train was already in the station near Tuskegee and peeping out the window of her sleeper car. The first thing she saw was the signs on the drinking fountains— "colored" and "whites only." Growing up in New York City, she knew such things existed but had never seen them. The warmth of the welcome at Tuskegee, where she was made to feel at home, mitigated that negative impression. As an adult, interested in the evolving field of strategic-venture philanthropy, Alice has found herself looking to her grandfather, Julius Rosenwald, as a "touchstone." She says she is "privileged" to be supporting the work of renovating schools. Each time she meets graduates of Rosenwald schools at National Trust conferences Alice is moved by their keen sense of purpose and warmed by their devotion to their communities. It surprises and humbles her to be asked, as she often is, to pose for pictures or sign autographs.

In the woods near Sperryville, in the foothills of the Shenandoah Mountains of Virginia, the one room Scrabble School served black children from the towns of Woodville, Sperryville, Slate Mills, and Peola Mills for first through seventh grades from 1921 until after segregation ended. For one year it was an integrated school, but in 1968 the children were sent to other, larger schools, and the building was boarded up. The county placed public trash containers on the grounds. Hidden behind a chain-link fence and surrounded by chest-high weeds, the schoolhouse deteriorated. That's when E. Franklin Warner decided to do something about it. After a career as a senior budget and program analyst for the Office of Management and Budget in Washington, D.C., he had returned to Rappahannock County to build a house on family land a half mile from the small school he had attended as a child. Warner convinced the County Board of Supervisors to remove the trash and then provided leadership for a group of alumni and community members, which became the Scrabble School Preservation Foundation. The group worked for years raising awareness of the school and seeking money to renovate it. Warner did not live to see it, but he was remembered fondly in April 2009, when sixteen alumni and a host of neighbors, local politicians, and representatives of Lowe's and of the National Trust for Historic Preservation gathered to celebrate the school's rededication as the Rappahannock County African-American Heritage Center and the County Senior Center at Scrabble School.

On that cloudy spring morning, the Scrabble graduate Nanette Butler Roberts stood in front of the school and sang the national anthem. Craig Barton, from the University of Virginia School of Architecture, spoke of the school's renovation and its tremendous resonance for the community around it, of how the children who attended Scrabble School "went out into the world strengthened by what they received here." Dorothy Warner, Franklin's widow, bustled about the school's new kitchen, its appliances donated by the local Lion's Club, of which her husband was a member, wearing a Scrabble School T-shirt and making ham biscuits. Her niece, Estelle Lewis, another graduate, poured punch. Samuel Glasker, one of thirteen siblings to go through Scrabble School, remembered how he and his sisters and brothers would walk three miles each way, there and back. They rarely missed a day of school. Their parents, neither of whom could read or write, insisted on hard work and regular attendance. Glasker went on to George Washington Carver High School in nearby Culpeper; to college at Virginia State University; and to a thirty-year career with the U.S. Army as an ordnance and automotive specialist (among many other things) that took him to Germany, Vietnam, and Saudi Arabia before he retired as a colonel. Outside, Glasker's nephew Robert Glasker, a special education teacher at Rappahannock High School, played the guitar and sang with a gospel quartet. The following spring many of the same people gathered again for the formal opening of the senior center. Dorothy Warner threw the switch that lit up the E. Franklin Warner Story Wall and the county administrator, John W. McCarthy, spoke of the importance of the history it tells. Men and women who attended the Scrabble School and who now meet at the senior center there shared fried chicken, cake, and fond memories. One recalled an old-fashioned punishment; he had to write six hundred times "I will not jump out the window any more."

The Shiloh School in Notasulga, Alabama, a few miles up the road from Tuskegee, was built in 1921, replacing one of the original six Rosenwald schools (which may have burned down, but the record is not clear). It cost $2,870, of which blacks contributed almost half, whereas public funds provided $900, and Rosenwald gave $800. The building served several generations of children as a school and went on to further significance in the 1940s and 1950s because participants in the U.S. Public Health Service's infamous syphilis study were recruited at the church next door, and many had attended the school. Elizabeth Sims, the granddaughter of a man in the study, attended Shiloh and remembered being kept out of school during the months of September and October so she could help her family harvest cotton. She promised herself, with every row she picked, that she was going to get an education so she wouldn't have to work like that forever. When she died, in November 2010, Liz was remembered as "the mother of the movement to preserve Shiloh" and eulogized as a "visionary who understood the power of symbols." The sanctuary of Shiloh Baptist Church was filled to overflowing with mourners—family and neighbors; colleagues from Auburn University, where Liz had worked as a contracts administrator; and many from beyond the community who had come to know her through her dedication to the preservation of the school. The scholars Susan Reverby and Mary Hoffschwelle, authors respectively of studies of the Tuskegee syphilis study and the history of Rosenwald schools, remembered her with both respect and affection. Among the mourners were a dozen graduate students from Auburn's school of architecture. Like students from previous classes, they had become, as she once said, "like my own kids," as she and they worked together, studying the building and developing plans to turn it into a technology, community, and heritage center. They led Saturday-morning workshops so neighbors could help in the work of scraping and refinishing the school's original windows. The project taught them a piece of history, they said, one they hadn't known. "The connections I made with my fellow workers and with members of that community," one of them recalled, "will last through my entire life." In fact, he added, it was the sense of community connection that most strongly impressed him about the history of Rosenwald schools: "Not often are communities united around a common theme as strongly as when they are asked to contribute not only finances but also labor." On the day of the funeral a black mourning wreath adorned the new historical marker in front of the schoolhouse.

In Stokes County, North Carolina, tobacco-farming country north of Winston-Salem, the four-teacher Walnut Cove Colored School was first converted into an apartment building and then was scheduled for demolition when Dorothy Hairston Dalton, a former student, decided to save it. In 1994 she founded a savings club and raised more than $10,000 to stabilize the building, organized volunteers to clean it out, and secured a low-interest loan to buy it. The project captured the interest of the builder Angelo Franceschina and his nonprofit Rural Initiative Project, which helped raise $500,000 from grants, individual contributions, and in-kind donations from the International Brotherhood of Electrical Workers and from the Dan River Prison Work Farm, whose inmates installed new siding, roof, and floors. The building was designated a state senior center and now hosts daily hot lunches; exercise and line-dancing classes; and monthly meetings of the town council, school board, and local NAACP chapter. Along one wall a brightly colored mural painted by high school students shows pupils and teachers outside the school as its last principal, T. L. Williams, Julius Rosenwald, and Booker T. Washington look down from the clouds.

In Round Rock, just north of Austin, Texas, the restored Hopewell school sits on a corner of the county education administration complex. It was moved there from its more rural original location, where it had been rotting and was slated for demolition. Renovated thanks to volunteers who raised funds and donated labor, it is now used for meetings and ACT test-preparation classes, its walls lined with photos of students and transcripts of their memories. "The school existed during a period of segregation in America," writes Robert Organ, the first president of the Hopewell ex-students association, "but somehow all the obvious things such as violence, racial hatred and disdain were not apparent. Students at Hopewell received a quality education from dedicated and caring teachers and administrators who did their best in a separate and unequal environment to provide a good education for learning the tools for success." Another former student says that the excitement of going to integrated Round Rock High School was tempered for him by the sense of loss at leaving Hopewell.

Noble Hill Rosenwald School, near the town of Bartow, Georgia, to which blacks contributed 47 percent of the building costs in 1924, has become a museum dedicated to African American cultural heritage. Highland Park School in Prince George's County, Maryland, has an enthusiastic alumni group that ensured its dedication as a histori-cal landmark and has made it a Head Start center for the adjoining elementary school. In Spring Hope, North Carolina alumni purchased the Rosenwald teacherage and hope to see it become a heritage cen-ter as well as the headquarters for their two-hundred-member alumni association. Next they would like to renovate the large brick school next door (which replaced a Rosenwald school that burned down in 1931), which is standing empty and filled with debris. The graduate Carolyn Hodge Avent, active in fund-raising for scholarships and work on the buildings, came back to Spring Hope after forty years of working in New York because "this is home." Down the road, in Castalia, on a winding road lined with pine trees and kudzu, a por-trait of Julius Rosenwald still hangs in the front hall of the school building that alumni purchased from the county for $1 and are ren-ovating with the help of Franceschina; a Lowe's grant; and personal contributions from alumni, among them Eunice Williams. The edu-cation she began at Castalia continued through graduate work at Columbia University Teachers' College and led to a forty-year career as a first-grade teacher. "If it hadn't been for Rosenwald," her son John says, "she'd never have had that." Members of the community are working to make the old schoolhouse into a tutoring and mentor-ing center, a place for alumni to share with and encourage the next generation.

Rosenwald Street in Baton Rouge recalls Louisiana's 393 Rosenwald schools. In the tiny crossroads town of Catawba, North Carolina, the Rosenwald Education Center is just down the hill from Rosenwald School Street. And in the mountains of western North Carolina, in the small town of Brevard, a marker at the intersection of Main Street and Rosenwald Lane notes that that Brevard Rosenwald School "lives on into the present through the memories of former teachers, students, and their families." The substantial stone building across the street housing the local board of education replaced the original Rosenwald school, which was destroyed by fire in 1941. The neighborhood it sits in used to be called Colored Town; now it is known as the Rosenwald Community.

The list of the schools—and of the people they have touched—goes on and on. There are many more.

Booker T. Washington and Julius Rosenwald have been criticized for acquiescing in the unfair dictates of the Jim Crow era—which, by building segregated schools, they did. Who knows what might have happened if each of them had used his enormous talents and influence to more vigorously make the argument for black voting rights, to focus attention on the horrors of lynching, or to push for integrated schools.

On numerous occasions Washington did speak out with passion about the wrongs being perpetrated against blacks, but he is remembered less for them than for his steady efforts toward tangible, practical results not on the level of national policy but on the level of individual lives, efforts he was convinced would ultimately lead to the equal treatment and respect to which black people rightly aspired. Washington's complicated relationship with other, more outspoken black leaders and his web of sometimes secretive political connections contrasts with his powerful, straightforward relationship to more ordinary people, especially those from the country. He had grown up as one of them; he understood the dramatic deprivation that so many of them suffered and the intensity of their aspirations for something better. It was these rural people who turned out en masse to weep at Washington's graveside when he died, and they were the majority of those who built and benefited from Rosenwald schools. One alumnus of a Virginia school told of being at Tuskegee for the graduation of one of his children. His father-in-law, he said, made a point of "patting Booker T.," touching the statue there of a man he greatly revered.

Rosenwald, too, was a practical man rather than a philosopher. To him, a large mass of uneducated citizens was a threat to the future stability of the country, and it was initially in that spirit, as much as from a sense of justice, that he became interested in helping African Americans. His talks with Washington and his many visits to the South made that mass of uneducated citizens become real for him. He saw how resolute so many individuals were, determined to improve their own lives and to provide education so that their children would have more opportunities than they had. He felt that helping people build schoolhouses in their own communities was the obvious place for him to start, and, as when he offered matching grants to build black YMCAs, he never questioned the policy that kept students separated by race. He believed that working together on the schools, both at the administrative, state level and within the individual communities, would lead not just to better facilities but also to improved relations between blacks and whites. Getting to know Booker T. Washington and the many other black men and women he met at Tuskegee had opened his own eyes to the reality of their experience. He thought greater familiarity could do that for others, as well.

Washington and Rosenwald got along well at least in part because they were both pragmatists, eager to move forward not just with ideas and words but also with action. Both were men well grounded in the truths they had learned in their own lives—the centrality of hard work, self-reliance, and care for members of the immediate community, values reinforced by their families and by the Christian and Jewish religious traditions that surrounded them. Confronting the particular challenges of their lives—sudden, extreme wealth for Rosenwald, and personal sadness and the relentless harsh reality of segregation and racial hatred for Washington—each man resisted self-interest and kept faith with those values. Neither was much interested in religious dogma, yet both were sustained by faith in something beyond self. As Washington mentioned in one of his final articles, the fact that he did not express bitterness over the injustice he experienced did not mean that he did not feel it. But faith in the essential soundness of the course he had chosen sustained him.

Both men were personally committed to education and believed in its power to develop the best in people. Rosenwald always regretted the fact that he had never finished high school, and he pursued his own learning via eagerness to meet new people and hear new ideas and also with wide-ranging, lifelong reading. He once wrote to Tuskegee asking that someone retrieve and send back to him a book he had been reading and had left in his room there—it was called *Islam and Christianity*. Washington changed his own destiny by his sheer determination to become an educated person, not settling for the learning available to him in the small town where he lived but, literally, walking to Hampton. His daughter, Portia, named for a character in Shakespeare, remembered her father taking the bard's works with him on his travels and sending her *The Knights of the Round Table* and Aesop's *Fables* when she was away at school. Both men believed that, beyond what it could do for individuals, education is necessary to a well-functioning democracy; it is the right and even the duty of each and every one of its citizens. By insisting that the schools they built be part of the public school system, Rosenwald and Washington drew attention to the fact that black children, just like their white neighbors, were citizens, the children of taxpayers. As such, they had the right to go to school. This was not a negligible contribution to the conversation. In the estimation of Edwin Embree, "The most notable effect of the school-building program was in the stimulus it gave to public support of Negro education." Writing in 1949, in his history of the Rosenwald Fund, Embree emphasized that "education for the masses of rural Negroes was far from an accepted policy thirty years ago."

In fact, the schools that Washington and Rosenwald created left many of their students with a feeling not of inferiority or of having attended a second-rate place but with a warm sense of pride. The schools that grew out of the collaboration between Rosenwald and Washington were well-designed, well-built structures, quite beautiful in a simple way (and their designs were often copied for white schools). But it was not primarily their architecture that made them memorable. One graduate of the Scrabble School in Virginia described her sentiment for it as a "home" feeling. Home—a place where one is loved, valued, and accepted. Black students often had to walk several miles to their schools, sometimes passed on the road by school buses carrying their white neighbors to their better-equipped schools, but when the black students arrived, the Rosenwald schools were a haven from prejudice. Their black teachers and principals were loving and supportive. Many children knew that their parents and neighbors had raised money and in some cases had even done the physical work of building the schools. The Scrabble School graduate Chris Wallace proudly remembers that his uncle, Isaiah Wallace, was one of the people responsible for building the school in 1921. For many years at Scrabble Friday was "soup day," with parents providing homemade lunch. A graduate in Texas described the school as "the hub of our community. It's where everyone went, where everything evolved. That was the center of our life." In his memoir of growing up in Mississippi, Ralph Eubanks, whose parents met at Tuskegee, writes of the Rosenwald school he attended: "Because of segregation . . . there was no Little League, swimming pool or community center. The school was the community center."

At some schools families had Rosenwald acres and Rosenwald patches to raise money for repairs and supplies. Rosenwald school days, encouraged by the fund and observed by most of the schools, were annual work days to take care of the building, but they were also community festivities with fish fries, picnics, and visiting. The African American men and women who taught in Rosenwald schools, many of whom had been educated at Tuskegee, were admired, valued members of their communities, role models for many of the young people they taught. Rosenwald schools were, indeed, part of a demeaning, segregated system, yet they were evidence of the fact that individuals could contribute to their own success and to that of their children, of what a community could do if people acted together. As Mary Hoffschwelle observed in her definitive study of the schools, "Rosenwald schools became part of the cultural capital held by . . . communities, a productive investment in social change upon which community members could draw as they saw fit." Ralph Eubanks saw the school of his childhood as a place whose sports, plays, and assemblies "were not just for schoolchildren and their parents; everyone in the community was welcome and often came, whether they had children in the school or not. Like many black schools of the time, Lincoln School reached out to make all members of the community feel that they had a stake in the success of the children at the school, which historically they had." Karen Riles, who researched Texas Rosenwald schools, sees them as marking "a period of educational awakening, as well as a time when people ceased to think of the city as the only place for decent schoolhouses and communities began to realize the possibility of organized effort." John Hairston passed up the opportunity for a more lucrative job up north to stay in Stokes County, North Carolina, where he was principal of the black London School. His dignified, passionate public defense of the school when county officials deemed it inadequate and wanted to close it inspired a student walkout and demonstrations that helped end segregation in Walnut Cove. Writing of him and others like him, Henry Weincek says, "They were ordinary people who, because of their race, had to possess extraordinary courage to achieve seemingly ordinary goals. As a young man

John L. Hairston had held in his hands the ticket to a better life . . . but he had taken the harder path. He had let his dream go because he thought he could 'make a difference on his home ground'—and he did."

Students at Rosenwald schools learned more than the "arithmetic, history, spelling and what not" that one remembered. No lesson plan told them that there is strength in numbers and power in the spirit, but they learned that watching their parents saw wooden planks or cook for community dinners to raise money for their schools. It is perhaps not too much to say that the spirit that inspired many of the men and women who contributed land and money and energy to Rosenwald schools became the defining strength of the movement their children created in the 1950s and 1960s to push for an end to segregation and for full civil rights. "One thing I think the history books, and the media, have gotten very wrong," commented Diane Nash, one of the early leaders of that struggle, "is portraying [it] as Martin Luther's King's movement, when in fact it was a people's movement. If people understood that it was ordinary people who did everything that needed to be done in the movement, instead of thinking, I wish we had a Martin Luther King now, they would ask, 'What can I do?'"

Indeed, the dignity and resolve, the faith in the future and in themselves that their parents and teachers had brought to the issue of education, black men and women from all across the South—many of them graduates of Rosenwald schools—applied to the struggle for full integration into American life. Charles Morgan, Jr., the Birmingham lawyer who spoke out forcefully against hatred in that city and devoted much of his long legal career to civil rights issues, noted that from Rosenwald schools "came the parents of the generation who marched and sang and risked their lives in the revolution for equal justice under the law." Among the many memorable images from the early civil rights movement is grainy black-and-white film of men and women thronging the sidewalks, walking to work in Montgomery, Alabama, where for more than a year in 1956 they refused to ride the city's segregated buses. The private taxi plan they organized gave thousands of rides for just the ten cents it would have cost people to take the bus. The brilliant leadership of the twenty-seven-year-old Martin Luther King Jr. and others encouraged them, but it was the selfless determination of many hundreds of ordinary working people that made the bus boycott successful and gave the civil rights movement a critical push. Writing about her experience the following year as one of the nine teenaged students who integrated Central High School in Little Rock (the school she attended after Dunbar, the city's Rosenwald high school for black students), Carlotta Walls LaNier writes, "My family may have seemed unlikely candidates for involvement in a movement that would spark nationwide change. But . . . determination, fortitude, and the ability to move the world aren't reserved for the 'special' people." Eulogizing the civil rights leader Dorothy Height in April 2010, President Barack Obama said, "She understood that the movement gathered strength from the bottom up, from those unheralded men and women who don't always make it into the history books but who steadily insisted on their dignity, on their manhood and womanhood." When their idealism was needed to combat the bitter legacy of slavery and the racial prejudice that lingered on even as legalized segregation was being dismantled, extraordinary numbers of black men and women were equal to the challenge.

The movement certainly gathered strength from people like Franklin Warner, the former student who inspired the renovation of the Scrabble School, described by one of his friends as "a man of presence." A graduate of Howard University, Warner worked for the Office of Management and Budget and for many years lived in Washington, D.C. Always active in civic affairs, he was the first president of Neighbors, Inc., an organization dedicated to fostering friendly contact between whites and blacks in his Northwest D.C. neighborhood with social events and meetings. As an elder of the Fifteenth Street Presbyterian Church, he and his wife, Dorothy, helped host people who came from out of town churches for the 1963 March on Washington and were invited to stay in their church building. Church members cooked dinner the night before and breakfast the day of the march, then everyone walked downtown together. Warner's connections earned him a place on the speakers' platform looking out over the extraordinary sea of people around the reflecting pool and stretching as far as the eye could see. In retirement he used to visit local schools on Martin Luther King's birthday to recite the "I Have a Dream" speech.

During her childhood near Montgomery, Rosa Parks, whose refusal to give up her seat would be the spark that ignited the bus boycott, knew who Julius Rosenwald was. "[He] was president of Sears, Roebuck & Co. and he was a millionaire," she wrote in her autobiography. "He had a great interest in education, especially the education of black children in the South. Out in the rural areas he built one-room schoolhouses and people called them Rosenwald schools. My mother used to speak about it." The school Rosa Parks went to in Montgomery was not a Rosenwald school, but she remembered that he came to visit it "one time. We weren't introduced to him but we all knew who he was."

One of the towering figures of the civil rights movement, John Lewis, now a member of Congress from Georgia, grew up on an Alabama farm south of Tuskegee, an isolated place where life revolved around work and worship at a little Baptist church. The elementary school he attended, Dunn's Chapel, was a Rosenwald school. In his memoir, *Walking with the Wind*, Lewis recalls the fish fries, picnics, and carnivals that neighbors would organize to raise money for supplies for the school. He wrote that to his parents: "Education represented an almost mythical key to the kingdom of America's riches, the kingdom so long denied our race." Lewis's first field trip was a visit to Tuskegee Institute, where he learned about George Washington Carver and his research on peanuts. From Dunn's Chapel he went on to a county training school. Hearing the voice of Martin Luther King Jr. on the radio one Sunday morning in 1955 changed Lewis's life. King's application of the gospel to the bitter prejudice Lewis's family faced every day made sense to him. A few months later the murder in Mississippi of Emmett Till, who was just his age, furthered his resolve to work for change. While still in his teens, as a student at American Baptist Theological Seminary in Nashville (the only college he could find where he wouldn't have to pay tuition) and later at Fisk University, Lewis began studying nonviolence and leading lunch-counter sit-ins. He absorbed the concept that became a defining quality of King's crusade, that of working through and toward a "Beloved Community." At twenty-three, Lewis was one of the speakers at the March on Washington. He heard Martin Luther King's inspiring words and his challenge to Americans to judge each other "not by the color of their skin but by the content of their character."

Chapter 10

Booker T. Washington and Julius Rosenwald were men who judged each other not by the color of their skin but by the content of their character. Certainly each had something the other wanted—Julius had wealth and influence that Booker needed to further his work; Washington was connected to a segment of society Rosenwald wished to encourage but knew little about. But each judged—correctly—that the other had goals larger than himself. From their vastly different families and homes and conditions Booker T. Washington and Julius Rosenwald had taken similar lessons—the conviction that there is dignity in work and meaning in service to others, that the best way to serve people is to give them tools to help themselves. The qualities Washington and Rosenwald learned in their own, often besieged communities—strength of character, material and spiritual generosity—they encouraged in several generations of adults and children with their own powerful personalities and with the program they created to build country schoolhouses. Those schools assured people in otherwise forgotten corners of the rural South that they could offer their children opportunities they themselves had been denied. The Rosenwald schools provided for the children who attended them not just book learning but also a personal legacy from Booker T. Washington and Julius Rosenwald of faith in democracy, optimism, confidence, and hope.

Epilogue

May 2011

On a rainy fall morning in 2007, I climbed the stairs of a one-hundred-year-old public elementary school near my home on Capitol Hill in Washington, D.C., for the dedication of a newly renovated library there. The space was lively, with bright archways, comfortable chairs, shelves and bins loaded with books. On the freshly carpeted floor sat children reading while parents chatted with teachers and neighbors greeted each other. The mayor of Washington, a city council member, and a representative of the superintendent of schools were there, and so was a group of young men and women in khaki pants and red jackets, volunteers from the national service program City Year. A poster proclaimed the new library to be the result of a partnership formed when parents, teachers, and principals got together to talk about ways to improve their schools and brought to fruition by a community foundation, the public school system, local architects, law firms, and banks—an array of volunteers and donors large and small.

As I listened to the speeches, I felt a thrill of recognition. Surely, I thought, this was something like programs dedicating the Rosenwald schools. The details of the occasions were, of course, different, but the pride my neighbors and I felt in what we had accomplished and the way our connection to one another had been strengthened by working together must surely, I thought, be similar. Certainly, we all shared the conviction that had motivated the folks who created Rosenwald

171

schools—that there was nothing more fundamental to the well-being of our community than our children's education.

This is a distinctive strain in American culture, this community spirit, this living out of the freedom that we both idealize and actually possess. We come together in countless ways—as parents running cooperative nursery schools, as amateur musicians playing Brahms and as poll workers on Election Day, as elders and Sunday-school teachers, scout leaders, tutors, mentors, fund-raisers, and simply good neighbors. For the hundredth anniversary of the birth of Julius Rosenwald, the historian and former librarian of Congress Daniel Boorstin wrote an essay in which he singled out the notion of community as "one of the most characteristic, one of the most important, yet one of the least noticed American contributions to modern life," and Julius Rosenwald as an example of the way that spirit played out in a distinctively American kind of philanthropy, giving that is not simply charitable but "a prudent social act." It is an investment in the national life shared by all, rich and poor alike, what President Barack Obama has often spoken of as "the common stake we all have in one another."

Booker T. Washington and Julius Rosenwald both came from groups with distinct identities, yet each understood that, in John Donne's words, "No man is an island entire of itself; every man is a piece of the continent." That continent was the American nation—a place that had lured the immigrant, had enslaved and then despised the black while holding out to each the ideal of equality and freedom. Both Washington and Rosenwald embraced that ideal; they believed in it. "Black people loved and kept faith with this country when white people did not love and keep faith with them." This observation by the former secretary of state Condoleezza Rice, who grew up under segregation not far from Tuskegee, would certainly describe Booker T. Washington. He stressed to his students not the bitterness to which they were entitled, and which he himself felt but did not publicly express, but ways they could take responsibility for their own lives and continue to have faith in their country even at a time when their rights were being curtailed.

Neither Washington nor Julius Rosenwald confronted segregation directly, but by building up significant numbers of men and women, they did help pave the way for a more equal and fair society. Washington urged his students to sing the spirituals their forebears sang, not in meek submission to injustice but in proud remembrance of the way they had survived hardship and had been sustained from generation to generation by faith and by each other. It must have been tempting to give in to anger, to lose heart and despair, but so many—Booker T. Washington, Martin Luther King Jr., John Lewis, Carlotta Walls LaNier, Dorothy Height, Franklin Warner—the vast majority of African Americans, did not. Like Julius Rosenwald, they took faithful steps in trying times without knowing just where they would lead.

ACKNOWLEDGMENTS

The professional staffs at the Manuscript, Periodicals, and Prints and Photographs divisions of the Library of Congress, the Special Collections of the Regenstein Library of the University of Chicago, the Tuskegee University Archives, The Jewish Museum of Baltimore, the Illinois State Historical Library, and the John Hope and Aurelia Elizabeth Franklin Library at Fisk University were knowledgeable and unfailingly helpful to me in the archival research I did on Booker T. Washington and Julius Rosenwald. I am so grateful to Henry Carrigan Jr. at Northwestern University Press for seeing value in this work and for offering it a home and to Gianna Mosser and Katherine Faydash for their thorough and thoughtful editing.

In addition, I was fortunate to have many people outside these institutions help and encourage me during the fifteen years of research, thinking, and writing that finally produced this book. In particular, I would like to express my gratitude to Peter Ascoli, who shared much information and insight about Julius Rosenwald and who, along with his wife, Lucy, offered me a place to stay on many trips to Chicago; to Adele Alexander, who read my entire manuscript twice and has encouraged me over the years with both scholarly comments and lively street-corner chats; to my niece Emily Colette Wilkinson, who offered a fresh eye and an insightful, careful reading of the manuscript at exactly the right moment; and to my sister Claudia Anderson, a superb editor and a cherished sounding board.

Early readers offered encouragement and comments that helped keep me going and refining my ideas—Noah Deutsch, Debbie Thawley, Charles Agle, Paul Abernathy, Maurice Jackson, Marguerite Kelly, and the late Tom Kelly. Alice Rosenwald, Julius Rosenwald's granddaughter, entertained me with a sumptuous tea and offered helpful insights. Erika Scott shared with me her undergraduate thesis about

her great-great-grandfather's philanthropy and many happy hours of Rosenwald-related conversation and travel. Margaret Wood was always ready to help me find articles at the Library of Congress. I am grateful, too, for help and encouragement from Julian Bond, Alan Cherrick, Christine Colburn, Patrick Coyne, Nicky Cymrot, David Dalin, Christopher Deutsch, Noemie Emery, Angelo Franceschina, Rob Hall, Bill Hess, Betsy Kleeblatt, Christopher Levenick, Adam Meyerson, the late Evelyn Sinclair, Susanna Spencer, Dorothy Warner, Yohuru Williams (many years ago), and Ellen Roberts (even longer ago) and from members of the Washington Biographers group, who offer a sympathetic ear to all projects and whose lively discussions helped me fend off discouragement and find the right shape for this work. Bonny Wolf and I have been talking about books (and many other things) for twenty-five years, and her friendship has been invaluable. William Rosenwald, Armand Deutsch, and my father-in-law Richard Deutsch encouraged this work, and I am saddened that they are not alive to see its completion.

As I worked on this book, I always kept in mind the next generation, especially my children and my many nieces and nephews. Sarah, Martin, Noah, Christopher, and Anna Katherine—I wrote this for you and for your cousins and your friends, all the young people who have brought so much into my life.

My husband, David Deutsch, is generous, enthusiastic, and loving, and he has believed in this book from the start and in me for even longer. He is the one person without whom I truly could not have written it, and I am deeply grateful to him. That he shares his great-grandfather's quirky sense of humor is an added blessing, one that brightens my every day.

NOTES

Introduction

xi   "the longest and most painful": David Remnick used these words often, including in an interview with Brian Williams on NBC *Nightly News*, April 5, 2010. Accessed May 9, 2011. http://www.newsbusters .org/blogs/brent-baker/2010/04/06/nbc-nightly-news-mohammad-ali -walt-whitman-annie-oakley-and-now-barack-?quicktabs_1=1.

Prologue: May 1911

4   "his personality radiated": Reuben Brainin, quoted in M. S. Werner, *Julius Rosenwald: The Life of a Practical Humanitarian* (New York: Harper and Brothers, 1939), 105.

4   "like a fighting cock": Julius Rosenwald (hereafter JR) to his wife, Augusta Nusbaum Rosenwald, always known as Gussie, 1910. The originals of many of the letters between Julius and Gussie Rosenwald I quote are in the collection of Longue Vue House and Gardens, the home of Edith Rosenwald Stern in New Orleans.

5   "dazed": Booker T. Washington (hereafter BTW) to Seth Low, September 14, 1911, in *The Booker T. Washington Papers*, ed. Louis R. Harlan and Raymond W. Smock (Urbana: University of Illinois Press, 1980), 11:91 (hereafter *BTW Papers*).

Chapter 1. "No White Man . . . Could Do Better"

My account of BTW's childhood is based primarily on Washington's own *Up from Slavery* (New York: Penguin Books, 1986; first published by Doubleday, Page in 1901) (hereafter *UFS*); on his earlier *The Story of My Life and Work*, in *BTW Papers*, 1:1–210; and on Louis R. Harlan's *Booker T. Washington: The Making of a Black Leader, 1856–1901* (New York: Oxford University Press,

1972). See also Robert J. Norrell, *Up from History: The Life of Booker T. Washington* (Cambridge, Mass.: Belknap Press of Harvard University Press, 2009).

7   "I was born": *UFS*, 1–2.

8   "about as near to Nowhere": Washington, *The Story of My Life and Work*, in *BTW Papers*, 1:10.

8   The property list is in Harlan, *Making of a Black Leader*, 8.

8   "I do not even": *UFS*, 2.

9   "on my boyish heart": *BTW Papers*, 1:10.

9   "by the way, a good one": Harlan, *Making of a Black Leader*, 14.

9   "very much as dumb animals": *UFS*, 9.

9   "about the same as getting into paradise": Harlan, *Making of a Black Leader*, 14.

10   "They didn't want us to learn": Peter Irons, *Jim Crow's Children: The Broken Promise of the Brown Decision* (New York: Penguin Books, 2004), 3.

10   "not exceeding fifty lashes": Charles M. Christian, *Black Saga: The African American Experience, a Chronology* (Washington, D.C.: Civitas, Counterpoint, 1995), 97.

10   "If you teach that": Frederick Douglass, *Narrative of the Life of Frederick Douglass* (New York: Dover Publications, 1995), 20.

11   "I have never seen": *UFS*, 15.

11   "wild rejoicing," "feeling of deep gloom": *UFS*, 22.

12   The story of BTW's baptism is recounted by Father Rice, in *BTW Papers*, 8:55.

12   "a long distance under the mountain": BTW, *The Story of My Life and Work*, in *BTW Papers*, 1:17.

12–13 "an old copy": *UFS*, 27.

13   "homespun": *UFS*, 33.

13   "One day, while at work": *UFS*, 42–43.

14 "always ready": Viola Ruffner in 1899 letter to Gibson Willetts, quoted in Harland, *The Making of a Black Leader*, 40.

14 "there was no hope": *UFS*, 78.

14–15 "patrollers . . . lost their lives": *UFS*, 78.

15 "nickel, a quarter, or a handkerchief," "rather weak": *UFS*, 46.

15 "first experience in finding out," "walking about": *UFS*, 47.

17 "convincing and unanswerable": Harlan, *Making of a Black Leader*, 69.

17 "a very terse, logical and lawyer-like": *New York Times*, June 15, 1875, quoted in Harlan, *Making of a Black Leader*, 75, 76.

17 "a conqueror who had won": Mary Mosely Lacy to BTW, quoted in Harlan, *Making of a Black Leader*, 76.

17 BTW on teaching algebra, in Harlan, *Making of a Black Leader*, 83.

18 BTW on the issue of West Virginia's capital, in Harlan, *Making of a Black Leader*, 95.

18 "I have always had more": *UFS*, 199.

18 "a remarkable man" "manifest such dignified ease": Unidentified reporter for the *Boston Congregationalist*, May 28, 1879, quoted in *BTW Papers*, 2:76n.

19 "a well qualified white man . . . send him at once": *BTW Papers*, 2:127; also quoted in Harlan, *Making of a Black Leader*, 110.

19 "I think I shall like it," "a beautiful, quiet little town": BTW to James Fowle Baldwin Marshall, June 29, 1881, in *BTW Papers*, 2:134.

20 "manly bearing": Harlan, *Making of a Black Leader*, 117.

21 "The colored people here are very anxious": BTW to James Fowle Baldwin Marshall, June 29, 1881, in *BTW Papers*, 2:135.

21 "an earnest and willing": *UFS*, 123.

22 "Think of it . . . can never forget": Olivia Davidson to Mary Berry, September 12, 1881, in *BTW Papers*, 2:147–48.

24   "in true picnic style," "what I have witnessed here today," "the time is near": account of Tuskegee closing exercises by BTW and Olivia A. Davidson, *Southern Workman*, May 11, 1882, in *BTW Papers*, 2:185–89.

24   "adds much to our happiness": BTW to James Fowle Baldwin Marshall, July 23, 1883, in *BTW Papers*, 2:235.

25   "As hard as it is," "I cannot be away": BTW to Samuel Armstrong, April 21, 1889, in *BTW Papers*, 2:525; BTW to Warren Logan, April 4, 1889, in *BTW Papers*, 2:528.

25   "she literally wore herself out": *UFS*, 199.

26   "deep, deep affliction . . . tell you about it sometime": BTW to General Samuel Armstrong, April 21, 1889, in *BTW Papers*, 2:525.

26–27 "Davidson had run in the drizzling rain," "tells me her nose bleeds": Margaret Murray to BTW, July 10, 1892, in *BTW Papers*, 3:245.

27   "Miss Murray and I": BTW to Emily Howland, September 29, 1892, in *BTW Papers*, 3:265.

27   "I love to work": Margaret Murray to BTW, July 1892, in *BTW Papers*, 3:254.

27   "in wagons, in carts": Account from *Southern Workman*, July 21, 1892, in *BTW Papers*, 3:231.

28   "so far as it": Account by E. W. Black, *Southern Workman*, July 21, 1892: 122, in *BTW Papers*, 3:231.

28   "Let us alone": William S. McFeely, *Frederick Douglass* (New York: W. W. Norton, 1991), 363; speech also in *BTW Papers*, 3:230–31.

Chapter 2. Peddler's Son

Biographical information on Rosenwald is drawn from Peter M. Ascoli, *Julius Rosenwald: The Man Who Built Sears, Roebuck and Advanced the Cause of Black Education in the American South* (Bloomington: Indiana University Press, 2006); Werner, *Julius Rosenwald*; and from sixteen family scrapbooks and other materials in the Julius Rosenwald Papers, University of Chicago, Regenstein Library Special Collections (hereafter Rosenwald Papers UC); and from a collection of family letters at Longue Vue House and Garden, Edith Rosenwald Stern's home in New Orleans (hereafter LV).

29   In a letter to German relatives in 1881 (quoted by Ascoli, *Julius Rosenwald*, 4, and by Werner, *Julius Rosenwald*, 11), Samuel Rosenwald wrote, speaking of anti-Semitism in America: "In business one hardly ever hears anything like that, but the children often hear about it, and that is unpleasant enough."

30   *Push-pull* was first used by Ernest G. Ravenstein, in *Laws of Migration* (1885; repr., New York: Arno Press, 1976).

30   "One hardly realizes," "The land is so 'fat'": Mark Wyman, *Immigrants in the Valley: Irish Germans, and Americans in the Upper Mississippi Country, 1830–1860* (Chicago: Nelson-Hall, 1984), 60, 73.

31   Baltimore's early Jewish community is discussed in Isidor Blum, *The Jews of Baltimore: An Historical Summary of their Progress and Status as Citizens of Baltimore from the Early Days to the Year Nineteen Hundred and Ten* (Baltimore: Historical Review Publishing Company, 1910); Isaac M. Fein, *The Making of an American Jewish Community: The History of Baltimore's Jews from 1773 to 1920* (Philadelphia: Jewish Publication Society of America, 1971).

31   "In as much as we know": *Baltimore American*, February 21, 1856, quoted in Fein, *Making of an American Jewish Community*, 75.

31   "in those early days": Blum, *Jews of Baltimore*, 9.

32   "Jews of good habits ... making money fast": R. G. Dun and Co. Collection, Harvard Business School, Baker Library, 198:112. *Pizzle* is an old English word for "penis."

33   The Rosenwald home is still standing and is owned by the National Park Service.

34   "representative citizen," "rather independent": *History of Sangamon County, Illinois* (Chicago: Interstate Publishing, 1881), 709–10.

35   "It has taken a long time": Rosenwald Papers UC, box 48, folder 7.

35   "live, active, energetic boys": This and other quotes from the *Illinois State Journal* are from notes that M. R. Werner used for his book *Julius Rosenwald*. The notes are part of the Rosenwald Papers UC, "Subseries 3: Chronological Notebooks," box 48, folder 7.

35   "He was the first man ... never forgotten them": James B. Morrow, "The Making of a Mail Order Menace," *The Nation's Business*, December 1917, Rosenwald Papers UC, box 55, folder 7.

35   "neither absent nor tardy": *Springfield Register*, quoted in "Chronological Notebooks," Rosenwald Papers UC, box 48, folder 7.

36   Shopping in New York is described by James D. McCabe Jr., *Lights
and Shadows of New York Life or the Sights and Sensations of the Great
City* (Philadelphia: National Publishing, 1872).

36   "only doing fairly well": Samuel Rosenwald to Mrs. Bernhard Rosenwald, March 11, 1894, quoted in Ascoli, *Julius Rosenwald*, 7.

37   The anecdote about waking up at night was told in an interview with
Ladies Weekly, "Men Who Are Making America," December 17,
1916, Rosenwald Papers UC, scrapbook 5, p. 32.

38   "I will never forget how bitter cold": quoted in Ascoli, *Julius Rosenwald*, 11.

38–39   Information about membership and contributions to Sinai congregation is from the American Jewish Archives at Hebrew Union
College, Cincinnati, Ohio, ser. A, collection no. 56.

40   "my darling . . . Gestopfe Ganz": Rosenwald Papers UC, box 48, folder 9.

40   "almost fainted": JR to Augusta Nusbaum Rosenwald (hereafter
"Gussie"), September 14, 1891, quoted in Ascoli, *Julius Rosenwald*, 16.

40   "A real nice [cloth] coat . . . why all extra expense worries me":
Gussie to JR, LV.

40–41   "If present conditions are . . . answered by us": Hirsch, *My Religion*, 131.

41   "the outcry for justice": Hirsch, *My Religion*, 75.

41   "$5,000 to be used for": Edwin Embree and Julia Waxman, *Investment
in People: The Story of the Julius Rosenwald Fund* (New York: Harper
and Brothers, 1949), 12.

Chapter 3. A Lucky Chance, a Daunting Task

44   "since . . . the fleet of Columbus": Frederick Jackson Turner, *The
Frontier in American History* (New York: Henry Holt, 1921), available
at http://xroads.virginia.edu/~hyper/turner/.

44   "as degraded as animals . . . American Negro": Quoted in Paula J.
Giddings, *Ida, a Sword Among Lions: Ida B. Wells and the Campaign
Against Lynching* (New York: Amistad, 2008), 273–74.

45 "Columbian Ode," in Paul Laurence Dunbar, *Oak and Ivy,* available at the Paul Laurence Dunbar Digital Collection, Wright State University Libraries, http://www.libraries.wright.edu/special/dunbar /poems/oak_and_ivy/columbian_ode.html.

45 "Men talk of the Negro problem": McFeely, *Frederick Douglass,* 371.

45 "No one who listened": BTW, *Frederick Douglass* (Honolulu, Hawaii: University Press of the Pacific, 2003), 336.

46 "repentance . . . shame . . . home of the brave": Ida B. Wells, *The Reason Why the Colored American Is Not in the World's Columbian Exposition* (Urbana: University of Illinois Press, 1999), 4, 13 (page numbers are from the microfilm version of the original edition of the pamphlet).

46 *Darkies Day at the Fair,* lithograph by Frederick Burr Opper, from Library of Congress, LC-USZC4-2096, reproduced in Giddings, *Ida, a Sword Among Lions.*

47 "at white heat": Graham Taylor, a Protestant minister, sociologist, and believer in the social gospel movement, a friend of Julius Rosenwald, quoted in Donald L. Miller, *City of the Century: The Epic of Chicago and the Making of America* (New York: Simon and Schuster, 1997), 536.

47 William T. Stead, *If Christ Came to Chicago* (1894; repr., New York: Living Books, 1984).

47 The story of Aaron Nusbaum's adventure is recounted in Ascoli, *Julius Rosenwald,* 25, and elsewhere.

47 The author remembers seeing such a device for sending money, receipts, and change through overhead tubes between floors at Le Bon Marché department store in Paris in the 1960s; they were also common in news rooms.

49 "a decision made": Werner, *Julius Rosenwald,* 45.

49 "a lucky chance": JR interview with Ira Mitchell, Rosenwald Papers UC, box 55, folder 3.

51 "tight place," "as I suppose," "the heat, together": *UFS,* 213.

51 "A sudden chill": W. J. McGee, interviewed in London *Daily News,* reprinted in Indianapolis *Freeman,* July 29, 1899, quoted in Harlan, *Making of a Black Leader,* 216.

51–52   All quotes of BTW's speech are from *UFS*, 218–25, which presents it in full.

52   "When the Negro finished": James Creelman writing in *New York World*, September 18, 1895, quoted in Harlan, *Making of a Black Leader*, 217.

52–53   "most of the Negroes," "That man's speech": *BTW Papers*, 4:3.

53   "phenomenal success," "a word fitly": Harlan, *Making of a Black Leader*, 225.

53   "Olivia was with you": Mary Stearns to BTW, September 19, 1885, in *BTW Papers*, 4:18.

53   "our Moses," "Upon you has fallen": William Cansler to BTW, September 26, 1895, in *BTW Papers*, 4:30.

53   "It looks as if you are our Douglass . . . the term Afro American": T. Thomas Fortune to BTW, September 26, 1895, in *BTW Papers*, 4:31.

54   "I told him . . . humiliated, disgraced": R. W. Taylor to BTW, in *BTW Papers*, 4:22.

54   "take proper steps," "I have heard nothing": William Baldwin to BTW, October 4, 1885, in *BTW Papers*, 4:47–48.

54   "a huckleberry in a bowl": *BTW Papers*, 14:185n.

54–55   "In the economy of God . . . previous condition": *UFS*, 300.

56   "to prevent the Democratic": C. Vann Woodward, *Origins of the New South, 1877–1913* (1951; repr., Baton Rouge: Louisiana State University Press, Littlefield Fund for Southern History of the University of Texas, 1971), 237.

56   "I believe as truly": Woodward, *Origins of the New South*, 340.

56   "true philosophy of the movement": Woodward, *Origins of the New South*, 331.

56   "the policy": Woodward, *Origins of the New South*, 324.

57   "an interesting coincidence": *The Nation* 66 (1898): 398–99, quoted in Woodward, *Origins of the New South*, 324.

57   "If one race be": *Plessy v. Ferguson*, 163 U.S. 537 (1895), quoted in Christian, *Black Saga*, 282.

58   "Whites' pursuit": Robert Norrell, *The House I Live In: Race in the American Century* (New York: Oxford University Press, 2005), xii.

Chapter 4. "You Need a Schoolhouse"

61   "permanent cure": BTW to *Birmingham Age-Herald*, April 26, 1899, in *BTW Papers*, 5:91, quoted in Harlan, *Making of a Black Leader*, 262–63.

61   "I have invariably found": Interview with BTW, *Washington Post*, June 21, 1896, in *BTW Papers*, 4:180.

62   "Any law controlling . . . open the schoolhouse": BTW letter to Louisiana Constitutional Convention, February 19, 1899, in *BTW Papers*, 4:381–82.

62   "There remains one other victory . . . massive building tremble": Speech and account quoted in *BTW Papers*, 4:491–92.

62   "When he escapes": *Atlanta Constitution*, October 18, 1898, quoted in Norrell, *Up from History*, 165.

63   "Within six years . . . I should hope so": Interview with Frank George Carpenter in *Memphis Commercial Appeal*, in *BTW Papers*, 5:279.

63   "on a tightrope": Norrell, *Up from History*, 109.

63   "Art . . . gayity": BTW outline for speech, October 28, 1899, in *BTW Papers*, 5:252.

64   "feasted our souls . . . the dear old Queen": Margaret Washington to Francis Jackson Garrison, August 7, 1899, in *BTW Papers*, 5:170.

64   "You need a schoolhouse . . . the people will help you": *Saturday Evening Talk*, April 28, 1895, in *BTW Papers*, 3:550.

64   "Go out and be a center": *Saturday Evening Talk*, April 28, 1895, in *BTW Papers*, 3:550.

65   "Despite superficial": UFS, 318.

65   "sets forth more graphically": Mary Fletcher Mackie to BTW, November 21, 1900, in *BTW Papers*, 5:675–77.

65   "has lived heroic poetry": William Dean Howells, review of *Up from Slavery*, by Booker T. Washington, *North American Review* 173 (August 1901): 280–88, quoted in *BTW Papers*, 6:192.

66   "When are you coming north . . . our last conversation": Theodore Roosevelt to BTW, September 14, 1901, in *BTW Papers*, 6:206.

66   "Washington is probably": *Atlanta Constitution*, October, 16, 1901, quoted in *BTW Papers*, 6:246.

66   "the most damnable": *Memphis Scimitar*, quoted in H. W. Brands, *TR: The Last Romantic* (New York: Basic Books, 1977), 423.

66   "the President is willing": Quoted in Philip Dray, *At the Hands of Persons Unknown: The Lynching of Black America* (New York: Random House, 2002), 161.

67   "The action of President Roosevelt": Quoted in Edmund Morris, *Theodore Rex* (New York: Random House, 2001), 55.

67   "are not taking": Monroe Trotter in *New York American*, November 4, 1902, quoted in Harlan, *Wizard of Tuskegee*, 110.

68   "very anxious": Portia Washington interview, *Boston Globe*, October 2, 1901, quoted in Harlan, *Wizard of Tuskegee*, 108–9.

68   "the most distinguished southerner . . . civic inferiority": W. E. B. Du Bois, *The Souls of Black Folk* (1903; repr., New York: Dover Publications, 1994), 31. Other quotes in this paragraph are from the same work.

68   "Is the rope and the torch": *Boston Advertiser*, July 31, 1903, quoted in Harlan, *Wizard of Tuskegee*, 44.

69   "We refuse to allow": "Declaration of Principles," in David Levering Lewis, *W. E. B. Du Bois: Biography of a Race* (New York: Henry Holt, 1993), 321.

69   *Giles v. Harris*, 89 U.S. 475 (1903).

69   On BTW's payment to Smith, see Harlan, *Wizard of Tuskegee*, 297.

70   "The man who dies rich": Andrew Carnegie, "Wealth," *North American Review*, no. 391 (June 1889).

70   On Booker Jr.'s exploits, see Harlan, *Wizard of Tuskegee*, 113, 116.

71   "Be careful": BTW to BTW Jr., May 27, 1907, in *BTW Papers*, 9:274.

71   "never learned to study": BTW to John Fisher Peck, December 28, 1909, quoted in Harlan, *Wizard of Tuskegee*, 116.

71   "Try to write legibly . . . your health will break down": Booker T. Washington Papers, Manuscript Division, Library of Congress (hereafter Manuscript Division, LC). Letters between BTW and BTW Jr. are found on reel 6.

71   "I have found": BTW writing in *UFS*, 51, quoted in Elizabeth Brownstein, *If This House Could Talk: Historic Homes, Extraordinary Americans* (New York: Simon and Schuster, 1999), 96.

72   "There are no peas, no turnips . . . economic element": BTW, "Chickens, Pigs and People," *Outlook*, June 1901, in *BTW Papers*, 6:124–38.

72   The story of BTW and Baldwin Sr. meeting in Boston is recounted in Werner, *Julius Rosenwald*, 107, and no source is given. Quite by accident, as I was finishing this work, I came across a report in the front page of the *New York Times*, from April 18, 1903, of Washington telling in a speech of Edward Everett Hale helping him to carry a heavy bag! I do not know which version is correct.

72   John D. Rockefeller Jr. was twenty-seven at the time of the train trip. According to Ron Chernow's biography of Rockefeller Sr., *Titan* (New York: Random House, 1998), 482, Rockefeller Jr. said later that it was "the most instructive experience of my life."

73   "very interesting meetings . . . gathering fast": Quoted in Eric Anderson and Alfred Moss Jr., *Dangerous Donations: Northern Philanthropy and Southern Black Education, 1902–1930* (Columbia: University of Missouri Press, 2001), 74–75.

73   "white ignorance and lawlessness": Quoted in Anderson and Moss, *Dangerous Donations*, 79–81.

73   "It seems to me": BTW, *My Larger Education* (New York: Humanity Books, 2004), 35.

74   "He is of more importance": *Outlook*, January 14, 1905, 115, quoted in Anderson and Moss, *Dangerous Donations*, 83.

74   "dwell too much": BTW to Portia Washington, November 15, 1906, in *BTW Papers*, 6:127.

74   The episode of the visit to Washington Monument is recounted by Portia Washington Pittman, in Harlan, *Wizard of Tuskegee*, 119–20.

Chapter 5. An American Citizen

75 Werner, in *Julius Rosenwald*, reports that it was Julius's friend Paul Sachs who gave him both books. Sachs was friendly with William Baldwin's widow, Ruth.

75 "busiest place I had ever seen": Robert P. Sniffen, "An Address Before the Men's Forum of Yonkers, N.Y.," 1919, Rosenwald Papers UC, box 55, folder 10.

76 "trinkets and notions": From Eva Sears's memoir; quoted in Werner notes, Rosenwald Papers UC, box 55, folder 5.

76 The episode of the miniature furniture, famous in Rosenwald family lore, is told in Werner, *Julius Rosenwald*, 36.

77 "Don't be afraid . . . promptly sent to you": From an early Sears catalog, quoted in Louis Asher, *Send No Money* (Chicago: Argus Books, 1942), 6.

77 "I am in the store": JR to Louis Rosenwald, December 7, 1900, Rosenwald Papers UC, box 55, folder 3.

77 "the great objector": Boris Emmet and John E. Jeuck, *Catalogues and Counters: A History of Sears, Roebuck and Company* (Chicago: University of Chicago Press, 1950), 125.

78 "felt himself ready": Emmet and Jeuck, *Catalogues and Counters*, 125.

79 "I regretsky to reportsky": JR to Richard Sears, February 25, 1905, LV.

80 "plain and even severe . . . slightest pretension": *Architectural Digest*, July 1905, 27–32. The same issue of the magazine reviewed the Fifth Avenue apartment of the prominent businessman and philanthropist Jacob Schiff, an interesting contrast with Rosenwald's home. The "prevailing character" of Schiff's residence is described as "that of an impersonal and stately magnificence" with "raised gold mouldings," "carved Istrian marble," and "wall coverings of crimson moiré silk."

80 "getting the old French royalties": JR to Gussie, LV.

80 "of course, they thought": Augusta Rosenwald to family, LV.

81 "I was a little extravagant . . . up to $225": LV.

81 "frenzied and bloodthirsty mob . . . all over the city": "Jewish Massacre Denounced," *New York Times*, April 28, 1903, 6.

82   On details of the evening at the Star Theater, see Werner, *Julius Rosenwald*, 94.

82   Werner attributes Horowitz's immediate liking of and trust in Rosenwald to a personal interview he had with the builder Louis J. Horowitz; Werner, *Julius Rosenwald*, 72n.

84   "When Jule gets excited . . . little we all know": Gussie to "Dear Ones," June 26, 1907, LV. This love of word play is a trait that lives on in several Rosenwald descendants with whom I am familiar, notably my son, Christopher, my husband, David, his brother Woody, and his cousins Erika Scott and Betsy Kleeblatt.

84   "You know, I am too optimistic": JR to Richard Sears and Alfred Loeb, August 16, 1907, Rosenwald Papers UC, box 55, folder 6.

84   "I am handing you these things": Sears to JR, August 8, 1907, LV.

85   "a mail order Barnum," "could sell a breath of air": Werner, *Julius Rosenwald*, 44.

85   "intoxicated": Emmet and Jeuck, *Catalogues and Counters*, 67.

85   "the most beautiful place": Richard Sears to JR, March 31, 1907, LV.

85   Fred L. Isreal, ed., *Sears, Roebuck and Company Catalogue 1897* (New York: Chelsea House Publishers, 1968).

86   "in the hands of a mob . . . friend of Abraham Lincoln": "Illinois Capital in Hands of Mob," *Chicago Tribune*, August 15, 1908; "Aged Negro, Once Friend of Abraham Lincoln, Hanged by Mob," *Chicago Tribune*, August 16, 1908.

87   "So far as I know": Claude Barnett ms., Barnett Papers, Manuscript Division, Library of Congress. Barnett later attended school at Tuskegee. He returned to Chicago, where he worked at the post office and ran a mail-order business selling portraits of famous black figures. In 1919 he founded the Associated Negro Press. In 1963 *Ebony* magazine named him one of the hundred most influential black Americans in its issue commemorating the centenary of the Emancipation Proclamation. *Ebony Magazine*, September 1963, 207, 228.

87   On JR's wishing to hire more blacks, see Edwin Embree and Julia Waxman, *Investment in People: The Story of the Julius Rosenwald Fund* (New York: Harper and Brothers, 1949), 26.

87   "Your father is too busy": JR to Lessing, Rosenwald Papers UC, box 52. All other quotes in this paragraph are from the same source.

88   "May my character": The words appear in the statements of belief, confessions, and prayers of contrition of many churches. These words are drawn from Arthur Bennett, ed., *The Valley of Vision: A Collection of Puritan Prayers and Devotions* (Edinburgh: Banner of Truth Trust, 1975), 78.

88   "Never be afraid," "Humble modesty": *McGuffey's Third Eclectic Reader*, rev. ed. (New York: John Wiley and Sons, 1997), 78, 74.

89   "Because then maybe": Author interview with William Rosenwald, New York, N.Y., October 1996.

89   "have some place to go": William Baldwin quoted in John Graham Brooks, *An American Citizen: The Life of William Henry Baldwin, Jr.* (Boston: Houghton Mifflin, 1910), 96.

89   "It is a glorious story . . . helpful lines": JR to Adele and Edith, September 10, 1910, quoted in Ascoli, *Julius Rosenwald*, 79.

Chapter 6. Lunch at the Blackstone

92   "No philanthropy in Chicago": JR in *Chicago Tribune*, April 7, 1910, quoted in Ascoli, *Julius Rosenwald*, 77.

92   "clubhouse," "undemocratic": JR to Lessing, January 10, 1910, Rosenwald Papers UC, box 49, folder 3.

92   "I think": Rosenwald Papers UC, box 32, folder 15.

93   "Well, I guess": Accounts of the meeting between JR and Messer found in Ascoli, *Julius Rosenwald*, 80–81, and Werner, *Julius Rosenwald*, 119, are based on an account of the meeting by Jesse Moorland in a letter to Tobias Channing, January 8, 1932, copy in the Rosenwald file, Kautz Family YMCA Archives, University of Minnesota.

93   "I do not want you . . . conditions of American life": From newspaper clipping, Jesse Moorland Papers, box 126–42, Moorland-Spingarn Center, Howard University.

93   Details of the fund-raising drive are in Ascoli, *Julius Rosenwald*, 82.

94   "a hell of a long time": JR to "Dearest Mother," February 14, 1911, Rosenwald Papers UC, box 49, folder 5.

94   "'black belt' and Jewish": JR to Gussie, March 19, 1911, Rosenwald Papers UC, box 49, folder 5.

94   "I've never felt worse": JR to Gussie, Rosenwald Papers UC, box 49, folder 5.

94   "You are spoilt": Gussie to JR, April 20, 1911, LV.

94   "I have been accustomed": Gussie to JR, May 11, 1911, LV.

94   "homesick and blue": Gussie to JR, April 14, 1911, LV.

95   "I can't under any circumstances . . . cooperation and helpfulness": JR to Gussie, April 4, 1911, Rosenwald Papers UC, box 49, folder 5.

95   "I have my hands full again": JR to Gussie, May 4, 1911, Rosenwald Papers UC, box 49, folder 6.

95   My account of the assault on BTW is based on Harlan, *Wizard of Tuskegee*, 379–404.

96   "Whether it is because": Transcript of JR and BTW remarks, lunch and dinner, Rosenwald Papers UC, box 49, folder 6. All other quotes in this paragraph and the following paragraphs are from the same source.

98   "Six Negroes Are Lynched": "Six Negroes Lynched," *Chicago Tribune*, May 22, 1911.

99   "a 'culled' gentleman . . . don't you?": JR to Gussie, Rosenwald Papers UC, box 49, folder 6.

99   The incident with the chauffeur is recounted, unsourced, in Werner, *Julius Rosenwald*, 121–22.

99   "happy to see": JR to Gussie, Rosenwald Papers UC, box 49, folder 5.

99   "the very great and helpful": BTW to JR, May 23, 1911, in *BTW Papers*, 11:165–66.

100   "I was greatly": Rosenwald Papers UC, box 49, folder 6.

100   "nothing could be more useful": William Howard Taft to Wilber Messer, January 9, 1911, quoted in Ascoli, *Julius Rosenwald*, 83.

100–101 "I told them . . . separate class": JR to Julian Mack, May 21, 1911, quoted in Ascoli, *Julius Rosenwald*, 84.

101   "full of mischief about": Gussie to Edith, LV.

Chapter 7. Between Chicago and Tuskegee

104 The story of the founding of Meharry is interesting. During Reconstruction a white man named Samuel Meharry was traveling along
a Kentucky road when his wagon careened into a ditch. A nearby
black family helped him pull it out and sheltered him for the night.
Meharry said he had no money to pay them but that he would do
something for their race. In 1875, he and his brothers kept this
promise with a large donation to found a medical department at the
black Central Tennessee College. Later, this became Meharry Medical College, offering medical, dental, and pharmaceutical education
to blacks. Today, Meharry Medical College is a major educator of
African American doctors and dentists and has a large public health
program.

105 "Southern darkey": JR to My Dear Children, February 20, 1912, Rosenwald Papers UC, box 55.

105 "those old, sweet, slave songs . . . to the students": BTW, *The Story of
My Life and Work*, in *BTW Papers*, 1:176.

106 "If anyone again claims . . . more people knew!": Rosenwald Papers
UC, box 55.

106 "Accept our sincerest . . . for our fellows": Booker T. Washington
Collection, Manuscript Division, LC, reel 76.

106 "I was astonished": *Chicago Tribune*, October 29, 1911, Rosenwald
Papers UC, box 53, folder 5, quoted in Ascoli, *Julius Rosenwald*, 89.

107 "a harelip is a misfortune": Speech to American Missionary Association, October 18, 1911, quoted in *Chicago Record Herald*, clipping in
Rosenwald Papers UC, scrapbook 1, p. 40.

107 "The horrors that are due to . . . in Russia": Quoted in Alfred Jarrette,
Julius Rosenwald: Benefactor of Mankind (Greenville, S.C.: Southeast-
ern University Press, 1975).

107 "I think you will be glad to know": BTW to Theodore Roosevelt,
December 12, 1911, in *BTW Papers*, 11:415.

108–9 The story of this first view of a Southern school is from a speech by
Channing Tobias, February 7, 1932, Rosenwald Collection, Kautz
Family YMCA Archives, University of Minnesota, box 7.

109   "Just think of it . . . unpacked and laid out": JR to Gussie, February 28, 1912, Rosenwald Papers UC, scrapbook 3, pp. 35–36.

110   "We are, of course": JR to BTW, February 9, 1912, Manuscript Division, LC, container 75, reel 68.

110   "Poor fellow": Margaret Washington to Gussie, Rosenwald Papers UC, scrapbook 14, p. 47.

110   "This week . . . get over it": Gussie to Adele and Armand, March 10, 1912, LV, quoted in Ascoli, *Julius Rosenwald,* 91.

110   "Noted Negro Educator": Rosenwald Papers UC, scrapbook 14, p. 48.

110   "Dr. Hirsch gave a splendid": Gussie to Adele and Armand, March 10, 1912, LV.

110   "unpleasantness with the help": Gussie to Adele and Armand, March 17, 1912, LV.

111   "How very much I enjoyed my stay . . . away with me": BTW to Gussie, March 20, 1912, Manuscript Division, LC, reel 75.

111   The story of Edith Goodkind Rosenwald's trip home is from Lessing Rosenwald's oral history, Archives, Sears, Roebuck and Company, Hoffman Estates, Illinois (photocopy in possession of the author).

112   "Charlie," "wild": BTW to JR, September 12, 1912, Manuscript Division, LC, reel 69.

112   "I make it a point": JR to BTW, April 11, 1912, Manuscript Division, LC, reel 68.

112   "manifestation of faith": Victor Tulane to JR, September 16, 1912, Manuscript Division, LC, reel 185.

112   "The coming of you two": Margaret Washington to Gussie, March 4, 1912, Rosenwald Papers UC, box 53, folder 11.

112   "a wonderful book . . . her own suffering": BTW to Sophie Adler, July 9, 1912, in *BTW Papers,* 11:558.

112–13 "I have considered . . . place responsibility on them": BTW to JR, June 21, 1912, in *BTW Papers,* 11:552–54.

114   "If you had a": JR to BTW, July 15, 1912, Manuscript Division, LC, container 76.

114   "Godsend": BTW to JR, June 20, 1912, in *BTW Papers*, 11:562.

114   "Rosenwald Gives $687,000": *Chicago Tribune*, August 12, 1912.

115   "all the works of real value": William Graves to BTW, October 3, 1912, Manuscript Division, LC, reel 69.

115   "valuable . . . as showing the sentiment": BTW to William Graves, October 9, 1912, Manuscript Division, LC, reel 69.

115   "Didn't we have": William Graves to BTW, August 28, 1914, Manuscript Division LC, reels 76–77.

115   "all of us are at home again": BTW to JR, August 13, 1912, Manuscript Division, LC, reel 69.

115–16 "bearing upon," "providing school buildings": BTW to JR, August 31, 1912, Manuscript Division, LC, reel 395.

116–17 "a plan for the helping . . . One thing I am convinced of": BTW to JR, September 12, 1912, Manuscript Division, LC, reels 390–91.

117   "My dear Papa": BTW Jr. to BTW, January 1912, quoted in Basil Mathews, *Booker T. Washington: Educator and Interracial Interpreter* (College Park, Md.: McGrath Publishing, 1969), 196.

117   "You got some talent": Quoted in Ruth Ann Stewart, *Portia: The Life of the Daughter of Booker T. Washington* (Garden City, N.Y.: Doubleday, 1977), 73.

117–18 The account of Portia's wedding is from *Tuskegee Student*, in *BTW Papers*, 9:392–93.

118   "My dear brother . . . how much to get": Amanda Johnson to BTW, in *BTW Papers*, 6:212–13.

118   "It is often true": BTW to JR, September 30, 1912, Manuscript Division, LC.

119   "there seems to be a feeling": Quoted in Mary Hoffschwelle, *The Rosenwald Schools of the American South* (Gainesville: University Press of Florida, 2006), 37.

119   "I do not want": JR to BTW, December 26, 1912, quoted in Hoffschwelle, *Rosenwald Schools*, 32.

119   "good and interesting . . . cheaper": BTW to JR, February 7, 1913, Manuscript Division, LC, reel 69.

119   "I cannot find words": BTW to JR, February 24, 1913, Manuscript Division, LC, reel 69.

120   "Mr. Eisendrath said": BTW to JR, April 2, 1913, UC, box 53, folder 12.

120   "You do not know what joy and encouragement": BTW to JR, May 31, 1913, Manuscript Division, LC, reel 69.

Chapter 8. Swing Low, Sweet Chariot

121   Edith's marriage is discussed in Gerda Weissmann Klein's *A Passion for Sharing: The Life of Edith Rosenwald Stern* (Chappaqua, N.Y.: Rossel Books, 1984), 30.

122   "Well, we are going to be dead": Julian Hart, Rosenwald Papers, UC, box 49, folder 12.

123   "Got up at five . . . garden and chickens": BTW postcard to family, quoted in Matthews, *Booker T. Washington*, 198.

124   The fascinating story of the *Clotilda* and the men and women it illicitly delivered to Alabama as slaves in 1860 is told in Sylviane A. Diouf, *Dreams of Africa in Alabama* (Oxford: Oxford University Press, 2007).

124   "I am not in favor": BTW to Tom Johnson, March 5, 1914, in *BTW Papers*, 12:468.

124   "Yesterday I spent": BTW to JR, June 1, 1914, in *BTW Papers*, 13:39–40.

125–26 All quotes are from letters in Manuscript Division, LC, reel 606.

126   "Plan for Erection of Rural Schoolhouses . . . themselves may do": Manuscript Division, LC, reel 90.

127–28 "Our Tuskegee trip. . . novel experiences": JR to Julian Mack, March 1, 1915, quoted in Ascoli, *Julius Rosenwald*, 146.

128   "At each place": Account by JR's guest Jenkin Lloyd Jones, head of Abraham Lincoln Center in Chicago, in *Unity*, February 18, 1915, quoted in Ascoli, *Julius Rosenwald*, 144.

128–29 Account of visit in *Montgomery Advertiser*, February 22, 1915, Rosenwald Papers UC, scrapbook 14.

128   JR's reaction to girl with flowers described by Robert Moton in speech after JR's death, reported in *Tuskegee Messenger*, February 1932, 16.

129   "those poor little children": *Boston Transcript*, March 24, 1915, quoted in Ascoli, *Julius Rosenwald*, 147.

129   "Unless you have lived": BTW to JR, February 2, 1915, Manuscript Division, LC, reel 69.

130   "The good fellowship": William Parker to JR, Manuscript Division, LC, reel 396.

130   "In accepting this . . . love this work": Rosenwald Papers UC, addendum III, box 1.

130–32   "the designs for the buildings": All quotes in this paragraph and the following are from Extension Department, Tuskegee Normal and Industrial Institute, *The Negro Rural School and Its Relation to the Community* (Tuskegee, Ala.: Tuskegee Normal and Industrial Institute Extension Department, 1915).

132   "The black man has": Clement Richardson, *Southern Workman*, January 1916, Rosenwald Papers UC, box 53.

132   "One old man": Quoted in Daniel Boorstin, "From Charity to Philanthropy," in *Hidden History: Exploring our Secret Past* (New York: Harper and Row, 1987), 206.

133   "to see how nicely": BTW to BTW Jr., in *BTW Papers*, 13:414.

133   "which I hope you will read . . . constantly": BTW to Laura Murray, October 15, 1915, in *BTW Papers*, 13:387.

133   Quotes from Booker T. Washington, "My View of Segregation," *New Republic*, December 1915, in *BTW Papers*, 13:357–60.

133   "There is sometimes . . . very well": BTW speech to the American Missionary Association and the National Council of Congregational Churches, New Haven, Conn., October 25, 1915, in *BTW Papers*, 13:413.

134   "He is a fine chap . . . yelling and singing": JR to Gussie, November 12, 1915, Rosenwald Papers UC, box 54, folder 1.

134   "The doctors all agree . . . you are to us all": Margaret Washington to JR, November 12, 1915, in *BTW Papers*, 13:435.

135   "I was born in the South": Harlan, *The Wizard of Tuskegee*, 454.

135   "shake the hand": William H. Jackson to BTW, November 1, 1915, in *BTW Papers*, 13:422.

135   "My heart is too sad": JR to Margaret Washington, November 14, 1915, in *BTW Papers*, 13:441–42.

135–36   Moton visit with bedridden BTW described in Robert W. Moton, *Finding a Way Out* (College Park, Md.: McGrath Publishing, 1920), 191.

136   "has great strength, and yet": Theodore Roosevelt to JR, December 18, 1915, Rosenwald Papers UC, box 54, folder 1.

Chapter 9. A School in Every County

I took the title of this chapter from an unpublished monograph by Jeffrey Sosland, who was sponsored by the Goldmuntz Family. He, in turn, was quoting the Rosenwald Fund's director Edwin Embree who expressed the goal for the Julius Rosenwald Fund of providing a school in every county of the South with significant numbers of black children.

137   "Inadequacy and poverty": Thomas Jesse Jones, "The Jones Report," quoted in Adam Fairclough, *A Class of Their Own: Black Teachers in the Segregated South* (Cambridge, Mass.: Belknap Press of Harvard University Press, 2007), 14.

139   "General Merchandise": Ascoli, *Julius Rosenwald*, 201.

139   "very friendly and democratic": Quoted in Howard Vincent O'Brien, *Wine, Women and War: A Diary of Disillusionment* (New York: J. H. Sears and Company, 1926), 180.

139   "made a fuss over the Chicago boys": JR to "Dear Ones All," August 29, 1918, quoted in Ascoli, *Julius Rosenwald*, 205.

139   "I speak of civic matters . . . like to have": "The Man the Boys Call Rosy," *Survey*, November 2, 1918, quoted in Ascoli, *Julius Rosenwald*, 207.

139   "All my speeches . . . my sentiments": *Chicago Record-Herald*, January 26, 1922, Rosenwald Papers UC, scrapbook 5, p. 36.

140–41 "race contacts ... element": Chicago Commission on Race Relations, *The Negro in Chicago: A Study of Race Relations and a Race
Riot in 1919* (Chicago: University of Chicago Press, 1922). This is
a remarkable 667-page document that describes in great detail what
happened during the Chicago riot and the racial situation in Chicago. It includes practical suggestions about ways to improve it.

141   "We have had the good luck ... of Europe": Rosenwald Papers UC,
scrapbook 8, p. 57.

141   JR's donations discussed in Ascoli, *Julius Rosenwald*, 215, and Werner, *Julius Rosenwald*, 185.

141   The loving cup is in the collection of the Museum of Science and
Industry in Chicago.

142   "the well-being of mankind": Bylaws of the Julius Rosenwald Fund,
article 2, in Edwin Embree and Julia Waxman, *Investment in People:
The Story of the Julius Rosenwald Fund* (New York: Harper and Brothers, 1949), 223.

143   "Slowly, doubt and antagonism": Embree and Waxman, *Investment in
People*, 44.

144   "I know of nothing in connection ... in their hearts": E. C. Roberts
to R. R. Moton, July 19, 1919, Tuskegee University Archives, R. R.
Moton Papers, box 51, folder 336.

144   "Truly, you are a noble chap": Bernard Baruch, quoted in Ascoli,
Julius Rosenwald, 224.

145   Lessing Rosenwald's desire to succeed his father is discussed in
Emmet and Jeuck, *Catalogues and Counters*, 330–31, and in Lessing's
Sears oral history, photocopy in possession of author. Archives, Sears,
Roebuck and Company Archives, Hoffman Estates, Illinois.

146   "saved hundreds of persons from immediate bankruptcy": Werner,
Julius Rosenwald, 240.

146   JR to Sears department heads, quoted in Werner, *Julius Rosenwald*,
242.

147   On William Rosenwald visit to Soviet colonies, author interview,
New York, N.Y., October 1996.

147   Tuskegee Institute became Tuskegee University in 1937.

147–48 "what Mr. and Mrs. Rosenwald have meant" and other quotes: Gussie's letters to Robert Moton, R. R. Moton Papers, Tuskegee University Archives, box 52.

148 The episode with the Veterans' Administration hospital in Tuskegee is detailed in Pete Daniel, "Black Power in the 1920s: The Case of Tuskegee Veterans Hospital," *Journal of Southern History* 36, no. 3 (August 1970): 368–88.

148 "brought down the house . . . attractive speech": R. R. Moton to JR, April 19, 1929, Rosenwald Papers UC, box 54, folder 7.

148–49 "better buildings and equipment . . . best buildings today": O. H. Bernard, "The Julius Rosenwald Fund in Tennessee," Fisk University Library, Rosenwald Fund, box 76, folder 2.

150 "Forrest County has a very unique . . . in the state": "The Julius Rosenwald Fund in Mississippi," Fisk University Library, Julius Rosenwald Fund, box 76, folder 2.

152 "human and spiritual values . . . help defeat it": Ralph McGill, quoted in Leon Harris, *Merchant Princes* (New York: Kodansha International, 1994), 307.

152 "Without her inspiration": Ascoli, *Julius Rosenwald*, 364.

152 There is a historical marker in front of Julius Rosenwald's home at 4901 Ellis Avenue in Chicago.

152 "a glorified Tuskegee": Quoted in Werner, *Julius Rosenwald*, 364.

152–53 "I walked to Mr. Rosenwald's bedside . . . was that person": Harry Kersey, unpublished memoir, photocopy of manuscript in possession of the author.

153 "the greatest joy": JR quoted in *Tuskegee Messenger*, February 1932, 16.

153 "It was the hard common sense . . . trusted each other": *Tuskegee Messenger*, February 1932, 6.

Chapter 10. Rosenwald and Main: Sweet Home

156 For detailed statistics on the amounts raised in each state broken down into categories, see National Trust for Historic Preservation, "Rosenwald School Initiative," http://preservationnation.org/rosenwald.

157–58 I interviewed Alice Rosenwald in October 2007 in New York and again in November 2010.

165 "The most notable effect": Embree and Waxman, *Investment in People*, 43.

165 Quotes from Scrabble School graduates in this chapter are taken from an interview that aired on WMRA, a National Public Radio affiliate in Harrisburg, Virginia, in February 2006: Martha Woodruff, "Reporter's Notebook." Accessed May 9, 2011. http://www.jmu.edu/wmra/news/m022306a.html. See also the Web site "Scrabble School," http://www.scrabbleschool.org.

165 "the hub of our community": Connie Quarles, quoted in Joshua Zeitz, "Rosenwald's Gift," in *Legacy: The Magazine of African American History and Culture*, Spring 2003, 23–29.

165–66 "Because of segregation": Ralph Eubanks, *A Journey into Mississippi's Dark Past* (New York: Basic Books, 2003), 55.

166 "Rosenwald schools became part of the cultural capital": Mary S. Hoffschwelle, *Rosenwald Schools*, 273.

166 Karen Riles, text on wall at Hopewell School, Round Rock, Texas.

166–67 "They were ordinary": Henry Weincek, *The Hairstons: An American Family in Black and White* (New York: St. Martin's Press, 1999), 247.

167 "One thing I think the history books": Diane Nash, quoted in David Remnick, "The Promise," *New Yorker*, February 15, 2010, 95.

167 "came the parents": Charles Morgan Jr., quoted in Jeffrey Sosland, *A School in Every County: The Partnership of Philanthropist Julius Rosenwald and American Black Communities* (Privately published monograph, 1995), 62.

168 "My family may have seemed unlikely candidates": Carlotta Walls LaNier, with Lisa Frazier Page, *A Mighty Long Way: My Journey to Justice at Little Rock Central High School* (New York: Ballantine Books, 2009), xvi.

168 President Obama's eulogy of Dorothy Height, *New York Times*, April 30, 2010. Accessed May 9, 2011. http://www.nytimes.com/2010/04/30/us/politics/30height-text.html.

169   "[He] was president . . . we all knew who he was": Rosa Parks, with Jim Haskins, *Rosa Parks: My Story* (New York: Dial Books, 1992), 45.

169   "Education represented": John Lewis, *Walking with the Wind: A Memoir of the Movement* (San Diego, Calif.: Harcourt Brace, 1998), 41.

Epilogue

172   "one of the most characteristic": Daniel J. Boorstin, "From Charity to Philanthropy," in *Hidden History*, ed. Daniel J. Boorstin and Ruth F. Boorstin (New York: Harper and Row, 1987), 193–209.

172   "the common stake we all have in each other": Obama used the phrase often in speeches during the 2008 campaign. For example, see Al Giordano, "Full Circle," October 23, 2008, *The Field: Al Giordano Reports on the United States. Accessed May 9, 2011.* http://narcosphere .narconews.com/thefield/full-circle.

172   "No man is an island": John Donne, "Meditation XVII."

172   "Black people loved and kept faith with": Condoleezza Rice, in an interview with Nicholas Kralev, "Rice: Race Struggle Is America's 'Birth Defect,'" *Washington Times*, March 28, 2008, 1, Accessed May 9, 2011. http://www.cbn.com/CBNnews/347957.aspx.

SELECTED BIBLIOGRAPHY

Archives

Fisk University, John Hope and Aurelia Elizabeth Franklin Library, Julius Rosenwald Fund Archives.

Library of Congress, Manuscript Division, Booker T. Washington Papers.

Tuskegee University Archives, Booker T. Washington Collection, Robert W. Moton Papers.

University of Chicago, Regenstein Library Special Collections, Julius Rosenwald Papers.

Books

Anderson, Eric, and Alfred A. Moss Jr. *Dangerous Donations: Northern Philanthropy and Southern Black Education, 1902–1930*. Columbia: University of Missouri Press, 1999.

Anderson, James D. *The Education of Blacks in the South, 1880–1935*. Chapel Hill: University of North Carolina Press, 1988.

Ascoli, Peter M. *Julius Rosenwald: The Man Who Built Sears, Roebuck and Advanced the Cause of Black Education in the American South*. Bloomington: Indiana University Press, 2006.

Asher, Frederick. *Richard Warren Sears: Icon of Inspiration, Fable and Fact About the Founder and Spiritual Genius of Sears, Roebuck & Company*. New York: Vantage Press, 1997.

Asher, Louis E., and Edith Head. *Send No Money*. Chicago: Argus Books, 1942.

Birmingham, Stephen. *The Grandes Dames*. New York: Simon and Schuster, 1982.

Blum, Isidor. *The History of the Jews in Baltimore*. Baltimore: Historical Review Publishing, 1910.

Boorstin, Daniel J. *Hidden History*. New York: Harper and Row, 1987.

Brands, H. W. *The Reckless Decade: America in the 1890s*. New York: St. Martin's Press, 1995.

Bregstone, Philip P. *Chicago and Its Jews: A Cultural History*, with an introduction by Julian W. Mack. Chicago: Privately published, 1933.

Brooks, John Graham. *An American Citizen: The Life of William Henry Baldwin, Jr.* Boston: Houghton Mifflin, 1910.

Brownstein, Elizabeth Smith. *If This House Could Talk: Historic Homes, Extraordinary Americans*. New York: Simon and Schuster, 1999.

Chandler, Alfred D., Jr. *Strategy and Structure: Chapters in the History of the Industrial Enterprise*. Cambridge: Massachusetts Institute of Technology Press, 1962.

Chicago Commission on Race Relations. *The Negro in Chicago: A Study of Race Relations and a Race Riot*. Chicago: University of Chicago Press, 1922.

Christian, Charles M. *Black Sage: The African American Experience, A Chronology*. Washington, D.C.: Civitas, Counterpoint, 1995.

Cohen, Naomi W. *Encounter with Emancipation: The German Jews in the United States, 1830–1914*. Philadelphia: Jewish Publication Society of America, 1984.

Dedmon, Emmett. *Great Enterprises: 100 Years of the YMCA of Metropolitan Chicago*. New York: Rand McNally, 1977.

Deutsch, Armand. *Me and Bogie and Other Friends and Acquaintances from a Life in Hollywood and Beyond*. New York: G. P. Putnam's Sons, 1991.

Douglass, Frederick. *A Narrative of the Life of Frederick Douglass*. New York: Dover Publications, 1995.

Dray, Philip. *At the Hands of Persons Unknown: The Lynching of Black America*. New York: Random House, 2002.

Embree, Edwin, and Julia Waxman. *Investment in People: The Story of the Julius Rosenwald Fund*. New York: Harper and Brothers, 1949.

Emmet, Boris, and John E. Jeuck. *Catalogues and Counters: A History of Sears, Roebuck & Co.* Chicago: University of Chicago Press, 1950.

Eubanks, W. Ralph. *Ever Is a Long Time: A Journey into Mississippi's Dark Past*. New York: Basic Books, 2003.

Fairclough, Adam. *A Class of Their Own: Black Teachers in the Segregated South*. Cambridge, Mass.: Belknap Press of Harvard University Press, 2007.

Fein, Isaac M. *The Making of an American Jewish Community: The History of Baltimore's Jews from 1773 to 1920*. Philadelphia: Jewish Publication Society of America, 1971.

Giddings, Paula J. *Ida, a Sword Among Lions: Ida B. Wells and the Campaign Against Lynching*. New York: Amistad, 2008.

Harlan, Louis R. *Booker T. Washington: The Making of a Black Leader, 1856–1901*. New York: Oxford University Press, 1972.

Harlan, Louis R. *Booker T. Washington: The Wizard of Tuskegee, 1901–1915*. New York: Oxford University Press, 1983.

Harlan, Louis R., and Raymond W. Smock, eds. *The Booker T. Washington Papers*. Urbana: University of Illinois Press, 1981.

Harris, Leon. *Merchant Princes*. New York: Berkley Books, 1979.

Hirsch, Emil. *My Religion*. New York: Macmillan, 1925.

Hoffschwelle, Mary S. *The Rosenwald Schools of the American South*. Gainesville: University Press of Florida, 2006.

Irons, Peter. *Jim Crow's Children: The Broken Promise of the Brown Decision*. New York: Penguin Books, 2002.

Klein, Gerda Weissmann. *A Passion for Sharing: The Life of Edith Rosenwald Stern*. Chappaqua, N.Y.: Rossel Books, 1984.

LaNier, Carlotta Walls, with Lisa Frazier Page. *A Mighty Long Way: My Journey to Justice at Little Rock Central High School*. New York: Ballantine Books, 2009.

Lewis, David Levering. *W. E. B. Du Bois: Biography of a Race*. New York: Henry Holt, 1993.

Lewis, John, with Michael D'Orso. *Walking with the Wind: A Memoir of the Movement*. San Diego, Calif.: Harcourt Brace, 1998.

Mahoney, Tom, and Leonard Sloane. *The Great Merchants: America's Foremost Retail Institutions and the People Who Made Them Great*. New York: Harper and Row, 1949.

Mathews, Basil. *Booker T. Washington: Educator and Interracial Interpreter*. College Park, Md.: McGrath Publishing, 1969.

McCabe, James E., Jr. *Lights and Shadows of New York Life; or, The Sights and Sensations of the Great City*. Philadelphia: National Publishing, 1872.

McFeely, William S. *Frederick Douglass*. New York: W. W. Norton, 1991.

Miller, Donald L. *City of the Century: The Epic of Chicago and the Making of America*. New York: Simon and Schuster, 1996.

Norrell, Robert J. *Reaping the Whirlwind: The Civil Rights Movement in Tuskegee*. Chapel Hill: University of North Carolina Press, 1985.

Norrell, Robert J. *Up from History: The Life of Booker T. Washington*. Cambridge, Mass.: Belknap Press of Harvard University Press, 2009.

Ogden, Christopher. *Aaron's Gift*. New York: Abacus and Associates, 2009.

Reed, Betty J. *The Brevard Rosenwald School: Black Education and Community Building in a Southern Appalachian Town, 1920–1966*. Jefferson, N.C.: McFarland and Company, 2004.

Simonhoff, Harry. *Saga of American Jewry, 1865–1914: Links of an Endless Chain*. New York: Arco Publishing, 1959.

Smith, S. L. *Builders of Goodwill: The Story of the State Agents of Negro Education in the South, 1910–1950*. Nashville: Tennessee Book Co., 1950.

Smook, Raymond W., ed. *Booker T. Washington in Perspective: Essays of Louis R. Harlan*. Jackson: University Press of Mississippi, 1988.

Spencer, Samuel R., Jr. *Booker T. Washington and the Negro's Place in American Life*. Boston: Little, Brown and Company.

Steward, Ruth Ann. *Portia: The Life of Portia Washington Pittman, the Daughter of Booker T. Washington*. Garden City, N.Y.: Doubleday and Company, 1977.

Washington, Booker T. *Up from Slavery*. New York: Penguin Books, 2004.

Weisburger, Bernard. *Booker T. Washington*. New York: New American Library, 1972.

Weincek, Henry. *The Hairstons: An American Family in Black and White*. New York: St. Martin's Press, 1999.

Werner, M. R. *Julius Rosenwald: The Life of a Practical Humanitarian*. New York: Harper and Brothers, 1939.

Woodward, C. Vann. *Origins of the New South, 1877–1913*. Baton Rouge: Louisiana State University Press, Littlefield Fund for Southern History at the University of Texas, 1977.

Woodward, C. Vann. *The Strange Career of Jim Crow*. New York: Oxford University Press, 1957.

Wyman, Mark. *Immigrants in the Valley: Irish, Germans, and Americans in the Upper Mississippi Country, 1830–1860*. Chicago: Nelson-Hall, 1984.

Other Publications

Daniel, Pete. "Black Power in the 1920s: The Case of Tuskegee Veterans Hospital." *Journal of Southern History* 36, no. 3 (August 1970): 368–88.

Morris, Jerome. "Research, Ideology, and the Brown Decision: Counter-Narratives to the Historical and Contemporary Representation of Black Schooling." *Teachers College Record* 110, no. 4 (2008): 713–32.

Scott, Erika Elizabeth. "A Rare Legacy: Julius Rosenwald and the Jewish Charitable Tradition," Honors B.A. thesis, Wesleyan University, Middletown, Conn., April 2001.

Sosland, Jeffrey. *A School in Every County: The Partnership of Jewish Philanthropist Julius Rosenwald and American Black Communities*. Washington, D.C.: Economics and Science Planning, 1995.

INDEX

ABOUT THE AUTHOR

Stephanie Deutsch is a writer and critic living in Washington, D.C. She has written for the *New York Times*, the *Weekly Standard*, the Millions blog, the *Washington Times*, and neighborhood newspapers. She edited and wrote the introduction to *Capitol Hill: Beyond the Monuments*, a book of photographs published in 1996 by the Capitol Hill Arts Workshop.